Outdoor Life

GUNS AND SHOOTING YEARBOOK

1989

Published by
Outdoor Life Books, Danbury, Connecticut

Distributed to the trade by
Stackpole Books, Harrisburg, Pennsylvania

COVER: Facilities and technical expertise by National Rifle Association. **Photograph by Randy Lamson,** Director of N.R.A. Photography.

At top: A Ruger Super Blackhawk revolver, .44 Magnum, in stainless steel with Ruger's new cushioned grips. The scope is by Leupold, in Ruger mounts.

Second from top: This Remington Model–700 barreled action features one of the new generation "drop-in" synthetic stocks by Bell & Carlson. The scope is by Leupold in Weaver mounts.

Second from bottom: Parker Reproduction, 12-gauge waterfowl gun features barrels designed for use with steel shot. A faithful reproduction of the original Parker Classic updated for today's hunting needs.

Bottom: A modern-day classic is this reproduction of the legendary Kentucky rifle by Cecil Brooks. Entirely handmade, with silver fittings, Brooks-made rifles, such as this one, are presented each year to the keynote speaker at the NRA annual conventions.

Copyright © 1988 Grolier Book Clubs, Inc.

Published by
Outdoor Life Books
Grolier Book Clubs, Inc.
Sherman Turnpike
Danbury, CT 06816

Distributed to the trade by
Stackpole Books
Cameron and Kelker Streets
P.O. Box 1831
Harrisburg, PA 17105

Produced by Soderstrom Publishing Group Inc.
Book design: Jeff Fitschen

ISBN 1–55654–045–0
ISSN 0889–0978

Manufactured in the United States of America

Contents

Preface *by Jim Carmichel*   **5**

Part 1:   **QUITE A SHOWCASE**

Beretta: Five Centuries of Gunmaking   **6**
by Michael McIntosh

A Canvas of Steel   **14**
by R. L. Wilson & Edward R. Ricciuti

A $900-Dollar Air Gun   **24**
by Tim McMurray & Dennis O'Flaherty

The Double Rifle *by Alex Brant*   **31**

The Custom Gunmaking Survey   **36**
by Ron Frank

Part 2:   **RIFLES TODAY**

Synthetic Stocks Are Here to Stay   **41**
by Jim Carmichel

The Alaskan Rifle *by Finn Aagaard*   **47**

Light as a Feather *by Jim Carmichel*   **52**

Made in Japan *by Jim Carmichel*   **57**

Part 3:   **SHOTGUN CORNER**

Sporting Clays: The New Shotgun
Challenge *by Robert W. Hunnicutt*   **62**

Super-Fox: The Waterfowling Legend   **70**
by Michael McIntosh

Part 4:   **HANDGUNS**

Handguns and Cartridges for Long-range
Varminting *by Bob Milek*   **78**

.22 Handguns *by Jan Libourel*   **84**

The .44 Magnum: Still the King?   **92**
by Jan Libourel

Part 5:   **SHOOTING**

Triggers and Trigger Control   **102**
by Jim Carmichel

Optical Terms for the Shooter   **107**
by Hugh Birnbaum

A Guide to Muzzleloading   **114**
by Jim Carmichel

Lones Wigger: World-Level Shooting
Champ *by J. Scott Rupp*   **122**

Part 6:   **GUNS OF YESTERYEAR**

Guns of the Boxer Rebellion   **128**
by Pete Dickey

Keeping His Powder Dry   **135**
by Helmut Nickel

Targets of Yesteryear   **140**
by Ralph Lindsay

Part 7:   **AMMO AND RELOADING**

New Loads from Federal, Remington &
    Winchester *by Jim Carmichel*   **142**

Factory Ammo: Better Than Handloads?   **147**
    by Layne Simpson

When the Bullet Gets There   **153**
    by Jim Carmichel

The .22 CHeetah Mark II: One Hot
    Wildcat *by Layne Simpson*   **157**

The .338 Winchester Magnum   **162**
    by Finn Aagaard

Part 8:   **GUNSMITHING AND
MAINTENANCE**

Scope Mounting Made Easy   **167**
    by Bob Milek

How to Clean and Protect Your Firearms   **173**
    by Rick Jamison

Appendix: NEW GUNS   **178**
    by Jim Carmichel

Index   **188**

Preface

I'm not much of a gun trader. Now, don't get me wrong, I love trading guns, it's just that I'm not very good at it. Perhaps it's my generous spirit, or just that the lure of a gun causes me to abandon whatever atoms of common sense I normally possess. By my own reckoning, if I had refused every gun trade in which I've been involved and simply given the other party $20 to forget the deal, I'd be way ahead of the game. Yet I haven't always traded-in the family farm.

Quite a few years ago, when I was fresh out of college and seldom had anything in my pockets except holes and lint, I cashed my paycheck and headed for a weekend gunshow. In case you've never seen one, a gunshow is a combination flea market and gun exhibit. If you like guns there is no better place to be. There are rows and rows of guns, thousands of 'em. Everything from $2 owlheads to the guaranteed, absolute promised revolver used by Jesse James to hold up the Bittercreek Stage, with a letter of authentication from his great, great grand nephew. (Jesse must have owned thousands of guns and used them all on every robbery.)

There's a jewel at every gunshow and this time it was a delicious little 20-gauge double made by the classy Belgian firm of Francotte. For me, this was love at first sight. I felt that if I owned that shotgun I would never want anything more for the rest of my days. In a way I *already* owned it. Clearly, it had been made just for me and was being held for ransom. That was it! To set the beautiful gun free and thereby secure my eternal happiness, I *had* to pay the ransom.

To be fair, the asking price really wasn't that unreasonable, but it was more money than I had. Even if I had missed a car payment and gone for a week without eating, I still didn't have enough money. There was nothing I could do but haggle, so haggle I did. For two days. Finally, during the closing hours of the show, I wore the trader down and he accepted the total contents of my pockets for the little Francotte. As I was gathering it up and preparing to stuff it into a scuffed plastic case I carried for the purpose, the trader reached under his table and brought forth the most elegant gun case I'd ever seen. It was made of leather, filled with silver oil bottles, ivory handled tools, and an ebony cleaning rod—all fitted into neat compartments. Even in those lean years, that case was worth upwards of three hundred dollars, more than I'd paid for the gun. "Here," he said, "this goes with it."

So sometimes you get a better deal than you bargain for. Such is the case with this, the 1989 edition of the *Outdoor Life Guns & Shooting Yearbook*. Let me list a few of the ways you come out ahead on this deal: This yearbook is a compilation of the best and most informative articles written on guns and shooting during the preceding year, selected from magazines including *Outdoor Life, American Rifleman, Guns & Ammo, The Handloader, Shooting Times, Sporting Classics, Outdoor Life's Hunting Guns,* and even *Audubon.* That's a pretty good deal in itself, but we make the deal even sweeter by making some of the articles look better than they did originally! Sometimes we publish more illustrations than appeared originally. Typically, an author will submit anywhere from 10 to 20 photos or illustrations with an article, especially if it is a technical piece deserving that many. But many magazines are critically short on space and may only have room for a couple of illustrations. As appropriate we've added illustrations, thus giving you a more comprehensive grasp of many subjects. If good photos did not exist originally, we arrange to have them made and quite often publish color photos rather than the original black and white. That's why you'll see so much more color here than in most shooting journals. Not only is there more color, but it's usually better, thanks to the quality paper, making this book a handsome addition to anyone's library.

Another way you often get something extra is in the text. The space limitations of some magazines often make it necessary to trim text to fit. In the case of my articles, you may note that many are longer than originally published and with added information.

The really big bonus of this year's yearbook is some of the very finest articles we've ever collected. You'll recognize the names of a few authors featured in earlier yearbooks. Good writers and researchers have a way of always coming up with important new ideas and information. That's why Bob Milek, Pete Dickey, R. L. Wilson, and Hugh Birnbaum are here again. Their articles are the best written on the subject, and you'll find over 30 articles in this class.

Whatever your interest—rifles, handguns, shotguns, reloading or whatever—there's a special bargain for you here. You thought you bought just the gun, and here we're tossing in the leather case with silver oil bottles, ivory-handled tools, and an ebony cleaning rod. That's a good deal.

Jim Carmichel

PART ONE

QUITE A SHOWCASE

Beretta: Five Centuries of Gunmaking

Michael McIntosh

Trompia Valley is a narrow groove in the foothills of northeastern Italy, hewn by the Mella River. Through much of its length, which isn't far, there is scarcely a square yard of naturally level ground. It's a difficult place to grow crops, and in any case the growing season is short. Unlike other valleys in that part of the world, Val Trompia doesn't even grow first-rate grapevines. But inhospitable as it might be to agriculture or the luxury of a good local wine, Trompia Valley is a piece of geography upon which nature bestowed a particular gift.

The valley slopes are laced with rich veins of ore that yield nearly pure siderite, iron carbonate. It has some phosphorus and a healthy dose of manganese, and produces a tough, lightweight iron that's easily worked. In the days before steel, such amiable metal was immensely useful, and ore was being dug and smelted in the valley as early as the Middle Ages, perhaps even before.

With all that going for it, Trompia Valley can

lay a fair claim to being the oldest gunmaking district in the world. It's a claim that Suhl, Antwerp, Augsburg, and Nuremburg might well dispute, but there is no question that Val Trompia is the oldest arms-producing district to remain an important center even today. Brescia, which lies at the southern end of the valley, is home to some of the finest gunmakers in Italy, and Gardone, a few miles north, has Beretta, the oldest and most famous of all.

By the middle of the 16th century, an arms industry already thrived in Trompia Valley, supplying arquebuses, muskets, pike heads, breastplates, and myriad other items of military hardware to the courts of Europe. Gun barrels were a particular specialty among Val Trompian craftsmen, but the area was unique in that it could produce guns with a greater degree of self-suffi-

The Tuscan fowling piece (top), circa 1725, with barrel signed "Giovan Beretta," and a 1980 side-by-side attest to Beretta's enduring custom-grade tradition.

This article first appeared in Sporting Classics

ciency than anywhere else in the world. Ore and wood could be transformed into a finished gun without ever leaving the valley and without any component being imported.

As evidence of just how pervasive was Val Trompia's influence upon arms making, national museums all over Europe and Asia contain guns locally manufactured but fitted with barrels signed by the *maestri da canne* of Gardone. Bartolomeo Beretta was one of them, and he represents the beginning of a family of gunmakers that would remain active in the industry for an astonishingly long time.

Putting a date to the exact origin of the Beretta company probably never will be possible. There is suggestive evidence leading as far back as 1450. Bartolomeo Beretta was a working barrelmaker in the 1530s. His second son, Giovannino, was by 1577 a master maker with his own shop. Because both tradition and law held that only the son of a master could himself become a master, the current company considers 1530 its founding date. A few years more or less scarcely matter; what is most intriguing about Beretta is that it has survived as a family-owned business through at least 21 generations and is today one of the three or four preeminent gunmakers in the world.

Inasmuch as Europe was the scene of countless wars and endless political uproar over those 400-odd years, it's hardly surprising that Beretta has from the beginning built military arms. But through all that time, Beretta has produced sporting arms as well. From the 15th through the 18th centuries, the superb Gardonese barrels, lightweight and marvelously strong, were the heart of the finest sporting pieces in the world. A fair number of those bore the Beretta name.

Almost without exception, Gardonese barrels were smooth-bored. Beretta, in fact, made no rifled barrels until the beginning of World War I—which meant that military and sporting barrels could be made interchangeably, with no alteration of technique and without interrupting production. Since everything was built by hand, the shop could fill military orders and switch to sporting guns without stopping for breath.

Beretta's guns followed the same evolutionary stages as all the rest. There were matchlocks, wheellocks, and flint guns. Naturally, all were muzzleloaders, although like others, the Berettas experimented with breechloading designs. Giovanni Antonio, the third generation of gunmaking Berettas, in 1641 presented the Venetian government with a breechloading cannon of his own invention. After testing it, the government awarded Beretta 200 ducats, a 20-year annuity of ten ducats a month, and promptly forgot about the whole matter.

The Venetian Republic, which governed nearly the whole of northern Italy from 1426 until the rise of Napoleon, took a protectionist view of its industry, certainly including the arms industry in the Trompia Valley, and even though the valley itself was periodically wracked with internecine social struggle, the national economy remained stable. The gunmakers freely carried on their work, their rights of trade supported by the government. After 1797, when Napoleon annexed Lombardy and dismantled the old republic, Val Trompia was governed by the French, and the arms industry turned virtually all its resources to supplying weapons for Bonaparte's Armies of the Eagles.

Eighteen years later, Napoleon went down in final defeat, and Lombardy became part of the Austrian Empire. The market for military arms stopped instantly. For the gunmakers in the Trompia Valley, the world was a new and somewhat hostile place. The obvious course was to renew the civilian markets, but those were in sad disrepair. The vast Oriental market, to which the Val Trompia traditionally had supplied gun barrels, was gone altogether. Most of the others had been usurped by the French, English, and Bel-

BRESCIA
Milan
Florence
ITALY
Rome
Naples

Left: Brescia lies in Italy's Val Trompia, the oldest gunmaking district in the world. Pietro Beretta S.p.A. is headquartered at nearby Gardone. Right: Beretta's rugged and reliable centerfire rifles are the result of centuries of development of military weapons. The double-bore Express Rifles come in both boxlock and sidelock designs, and in calibers from .30/06 to .458 Win. Mag.

Pietro Beretta at the wheel of his DeDion–Bouton in 1906 with target-shooting companions. Under Pietro's leadership Beretta achieved international status.

gians. To make matters worse, the European economy was sluggish, and the Austrian government was hungry for taxes.

Beretta's position was no better than anyone else's. The family still had its workshops, but without some means of competing on a broad scale, its prospects were dim. But as sometimes happens, the right man was in the right place at the right time.

Pietro Antonia Beretta was born June 18, 1791, heir to eight generations of gunmaking tradition. Like his forebears, he had all the skills of a master barrelmaker, but he also owned an astute sense of how to meet the demands of a largely uncertain future. Almost before the cannon smoke had cleared from the battlefields at Waterloo, Pietro Beretta left the Trompia Valley to gather up the threads of a tattered market.

He met with wholesale dealers, retailers, and importers all over Italy. Inevitably, there soon was some demand for martial arms from the Hapsburgs in Austria and their allies, but it was scarcely a trickle compared with the old days of the Venetian Republic. No doubt Pietro Beretta was pleased that his workshops were turning out barrels of any kind, but he was shrewd enough to know that the Val Trompia industry and the Berettas in particular could hardly hope to prosper without a strong showing in sporting guns. His pursuit of that market, won largely through the network of contacts he forged over the next few years, would in time form the foundation upon which the company still stands.

Even the name he gave it in 1832 remains to-day—*Fabricca d'Armi Pietro Beretta*.

He would not live to see it come to full flower,

but Pietro Beretta virtually assured the firm's future. In 1850 he bought back a smithy that his father had sold in 1814. The two buildings, with their forges and workshops, were important enough, but along with them came the rights of use for such canals and watercourses as might provide both transportation and a source of power. The full significance of the purchase would not become apparent for more than a generation.

Pietro Beretta died in 1853, and in due course, control of the company devolved upon his son Giuseppe. Here, too, was a man who knew that merely manufacturing barrels or locks was no assurance of survival in a world grown increasingly complex. He strengthened and expanded the marketing network his father had put together and transformed Armi Beretta from what still was basically a barrel shop into a full-fledged manufactory.

The gunmaking industry in the Trompia Valley had always been largely cooperative. The Gardonese masters made barrels; craftsmen in other villages made locks, springs, mountings, screws, and other metal parts; the majority of guns were assembled, stocked and finished in Brescia. By about 1870, Beretta had consolidated all phases of gun manufacture into one operation. With that, Armi Beretta became unique. In an 1878 letter to *LaBorsa*, a newspaper published in Naples, Giuseppe Beretta claimed that his firm "alone possesses the remarkable quality of total production: that is, it brings to its premises raw iron and wood, and sends out finished guns . . ."

The majority of them, by about 1880, were sporting guns, although Beretta continued to pursue military contracts. A few simple statistics clearly show where Giuseppe Beretta was headed. From 1850 to 1860, Beretta produced about 300 sporting guns each year; by 1881, annual production was 8,000 finished shotguns and nearly 2,000 double-barreled pistols. Moreover, the firm

Coat of arms of the Beretta family. Berettas have manufactured firearms since the 15th century.

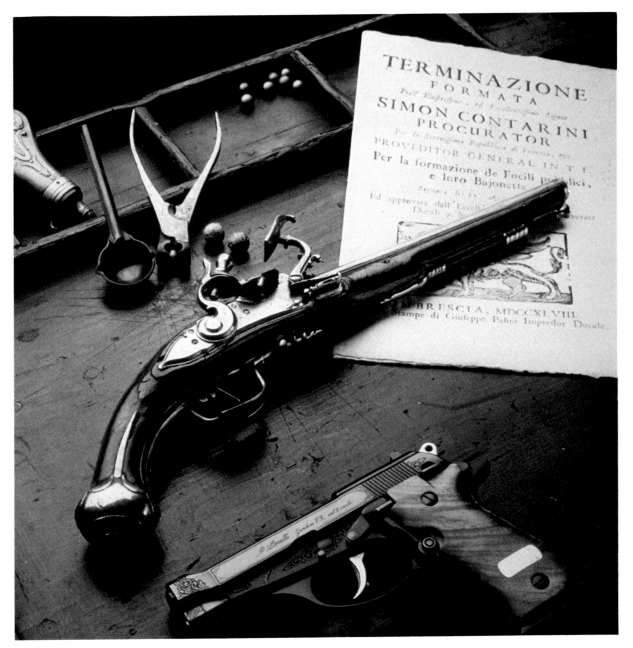

Here are a Beretta 200-year-old flintock pistol and a semi-automatic.

annually sold about 2,500 pairs of barrels and accompanying locks and small parts to other gunmakers. There were 200 employees in the factory that year, and the production rate was high enough that a good deal of work was contracted out to other firms around Gardone.

Beginning about 1873, primary emphasis went to breechloading shotguns, and before the decade was over, they were being sold in every corner of Italy, in Greece, Turkey, Tunisia, and Egypt. The 1887 catalog lists more than 100 different shotguns. About 70 are breechloaders of either centerfire or pinfire type; some 50 of these were of Beretta's own make, the others Belgian and English imports. There are sidelocks of various designs, with bolting systems ranging from top-lever snap actions to underlevers with wedge bolts.

The first hammerless guns appeared in the catalog of 1893, and these included boxlocks as well as sidelocks. The vast variety of Beretta sporting guns would continue to flourish until the beginning of World War I, when the firm made its first serious—and as it turned out, prophetic—foray

Facilities at Beretta's huge plant vary from space-age automation (see inset) to meticulous personal inspection of gunstock blanks. Claiming nearly 70 percent of the European firearms market, Beretta has established factories in several other countries, including one in the United States.

Beretta's 92F semiautomatic, which fires 16 rounds of 9mm ammunition, was selected by the United States military as its official sidearm in 1985.

into the design and manufacture of automatic weapons. The results of that make a story in itself, for Beretta continues to occupy an eminent place in the international military-arms industry.

Given Italy's involvement in the Great War, the demand for sporting guns naturally dwindled after 1914, only to revive shortly after the Treaty of Versailles. By then, Armi Beretta was in new hands.

Giuseppe Beretta died in June 1903, and leadership passed to his son, the second Pietro. In less than 30 years, building upon what his grandfather and father had begun, Pietro Beretta brought the firm international status. To ensure that production could keep pace with the world markets he so successfully curried, he expanded the factory, installed new machinery and, taking advantage of water rights the first Pietro had purchased long before, built two generating plants on the Mella River to secure his own source of electric power.

The proliferation of sporting-gun designs abated

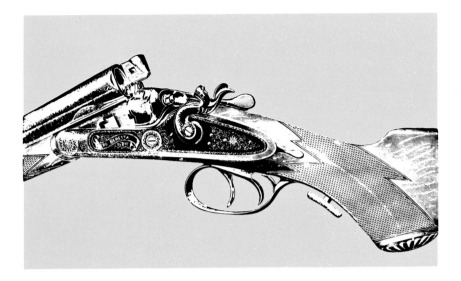

Fine double from Beretta's 1912 catalogue. From 1850 to 1860, Beretta produced about 300 sporting guns each year: by 1881, annual production was 8,000 shotguns.

somewhat between the two world wars, but there was variety enough to reach almost every niche in the market. Breechloaders naturally predominated, but muzzleloading percussion guns remained in production until 1923. The 1938 catalog even featured a special insert offering pinfire guns, ranging in finish from plain to lavishly ornate. As early as the mid-19th century and probably even before, Beretta had built a number of over/under muzzleloaders. No doubt well aware of John Browning's Superposed and probably sensing what an impact the over/under gun would have in the future, Pietro Beretta introduced his own version in 1932, called the Model SO. The name is still used for Beretta's best-quality sidelock over/unders.

Even with so great a diversity of types, virtually all of the Beretta double guns built in the 20th century share a common basic design. The monobloc system first appeared about 1903 and has been used ever since. The breeches of both barrels, the barrel lump, and rib extension are milled integrally from a single block of steel. The breeches are countered-bored to accept the barrels. The block is heated to about 350° Centigrade, and the barrels, their chamber-ends lathe-turned to form sleeves, are inserted. As the block cools, the shrinkage, combined with a special-alloy solder, bonds barrels and breech as firmly as if they'd been machined all of a piece.

Of itself, the monobloc system doesn't necessarily produce a stronger gun than one built the more traditional way, but it does offer some practical manufacturing advantages. If a break-action gun is to open, close, and lock up properly—and continue to do so for a lifetime—it's critical that the breech, barrel lump, and bolting notches all fit together in precisely the right way. Assembling them as separate parts is a demanding job; if

they're all made in one piece to begin with, the task is simpler, requires less handwork for fitting, and essentially amounts to higher quality at lower cost.

The monobloc system isn't the only way to build a high-quality gun, but it's an excellent way to build one that doesn't cost your left arm and your firstborn.

Providing quality is something that Beretta does very well indeed. Any Beretta gun—whether it's an assault rifle, a pistol, a pump, or autoloading shotgun, or a meticulously finished, best-quality double—is an admirable piece of work. The difference between a custom-built game gun and a production side-by-side or over/under is largely a matter of cosmetics and wood. Everything else, the steels and the functional mechanics, is identical. To my mind, that makes the lower-grade Berettas among the best buys on the world market.

And it's the world market that really tells the tale of Beretta's success. American sales of sporting guns are respectable but not remarkable; it's just the reverse nearly everywhere else. Over the past 20 years or so, the Italians have all but taken over the market for top-quality target guns, and Beretta is preeminent in almost every country except America, claiming a nearly 70-percent share of the European market. You won't see all that many Berettas on the firing lines at the big-time American tournaments, but don't let that fool you. The rest of the world shoots more Berettas than anything else.

The reason is simple: Beretta builds a superbly rugged, thoroughly reliable gun. That comes from a deep understanding of what a shotgun ought to be, a commitment to building it that way, and from having been around long enough to figure out how to do it.

A Canvas of Steel

R.L. Wilson &
Edward R. Ricciuti

Long, long ago, when massive glaciers still groaned over the lands that would one day be northern Europe, a man engraved the image of a woolly rhinoceros on the shadowed wall of a cave in what is now Dordogne, France. The vitality of the engraving suggests that the artist had a passionate feeling for the thunderous power of the animal he depicted. The extinct rhino—two horns hooking up from its snout, massive shoulders tensed, neck characteristically lowered—gives the impression of a primal force about to explode.

No one knows for sure just what compelled that ancient engraver to his task. Scholars theorize that the art had a ritualistic motivation—a desire to ensure success in the next hunt, perhaps, or to capture the fecundity that wild animals may have represented. But possibly he was moved by the same impulse that drives wildlife artists today—interest in, curiosity about, and admiration for wild animals. The engraver who handed us across the centuries his image of the woolly rhino was probably the artistic ancestor of craftsmen who today reproduce the likenesses of wildlife in the steel of sport-hunting firearms.

For the past five hundred years engravers have been turning firearms into canvases of steel, crafting them into pieces of fine art sometimes worth hundreds of thousands of dollars. Author and television nature commentator Roger Caras

This article first appeared in Audubon

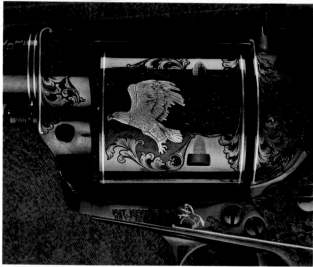

Beautiful images of wildlife, in gold inlay by Leonard Francolini, decorate cylinders of matched Colt Single-Action Army revolvers. (G. Allen Brown photos)

HIGHLY FINISHED WINCHESTER RIFLES.

A FANCY FINISHED MODEL 1894 WINCHESTER RIFLE.

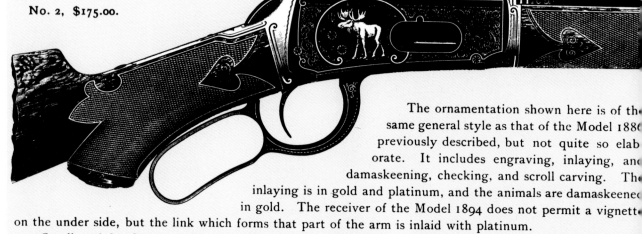

Style of Engraving

No. 2, $175.00.

The ornamentation shown here is of the same general style as that of the Model 1886 previously described, but not quite so elaborate. It includes engraving, inlaying, and damaskeening, checking, and scroll carving. The inlaying is in gold and platinum, and the animals are damaskeened in gold. The receiver of the Model 1894 does not permit a vignette on the under side, but the link which forms that part of the arm is inlaid with platinum.

Scroll and border engraving are prominent in the ornamentation of the receiver, it being set off by inlaid borders of gold and platinum. The barrel is engraved at the breech and muzzle, also inlaid with lines of platinum and gold. The hammer and rear sight base are engraved and inlaid with platinum.

As this catalog ad attests, Winchester's legendary lever-actions could once be ordered with elaborate ornamentation direct from the factory. The $175 catalog price for a fancy Model 1894 would become quite a bundle in today's money. (Courtesy of Winchester Museum, Buffalo Bill Historical Center, Cody, Wyoming.)

Action of a double rifle from the English gunmaker Holland & Holland has been engraved with detailed scenes of Old World ibex and urials. (Holland & Holland Ltd. photos)

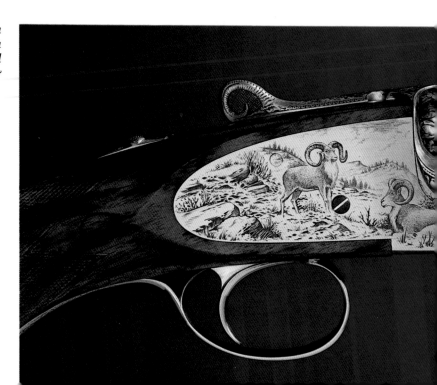

took note of this in his 1970 book, *Death as a Way of Life:*

"If the mechanical perfection of a firearm doesn't convince you that man loves his guns, perhaps art will. A modern rifle can cost anywhere from twenty-five dollars to several thousand, depending on style, place of manufacture, and embellishment. Older guns can sell for many, many thousands, and leading art museums display firearms as appropriate and significant works of art." Kings, presidents, and dictators, Caras observes, have been giving each other guns as gifts for centuries. "Gold-and-jewel-encrusted presentation models are sought after at auction today the way materpieces of painting and the choicest first editions are . . . Gold, silver, ivory, jade, stones both precious and semi-precious, have adorned endless examples of the gun craftsman's skill down through the centuries. Neither the can opener, the plow, nor even the automobile has been so honored. In plain fact man has ridden off to war and on his hunts with exquisite works of art for tools. It has not been an accident that this is so. It is a crystal-clear expression of a man's attitude toward his gun—love and respect.

Wildlife is certainly not the only theme of gun engravings. Guns have been decorated with all sorts of subjects. Many have only scrollwork, leafy patterns that Connecticut gun-engraver Leonard Francolini says originally may have represented foliage. But wild creatures probably have appeared in more firearms engravings than any other subject.

The hunter's desire for images of wild animals on his guns is probably akin to the one that prompted Ice Age cave art. Like him or not, the hunter possesses—or is even possessed by—a powerful fascination with the hunted. Some hunters will tell you that the ultimate reason they shiver with cold-numbed fingers on a deer stand or crouch pelted with sleet in a duck marsh is a yearning, difficult to articulate, to experience the quarry in a way that people who do not hunt will never understand.

From the beginning, gun engravers have portrayed the chase on metal. The images were generally quite stylized and frequently repeated from gun to gun: hunters and dogs pursuing stags, wild boar, or birds. The eagle was also a heraldic or symbolic animal on guns, appearing on American weapons since the Revolution.

Because hunting was a pursuit of the upper crust, not of craftsmen, early European engravers seldom saw in the flesh the animals they depicted. Instead they relied heavily on models, usually prints pulled from previously engraved arms. Some engravers, however, were able to observe animals in private zoos.

Most of today's gun engravers model their an-

imals after photographs in books and magazines and wildlife seen on television. Some of the very finest engravings are based on paintings by renowned artists that have been commissioned specifically for collaboration with the engraver.

In 1985, for example, the Southport, Connecticut, gunmaker Sturm, Ruger & Company announced a series of 21 rifles in its No. 1 model, each bearing gold inlays of a North American big-game species. The inlays are renderings of paintings by leading American wildlife artists, such as Gary Swanson, Greg Beecham, Leon Parson, Tom Beecham, Lee Cable, and Bob Kuhn.

Species shown on the guns, priced at $45,000 each, include grizzly bear, caribou, moose, mountain lion, mule deer, elk, and Rocky Mountain bighorn sheep. The bighorn was the motif for the initial gun in the series. The images inlaid on the gun by Phoenix engraver Franz Marktl were modeled after three sheep paintings by Gary Swanson. One scene decorates each side of the receiver, finished in gray. Another, the head of a magnificent ram, is on a cap atop the rifle's grip.

Among the painters whose work frequently is the basis for gun engravings is Guy Coheleach, who has roved the world observing wildlife in the field, lending outstanding vitality to his paintings. His insight into the behavior and anatomy of various wildlife species has been translated into truly

magnificent metal by a host of engravers.

Coheleach was commissioned by Safari Club International in 1984 to paint in oil a leopard resting on a tree limb. Australian-born Lynton McKenzie used the painting as the basis for his engraving of a customized Model 70 Winchester, a rifle which had its golden anniversary last year. The gun sold at auction for $201,000.

The "Leopard Gun," as it is called, is the last of a series of firearms engraved with the Big Five of African game—which also includes the elephant, rhinoceros, buffalo, and lion. Starting in 1982 a Big Five gun was auctioned each year at the club's International Hunters' Convention.

The auctions netted almost a half-million dollars, which went to the Safari Club International Conservation Fund. The fund has purchased habitat for bighorn sheep in California, supported reestablishment of moose in Colorado and antelope in Texas, helped finance the relocation of black rhinos in Zimbabwe, and provided equipment to Kenya's antipoaching effort.

One might expect that an organization devoted to hunting big game would make contributions to maintain the species its members prize, but the Safari Club has also sponsored research on non-game species. The club in 1979 and 1980 provided funds to the State of Michigan for controlled burning of the jack pines in which the Kirtland's

Guy Coheleach's leopard painting below served as the basis for the engraving (left) by Lynton McKenzie on the last of a series of firearms featuring the Big Five of African game. The Winchester Model 70 rifle was auctioned for $201,000 on behalf of the Safari Club International Conservation Fund, which has aided various types of wildlife ranging from black rhinos in Zimbabwe to Kirtland's warblers in Michigan. (Courtesy Safari Club International)

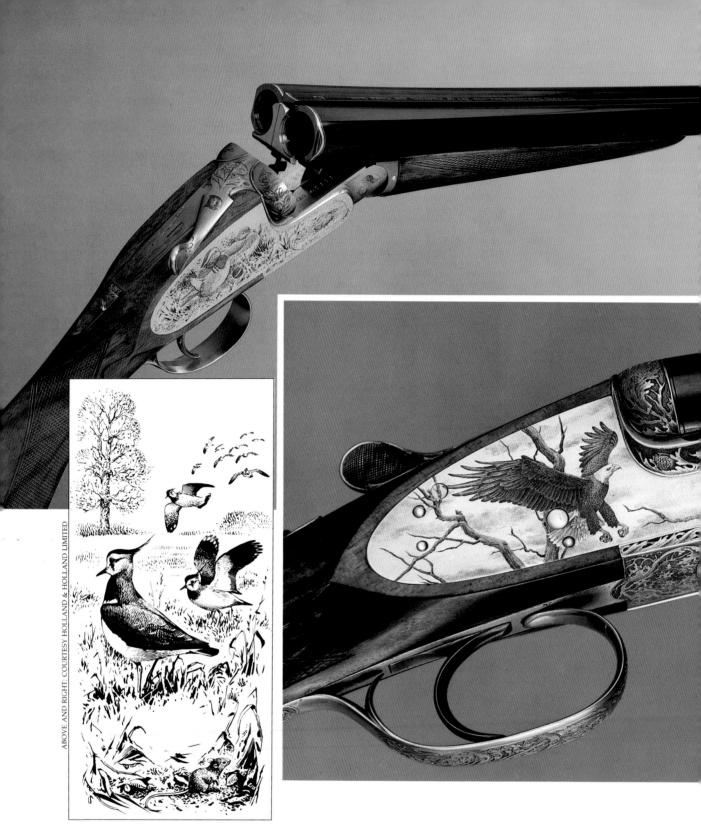

To commemorate the 75th anniversary of the 60,000-member British Association for Shooting and Conservation, Holland & Holland produced a set of six shotguns with engravings illustrating geese, ducks, wading birds, and shorebirds—plus mammals, fish, amphibians, and appropriate plantlife—from around the world. Original drawings, including landing lapwings with a field mouse in the grass (left), were by prominent British wildlife artist Roger McPhail. In addition to mandarin ducks on the lock, this side-by-side shotgun (above left) featured a woodcock, oystercatcher, shelduck, red-crested pochard, newt, and heathland plants. Above right: A shotgun built in Italy for artist Guy Coheleach was engraved by G. Pedersoli after the artist's own bald eagle drawings in a highly detailed technique with which each scene is composed of countless tiny cuts.

ENGRAVING BY G. PEDERSOLI; COURTESY MARIO ABBIATICO

warbler nests. The birds require trees about 6 feet high as nest sites, but forest-fire prevention has resulted in mature forests unsuitable for warbler breeding. Money contributed to the State of Wyoming was used for captive breeding of the peregrine falcon, part of an effort to reintroduce the bird into that state. The donation also helped defray the cost of obtaining areas for nesting sites once the falcons were freed.

Fine engraved guns have been used for conservation fundraising by several other organizations linked to sport hunting. The National Shooting Sports Foundation of Riverside, Connecticut, which is backed by firearms manufacturers, regularly auctions off prestigious engraved firearms. Money raised goes for educational programs, such as production and distribution of conservation filmstrips seen by more than 2.5 million schoolchildren yearly.

Many fine firearms have historical significance, but one auctioned off by National Shooting Sports last year had a history with an unusual twist. It was the two-millionth Automatic-5 shotgun to come off the Browning production line, an event which occurred in 1970. Removed from the line, the gun was placed in the hands of engravers who were to prepare it for presentation to President Richard M. Nixon. He, in turn, had agreed to donate it to the Smithsonian Institution. There it would become a part of a memorial to the famed gunmaker and designer John M. Browning, whose automatic rifle was carried by the infantrymen of two wars and, until the Vietnam era, was the anchor of Marine Corps fire teams. However, for political reasons, the presentation was never made, and the Smithsonian never received the gun.

The Browning arms company kept the gun in its vaults for fifteen years while looking for a meaningful use for it, then finally gave it to the National Shooting Sports Foundation for a sealed-bid auction. The gun brought $50,001.

The National Wild Turkey Federation, a major supporter of wild turkey restoration programs, is another organization that gains funds from engraved guns. In 1984 it auctioned for $25,000 a one-of-a-kind Ithaca Model No. 37 shotgun with gold inlays of wild turkeys by William H. Mains of Las Vegas.

Not all engraved guns sold to help wildlife are unique creations. Ducks Unlimited, which holds continual fund-raising dinners across the country, auctions and raffles guns that are of good quality and produced in limited numbers but that are by no means the stuff of which museum collections are made.

No matter. Ducks Unlimited does it big. All told, from 1973 to 1986, DU auctioned off 52,525 guns that raised almost $58 million. That's big

Gary Swanson paintings of bighorn rams were carved in relief and inlaid in gold on the first in a series of 21 Ruger No. 1 rifles portraying North American big game. This single-shot rifle brought $52,000 in a Christie's New York auction. The engraver was Frank Marktl.

RY R. SwANson
©'83

bucks for ducks, if you will, and an indication of how many people prize engraved firearms.

Most of the firearms produced in the United States today do not carry decorative engraving, although mass-produced guns did before 1850. The number of professional engravers working in this country, therefore, is small—about one hundred and fifty. Some engravers are employed by firearms manufacturers. Colt Firearms, for instance, has a Custom Gun Shop at its Hartford, Connecticut, plant. Others are freelancers, working for both manufacturers and private individuals.

A handful of American engravers are self-taught, but most served apprenticeships either under established engravers or while working for a manufacturer. Many did not begin their careers by working on firearms. Leonard Francolini, for instance, began as a die cutter.

The jewelry business has been the origin of some of the best-known engravers, including the so-called "dean of American engravers," A.A. White of Cape Cod, Massachusetts. White was trained in the jewelry trade in his native Attleboro, Massachusetts, and at the Rhode Island School of Design. He has produced presentation guns for five U.S. Presidents and many prominent personalities in industry, entertainment, and finance.

The process of engraving a gun is extremely detailed. First the engraver draws the image on the gun. The next step is to cut fine lines in the steel. These are made first with slender chisels, called scribers, of a steel slightly harder than that of the gun. The engraver carefully taps the handle of the scriber with a jeweler's hammer, and a fine shaving of steel peels away from the cut.

Scribers are used to produce the basic design and shading of an engraving. Details are made with a graver, which is a shortened scriber with a bulbous handle. Because steel is so hard, the engraver can attain much more detail than is possible, for instance, in wood.

Once the design is completed, the engraving may be inlaid with a precious metal such as gold. Lampblack is rubbed into the cuts. Beeswax on paper picks up the design when pressed on the lampblack and burnished. The image is transferred to a thin sheet of gold. Using the tools of a jeweler, the engraver cuts out the image and pounds it into the cuts on the gun. The inlaid gold is then sculpted into final shape.

The finest engravings—those on firearms such as the Leopard Gun—can take more than a thousand hours to complete. Many such firearms are destined to become museum pieces. As objects of fine art, they are treated as gingerly as a great painting. Ironically, most of the finest hunting firearms in the world are never fired, nor even cocked, much less taken into the field.

A $900-Dollar Air Gun

Tim McMurray & Dennis O'Flaherty

Until very recently, if you said "air gun" to the average American sportsman, the reaction would be predictable: "Ah . . . air gun? Sure, I had one of those when I was (eight) (ten), and my (Mom) (Dad) took it away when I shot the (kitchen window) (neighbor's dog) (Fuller Brush man)." For millions of sportsmen, their first shooting experience came with a Daisy, Crosman, or some other brand of air gun. Years ago, of course, everyone regarded BB guns and pellet rifles as "kid's stuff"—something youngsters could use to cut their shooting teeth before graduating to cartridge firearms.

Within the last couple of years, however, this situation has been changing drastically—so much so that over the next five years, virtually every serious American shooter will own at least one high-quality air rifle or air pistol.

So how do you explain this renaissance of air guns? Before we explore the weightier reasons behind the air gun's revival, let's state the bottom line first: Air guns are fun to shoot. In fact, for pure shooting pleasure, they are really hard to beat!

As for those weightier factors, most center around the shrinkage of elbow room that characterizes modern American life. Because of various demographic, legal, and just plain financial reasons, it's getting harder and harder to shoot cartridge firearms as freely as we used to.

For those of us who are incurable shooters and gun nuts, the air gun offers an inexhaustible source of shooting pleasure that's largely free of restrictions. The "hottest" air gun is, after all, less powerful than even the least powerful cartridge guns. While that may have some drawbacks on a sporting level, it does lead to a lower social perception of danger and a blessed reduction in the "busybody" factor.

Two hundred years ago, air guns were definitely not low-powered items. Back then, pneumatic rifles and pistols were easily capable of killing a stag or a man, propelling balls of as much as .60 caliber at lethal force to ranges of 100 yards or more. The fact that such a shot could be achieved with a somewhat smaller report than was possible with gunpowder, and even more important, with no telltale cloud of white smoke, gave the air gun a military potential which the Austrians who fought Napoleon at the Battle of Wagram exploited successfully. Of course, it took an enormous amount of physical labor to pump the reservoirs of those early pneumatic weapons to the point where they could fire 20 to 30 full-powered shots. This problem, along with the introduction of powder-firing guns, eventually led to the air gun's demise as a fighting weapon.

At the turn of the century, restrictions on the use of cartridge firearms in Europe and England made air guns increasingly popular. Unfortunately, governments then turned their attention to restricting the power of air guns themselves. This ended the widespread use of pneumatic power for sporting arms. Even the use of CO_2 guns, which had been pioneered in Europe in the 1880s and 1890s, fell to the regulators' axes.

In Europe, primary emphasis from the beginning of this century has been on spring-piston air guns. Familiar to us in its simplest form as the BB gun, this is the propulsion system in which a stroke of a cocking lever forces a spring-loaded piston along a compression tube until it's engaged by the sear assembly. Pulling the trigger allows it to zoom down the tube, compressing the air ahead of it until it blasts the pellet (or BB) out the barrel.

Until recently, the spring-loaded piston has been the lowest-powered of the three air gun systems. The other two are the pneumatic, which uses air that has been pre-compressed and then stored; and the CO_2, which uses the gas either in bulk form or in soda-syphon bulbs.

Over the past decades, European and English technicians have refined spring-piston guns until they are capable of anything from the kind of one-ragged-hole-at-33-feet shooting, which is accom-

This article first appeared in Sporting Classics

Not your ordinary air guns (from top): Sharp Model "Ace" Hunter Deluxe, .177 pump pneumatic with Bushnell 4× scope (about $300); Feinwerkbau Model 600, .177 single-stroke pneumatic, imported by Beeman Precision Arms (about $900); and Weihrauch 77K, .22 spring piston with 6× scope (about $800). (Art Carter photo)

plished with recoilless match rifles at the Olympics, to 100-yard hits on a 2-inch kill zone. (It should be pointed out, however, that to own an air rifle capable of that kind of performance in Europe generally requires some kind of firearms license, not easily obtained.)

Henry Marcus Quackenbush was America's first air gun manufacturer. The Quackenbush air

rifle became so popular in the 1870s and 1880s that it was introduced in Europe. There, its basic design laid the groundwork for many future developments in spring-piston airguns.

In the U.S., the spring-piston power plant was largely the domain of BB guns, most of which were intended for preteen shooters. The early teen, precartridge market was serviced by pneu-

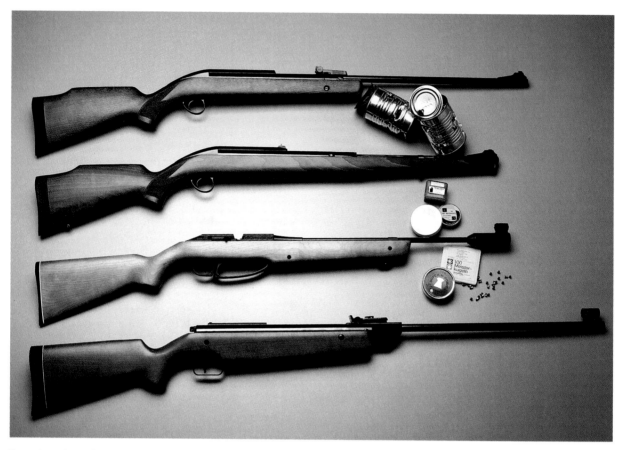

Ranging about $200 to $300, from top: BSA (Birmingham Small Arms) Mercury Challenger, .177 spring piston; BSA Airsporter Stutzen, .22 under-lever cock spring piston (does not have an iron sight, but comes with a shock resistant mounting rail for a telescopic sight); Daisy Powerline 953, .177 single-pump pneumatic; Dynamit Nobel RWS Model 45, .177 spring piston. (Art Carter photo)

matics and CO_2s, which were capable of greater power.

Some of the early American pneumatics and CO_2s were truly remarkable guns, such as the various models of the Sheridan pump-up and the Crosman CO_2 rifles produced under Philip Hahn. (His single-shot 160 was one of the finest sporting air rifles ever made, and his Model 400 10-shot repeater was a truly outstanding design.) Unfortunately, because these air guns were used primarily by kids, they tended to get pretty rough treatment and little maintenance. This led to a completely undeserved reputation for unreliability (in this case, consumers rather than producers were at fault.) In addition, stock design and triggers were generally poor enough to betray what were inherently very well-designed firing systems.

The fact is that many of these "youth market guns," when equipped with decent adjustable sights, improved stocks, and well-tuned triggers, can deliver standards of performance that equal top-of-the-line European spring guns. McMurray

& Son has been re-equipping various classic American designs for some years, and finally, other U.S. air gunsmiths are following suit. It is important to make this point, so that you won't assume that our discussion of quality air guns applies only to fancy European brands. Indeed, before you make a purchase, ask a local expert to show you what can be done with customized American air guns as well as with the European models.

The the first-time buyer of an adult air gun faces an almost stupefying variety of rifles and pistols—and more than a hundred kinds of pellets. To make things even more difficult, all of the different air gun models and calibers are enshrouded in a baffling smoke cloud of advertising hype and quasi-scientific information. One article can't quite cover all you need to know about air guns, but perhaps we can provide enough basic information to demystify the subject.

Prices for air guns range from about $100 for some of the less expensive, but still excellent offerings from Daisy, Crosman, Sheridan, and Benjamin to the $700-$900 range for some of the handcrafted European models. Surprisingly, a fine air rifle or pistol usually costs more than a comparable firearm. The reason is that it's more complicated to manufacture, with many more parts and much finer tolerances. For example, a Crosman CO_2 version of the Colt M1911 A1 automatic pistol (a six-shot gas-powered repeater) has three times as many parts as the cartridge gun.

To help you determine the type of power plant you'll want, try to shoot each of three air gun propulsion systems. Most air-gun dealers have indoor ranges which you can use for this purpose.

Spring-piston air guns include some of the most beautiful, sophisticated, and powerful models on today's market. At the very peak of the spring-gun range is the Venom conversion approach from Venom Arms of England, which takes the Weihrauch HW77 and HW80 (widely available here in their standard forms) and reworks them internally to increase their power and smoothness beyond all recognition. Their cosmetics are likewise excellent, with highly polished metal and well-designed stocks made of fine European walnut. Even the standard HW77, available from Beeman and others, or the R1 from Beeman (a close cousin of the newer HW80), are shooting machines of the highest order.

A number of fine English and German spring guns deserve serious consideration. The thing to remember here is that generally, increased power means increased weight due to heavier springs, larger compression chambers, heavier pistons, and so on.

Most of these heavier, high-powered air guns also have more recoil. Venom, however, has made some remarkable advancements in reducing recoil. Its latest HW77models deliver 15 to 18 ft./lbs. with virtually no kick. A number of production air guns give very good power with low recoil. Some models include the new BSA Mercury Magnum, the Feinwerkbau 124 and 127, and the Crosman Challenger 6500, which is none other than the Anschutz 335 under an American name. The Anschutz, incidentally, has always been underrated but is a delightful shooter of excellent quality.

When hunting, remember that spring-piston guns tend to become spring-bound if left cocked. Venom has discovered some mysterious process which makes it possible to leave their guns cocked; but quite frankly, veteran air gunners shudder at the thought, no matter what innovations have been devised in spring design. Best to develop the habit of carrying the gun broken, with a pellet in the breech, but not cocked. That way you can still get off a fast shot.

Pneumatics can be carried at a full charge with-

Tyrolean-style cheekpieces, valuable for consistent eye-to-sights alignment, have long been popular in Europe. Shown here are Venom conversions of the Webley Omega in .177 caliber (below, top) and the HW 80 in .22 caliber (center). Because of the adult market, current air-gun designs may also reflect hot firearms trends. The Daystate reservoir pneumatic in .22 caliber (bottom) has been "bullpupped" by Venom Arms.

This Crossman Challenger Model 84, .177 caliber CO$_2$ match rifle was used in Olympic competition.

out any danger to the gun. Along with the pump-up guns, they offer yet another advantage—variable power. A couple of pumps enables you to harry the local beer can population; pumping it to the maximum allows you to bring home a rabbit for the stewpot. Before you go afield, however, punch out some paper with varying numbers of pumps, but at a fixed distance. That way, you will know how different power levels affect the point of impact.

Crosman makes a high-quality, but low-priced .22 pump-up in its Model 1; Benjamin has a number of popular models including the 340 Series single shots and the 3100 and 3200 magazine rifles. We rather like the 3200 in .22 caliber, which has a rifled barrel and a magazine capable of holding 85 very hard-hitting balls. Sheridan has one of the all-time greats in its .20 caliber Blue Streak. Lastly, the Japanese firm Sharp has introduced a new rifle

called the Sharp Ace Target, which has an excellent adjustable trigger and offers considerable power with fairly reasonable pumping force. For example, four pumps will deliver 540 feet per second with a standard-weight, .22, six will give 640 fps (feet per second), eight will yield 705, and 12 will produce 820.

CO$_2$ air guns have been given a bad rap in this country. When foreign spring-guns were introduced, one of the marketing strategies was to fault CO$_2$ guns for unreliable seals. Not true! Anyone who can follow instructions and provide normal care will have a gun that works like a charm until he's too old to pull the trigger. In fact, if you can find any of the old CO$_2$ guns, buy them! Many local service stations can repair them, or you can send them to the Crosman factory in New York.

As for current production, the only sporting rifle available with CO$_2$ power is the Sheridan F, a handy, well-designed little gun that comes from the factory a little short-changed by its stock and sights, and a little underpowered with one CO_2 cylinder. McMurray & Son increases the Sheridan's power by using a dual-CO_2-bulb system. It also refits the rifle with a custom-designed Fajen stock and high-quality optics. But even as it comes from the factory, the Sheridan is an enjoyable and accurate backyard plinker and target gun.

At the opposite end of the spectrum in terms of price and sophistication is the Crosman 84 Match Rifle, one of the most innovative guns in recent times. Developed especially for the 1984 Olympics in which 10-meter air rifle shooting was included for the first time, the 84 is a super match rifle, capable of up to 750 fps, with variable power output, and a digital readout that monitors the amount of gas pressure. The rifle fills on bulk rather than using soda-type bulbs, and is capable of 100 shots before refilling.

The same might be said of the two CO_2 match pistols—the FWB Model 2 and the Walther CP2. Pistol champion Don Nygord used a CP2 to wipe up the opposition in the Championship of the Americas; meanwhile, the FWB has been doing well in Europe. It seems likely, in fact, that CO_2 will supplant both spring-piston power and single-stroke pneumatics for international pistol competition. We tend to favor the Walther. Its valve-release system is superior to the FWB's, plus it comes in a nice Samsonite case. Because of import quirks, the CP2 sells for $100 less than the FWB in the U.S., but $100 more in Europe. Both guns are superb, however.

Finally, don't ignore Crosman's delightful CO_2 lookalike pistols—the MKI and II standing in for the Ruger MKI and II, and the 357 for the Colt Python. The 357 is available with an 8-inch barrel, a simple, but functional pistol scope, and a supply of extra six-shot cylinders. It's quite accurate, with power approaching 500 fps in .177. Only somebody with a heart of pure stone could sit in the back yard with one of these and a supply of tin cans and not feel uplifted!

Whether you plink cans or hunt rabbits, you should know a few facts about air gun performance. A typical BB gun, for instance, shoots a five-grain steel ball at 350 fps, yielding about 1.4 ft./lbs. of muzzle energy. One of the new spring-piston air guns, like the .177 Venom HW 80 Vantage, can deliver a 10-grain Beeman Ramjet pellet at 950 fps, for an energy output of nearly 20 ft./lbs. The most powerful of the currently available air guns (the Daystate Pneumatic Reservoir Rifle) has a peak capacity in .22 caliber of 35-40 ft./lbs. of muzzle energy. By comparison, a standard-velocity .22 Long Rifle slug fired from a rifle will give you about 100 ft./lbs.

What counts in good air-gun ballistics is pellet

Today's air guns are capable of taking a wide range of small game in states where game laws permit air-gun hunting. This gobbler was taken with a head shot with a scoped Sheridan pneumatic.

Air-gun pellet design today reflects an effort to maximize efficiency from relatively low power of an air or gas charge. Pointed, rounded, flat-headed and hollow-point designs are designed for a wide range of air-gunning tasks.

speed *plus* weight. Despite the fact that U.S. shooters have traditionally used .177 caliber pellets, the .22 will do a much better job for outdoor shooting. The reason is that heavier projectiles have flatter trajectories, are less subject to wind deflection, and arrive on target with greater energy simply because they started with more kinetic energy due to their weight.

An air gun shooting a standard-weight .22 pellet with a minimum initial velocity of 625 fps will be quite dependable up to 60 yards. However, many fine air guns are capable of putting a pellet on target beyond that distance.

A number of first class scopes are available to enhance your marksmanship at longer distances. Tasco, for instance, makes a full range of air gun scopes, beginning with a 4×32 compact and ending with a $3\text{-}9 \times 50$ behemoth.

When selecting an air gun, keep in mind that extra power can be fun and useful, but it really isn't all that necessary. Many English air gunners are keen hunters (preferred quarry includes wood pigeons, rabbits, and squirrels), yet they are restricted by law to air rifles producing no more than

The German firm Feinwerkbau produces an Olympic-class target pistol powered by CO_2. The detachable CO_2 reservoir (shown with accessories and tools) permits several hundred shots in .177 caliber on one filling.

12 ft./lbs. and pistols producing no more than 6. (This means about 625 fps for rifles in .22 and 825 fps in .177, using standard-weight pellets.) Thirty yards is considered an average distance for a hunting shot, though 50-yard shots and longer are common. Regardless of the distance, a well-placed shot is essential when hunting small game—which brings us to the subject of accuracy.

The mere existence of Olympic-class .177 caliber target rifles has suffused the whole air-gun question with a mystic glow of micrometer-measured accuracy, all of which is patently silly. The only thing that really makes for accurate shooting is one hell of a lot of practice, no matter what sort of gun you use. Many kids who put three or four zillion rounds through their trusty Sheridans can outshoot grown-ups using European match rifles.

Here, to be sure, is the wondrous virtue of air guns: You can do precisely as much shooting as you please in your living room or back yard—just about anyplace where you can put up a good, nonrebounding backstop. And, you won't spend much money (about one penny per shot) or attract a lot of annoying attention.

This has been, of necessity, a perfunctory tour of one of the most vital, enjoyable, and creative areas in the whole shooting sports spectrum. Please believe that anything we've said is to be regarded purely as well-meant starting-point advice and is not "graven in stone." One of the nicest things about the air-gun scene is that it's a little less rigid, a lot more quirky, and considerably more open to argument and experimentation than the firearms scene.

We'll make you a bet: If you pick your first air gun carefully with an eye on how much you enjoy shooting it and nothing else, you will rapidly find yourself among one of the fastest-growing groups in American sports today—the adult air gunners!

Tim McMurray, proprietor of McMurray & Son in Inglewood, California, represents the third generation of McMurrays involved in air-gun research, modification, and merchandizing. Dennis O'Flaherty, McMurray's advertising manager, is a reformed academic and word mechanic who finds airgunning good medicine for a stressful existence.

The Double Rifle

Alex Brant

In the late 1700s, European settlers, who had lived on the fringes of sub-Saharan Africa since the days of Prince Henry the Navigator, began to look to the interior of their "Dark Continent." *Trekboeren*, Duch-African farmers of the 1760s, left the security of Capetown and pressed up the Great Karoo to settle in the vicinity of present-day Graf-Reinet. Portuguese and Spanish explorers charted the Limpopo and Zambezi rivers in the east and followed the Congo eastward to the shores of Lake Tanganyika. Englishmen worked from both ends of the continent, searching in the north for the source of the Nile and sending settlers up the Great Fish River in South Africa.

The risks incurred by these men, and by their women as well, were very real and very often fatal. Malaria, sleeping sickness, and a hundred other diseases took their toll. So did poisonous snakes and insects for whose venom there was no antidote. And most black Africans, particularly in the interior, associated nonblacks with the slave trade, and were understandably hostile.

But these courageous pioneers found things that made the risk worthwhile. The farmers found land to grow crops and build houses, to raise families, and to call "home." The scientists and adventurers found new areas to study and to map, new routes of commerce and new markets for their goods. And both groups found something truly grand—game animals in variety and numbers never before seen by European eyes.

They also found, whether settler or treasure seeker, that the guns that served so well at home were no match for African game animals. What would reliably defend against a marauding wolf or down a lordly stag would anger a leopard and drive a buffalo to seek terrible revenge. The problem even in the largest rifles was insufficient striking power.

The solution in those days of black-powder propellant and lead bullets was to increase bore diameter; to build guns of 8-, or 4-, or even 2 gauge firing round balls that weighed 2, 4, or 8 ounces

Built in the late 19th century, an 8-gauge double by Charles Osborne & Co., London, typifies the black-powdered heavy-game gun.

each. These earliest "smashers" were muzzle-loading, predating the introduction of breech-loading guns by about 15 years. Usually they were smoothbore (though we shall refer to them as "rifles") and of single barrel design.

Though their useful life was short, about 20 years, some of these small cannons continued to be used for quite a long time. Frederick Courtney Selous, who explored the area north of the Transvaal and south of the Congo basin between 1870 and 1890, used a Dutch-made 4-gauge rifle during his early travels.

This article first appeared in American Rifleman

Sir Samuel Baker, who began his explorations on the island of Ceylon, did so armed with a 4-gauge "rifle" that really was a rifle. Built to Baker's design, the rifle had two-groove rifling and used a 3-ounce belted ball or 4-ounce conical bullet that was also fitted mechanically to the bore. The charge for this behemoth was 16 drams of powder. The rifle weighed 21 pounds, and it was *not* Baker's legendary "Baby."

"Baby" was born nearly two decades later for use on the 1864 expedition into present-day Uganda, during which Baker discovered Lake Albert. The exact diameter of Baby's bore is uncertain. Baby was probably a 4-bore, though it is generally said to have been a 2-gauge. Baker described it as "firing a half-pound percussion shell." He also described the rifle as "an instrument of torture to the hunter," and complained that it weighed less than 20 pounds, which was too light for a gun firing a "charge of 10 drams of powder."

Baker also admitted to dreading his own rifle even though he was accustomed to firing heavy charges of powder and to severe recoil. His Arab guides, Baker wrote in an 1866 book telling of his trip, could not fire this rifle and looked upon it with awe. They called the gun "Jenna al Mootfah," meaning child of a cannon. Baker named the gun "Baby," and he noted that when "Baby" cried, the result was always fatal.

"Baby" notwithstanding, technology caught up with the extra-large bore rifles, and caught up quickly. The development of industrial processes for making steel enabled gunmakers of 1855 to '65 to build barrels strong enough to use conical bullets and prodigious powder charges, and to make them light enough that two barrels could be fitted

The earliest cartridge heavy-game guns used bulleted shotshells like Holland & Holland's famed Paradox.

together—something that shotgun makers had been doing for years. Breechloaders then coming into their own enabled makers to build rapidly reloadable, real rifles (with rifling the full length of the bore) and the so-called "rifled-muzzle" guns such as the Holland & Holland "Paradox" or Westley Richards "Explora." All using conical bullets, they brought a reduction in weight from 20 to 25 pounds for an 1850s vintage 4-gauge, to 14 or 16 pounds for a 10- or 8-bore of 1880.

The greatest advance in double rifle technology, after steel, was the perfection of smokeless rifle powder and, along with it, the development of jacketed bullets. From 1888, when the British government adopted Cordite as a propellant, guns and ammunition could be made that would duplicate—even exceed—the killing power of the 4-bores without the need for tremendous physical size. A .500 Nitro Express, 3 inch, for example, would propel a 570-grain jacketed bullet at 2150 feet per second, for 5850 ft.-lbs. (foot pounds) of energy. A 4-bore firing a 1250-grain round ball could achieve the same energy level using a charge of 328 grains of black powder, but at what cost? The .500 was a 10-pound double, with two shots instantly available, and either of its two bullets would penetrate better than the single lead ball launched from a 4-bore.

Between 1889, when Kynoch introduced ammunition loaded with "Axite"—the firm's proprietary version of government-used Cordite—and 1898, when the .450 Nitro was introduced, most of the lighter black-powder big-game loadings were adapted to the use of smokeless powder and bullets that were at least partially jacketed.

Neither the introduction of steel barrels in place of iron nor the advent of smokeless powder spelled instant doom for the super large-bore guns. The 4-bores particularly remained popular in many areas until well into the 20th century, and Kynoch loaded cartridges for 4-bore rifles using Cordite propellant into the 1920s.
—Editors

The .450 Nitro Express, 3¼ inch, introduced by John Rigby in 1898, was the first modern "elephant cartridge." Rigby's .450 used a 480-grain jacketed bullet at 2150 feet per second to deliver just less than 5000 ft.-lbs. of energy. Selous, who had by then long since retired his 4-gauge in favor of a pair of 10-bores, promptly put the 10s out to pasture and became one of the earliest proponents of Rigby guns and Rigby's new cartridge.

The British are a funny lot. Rigby's .450 was a great success, but instead of standardizing upon it, British arms makers raced to create a flood of proprietary rounds, each like Rigby's but different. Holland & Holland introduced the .500/.450 Magnum Nitro Express to compete with the Rigby offering. Jeffery came up with a real honey, calling it the .450 No. 2, Nitro Express, 3½ inch.

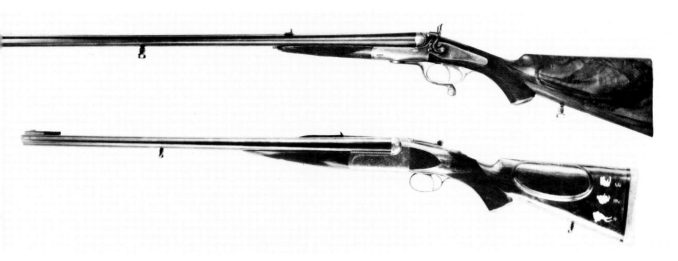

Double rifle evolution is evidenced in a Purdey .500 Black Powder Express (top) contrasted to a .577 Nitro Express from Westley Richards & Co.

The .450s were supplanted in rather short order, and for an odd reason. In 1907, in an attempt to deny rebels in India and in the Sudan a source of ammunition components for the Martini-Henry rifles they used, the British government banned use of .450-bore rifles in those locations. The .450s remained popular where permitted—in fact the Rigby-designed .450 Nitro Express was still in production when Kynoch ceased production of centerfire cartridges in the mid-'60s—but the effect of the ban was to spawn a new series of big-game cartridges over .45 caliber.

Rigby brought out a .470 said to have been designed by Joseph Lang. Holland & Holland went to a .465, like the Rigby/Lang cartridge, necked down from .500-3¼-inch cases. Westley Richards used the .500 case to make up its .476 Nitro Express, 3¼ inch. Jeffery offered the .475 Nitro Express, No. 2.

The proliferation of proprietary cartridges had its advantages as long as all the makers were active, but it was a long-run disaster. Consolidation of the British gunmaking industry, which began in the 1930s and continued following World War II, meant that orders for proprietary cartridges decreased both in frequency and in quantity. The ammunition makers, for sound reasons, discontinued manufacture of those calibers for which the demand was uneconomical until, by 1955, only four Nitro Express cartridges—the .450, .500/.465, .470, and .500, 3¼ inch—remained. After Kynoch ceased its production of centerfire metallic cartridges around 1966, the source—even of the four survivors—dried up until recently.

For about the last 10 years, Brass Extrusion Laboratories, Ltd. (B.E.L.L.) in Bensenville, IL. has made an increasing variety of basic cases from which the old African cartridges can be formed. B.E.L.L.'s founder, Jim Bell, got into the business because of his efforts to procure ammunition for a .369-inch Purdey double rifle, and he has done his best to satisfy all comers including owners of .577 and .600 Nitro Express rifles. Today, in addition to new brass cases, B.E.L.L. loads ammunition for the .500/.465 and the .470 Nitro Express and stocks Australian Woodleigh bullets.

Helping along in the struggle to keep the old double rifles working, Huntington Die Specialties, P.O. Box 991, Oroville, CA 95965, will make reloading dies. Randy Brooks of Barnes Bullets, P.O. Box 215, American Fork, UT 84003, makes softpoints and solids for most bore diameters from that of the .416 Rigby up to .620-inch-diameter 900-grain bullets for the .600 Nitro Express. Finally, there are a few commercial reloaders, among them A.F. Sailer, P.O. Box "L," Owen, WI 54460, and Gene Enterkin at The Powder Horn, P.O. Box 114, Patty Drive, Cusseta, GA 31805, who can provide reloaded ammunition for some of the old "African" calibers.

Now that the important components are once again available, I intend to save up my pennies until I have enough to have Shotguns of Ulm build me a .470 double rifle. With such a rifle in hand, or on order, I can justify buying enough B.E.L.L. brass and Barnes bullets to last three lifetimes. That way I'll be set for the one lifetime that is allotted to me. It's not that I fear scarcity, mind you; I simply believe in sufficiency. Another advantage to my plan is that I will be able to order, simultaneously, a set of light barrels for .30/06 or .300 Winchester Magnum, and a set of shotgun barrels, and get a lot of use and versatility out of one gun.

With all this talk of specially ordered guns, discontinued cartridges, and scarce components—not to mention cost—one might wonder, "Why?" Why go to all the trouble when a bolt rifle in .458 Winchester Magnum will do just as well?

The answer for those who have been bitten by the double bug is that there is something about a double rifle that a bolt gun, no matter how well contrived, just can't match. Handling is a big part of it. The gunmakers thought of it as reliability, and reliability was all-important to them. With a double rifle a hunter can get off two shots quicker than the fastest bolt gunner and with virtually no chance of a jam.

As Purdey put it, "It is one thing to shoot grouse and another to hunt dangerous game when, at times, the safety of the sportsman's own skin depends on the absolute efficiency and reliability of the gun he is handling."

Double rifles, whether from Purdey's or the creations of other masters like Boss, Holland & Holland, Rigby, or Westley Richards were built to satisfy those requirements. They were made to be handy. If they tend to be a bit barrel heavy, it is so that they come back on target faster, and

they swing like no bolt-action could ever do. Take a 26-inch barrelled side-by-side or over/under shotgun sometime and put it beside a bolt-action rifle with a similar-length barrel. See how much shorter the two-barrel gun is. Heft both guns, swing them both. See which is quicker. Balance, shortness of barrels, and weight of barrels all make the double quick. So does the tang safety found on virtually all British double guns.

The real art of making a double rifle lies in the maker's ability to regulate the barrels so that at a given range the bullets converge and shoot to the sights. Rigby, in an old catalog, gives the best explanation of how this is done.

"Many sportsmen," wrote Rigby, "think that all a gunmaker has to do when he builds a double rifle is to set the barrels together so that the two axes of the bores are parallel. . . . We only wish the matter were so simple, but in actual fact, the two axes are seldom, if ever, parallel.

"When the right barrel is discharged the recoil very naturally throws the rifle outward to the right. This means that the axis of the right barrel will be pointing to the right of the line of original

This Holland & Holland catalog drawing published about 1910–12 illustrated the need for firepower. As the rhino hunter fires, a second rifle is at hand.

aim when the bullet actually leaves the muzzle. When the left barrel is fired an identical movement takes place in the opposite direction. In other words, the two barrels naturally tend to shoot apart. In order to counteract this tendency, the barrels of all double rifles are set so that the axes are converging in the direction of the muzzle. The great difficulty in regulating a double is the determination of the correct amount of divergence. This will vary for every individual rifle, so no two barrels behave identically on firing.

"The barrels are first of all set at a slightly convergent angle and brazed together at the breech ends. They are then held together at the muzzle with a wedge, and lumps of packing are inserted at various points between the breech and muzzle.

"The attainment of the best possible shooting from each barrel is chiefly dependent on the positions of these pieces of packing, and can only be ascertained by experiment. There is no golden rule on which to work, merely experience and the skillful cunning of a master hand. When both barrels have been made to shoot their best, independently of each other they are regulated to shoot together by the alteration of the position of the wedge at the muzzle," the gunmaker wrote.

Rigby went on to explain how its system of regulation took into account the difference in conditions that might be encountered when a rifle made in England was used in the tropics, and to explain how changing velocity or bullet weight could adversely affect regulation.

Rigby waited until after barrels had been regulated, then sighted the rifle by adjusting the rear sight. The company recommended, also, that a purchaser shoot his rifle at its range to confirm that it was correctly zeroed.

The classic double rifle has detachable sidelocks, with a spare set in the best guns. The advantage of sidelocks is that they can be removed—however easily—and the innards cleaned in the field.

Boxlock double rifles are less expensive to manufacture than are sidelock guns, but they are more difficult to repair in the field. On the other hand, the extra wood in the stock makes a boxlock gun stronger and more robust than its sidelock counterpart. Westley Richards made a boxlock gun that did have removable locks. A hinged plate under the frame held the lock mechanisms in place and opening the plate allowed the locks to drop into the shooter's hand. This was a very sturdy design with all the best features of both systems.

Some double rifle users prefer plain extractors over automatic, selective ejectors—but the author does not. The big plus given for extractors is that they are quiet if one needs to open the gun. The hunter only opens his gun to reload and has already fired at least one disquieting shot when he does so. Besides, with ejectors, by holding two

extra cartridges between the fingers of his left hand, the double shooter can fire twice, open the gun, reload, close the gun, and be ready to fire twice more while the average gunner is getting the fired cases out of his non-ejector rifle.

The principal British makers of double rifles were Bland, Boss, Evans, Gibbs, Grant (independently and as partner with Joseph Lang), Greener, Holland & Holland, Jeffery, Powell, Purdey, Rigby, Westley Richards, and Woodward. Today most of these makers are inactive, but Holland, Rigby, Westley Richards, and Purdey are still in business.

Teddy Roosevelt chose a Holland & Holland .450 for his African hunting expedition of 1909 and waxed enthusiastic about it.

"For heavy game like rhinoceros and buffalo," he wrote, "the heavy Holland .450 was unquestionably the proper weapon."

Roosevelt's confidence to the contrary, the Indian gun law that banned the .450 was probably a blessing in disguise because it brought about cartridges like the .465 Holland and .470 Nitro Express. Most think of the .470 as *the* double rifle cartridge, with the .465 almost as popular. In fact both John "Pondoro" Taylor and Sanchez-Arino preferred the .465. John Hunter, who probably killed more of the "Big Five" dangerous game animals than any other 20th-century hunter, was most comfortable with a .500.

Neither is the .577 a gun to sneeze at. Sir Samuel Baker, whose "Baby" started the whole thing, is reputed to have purchased the first .577 ever produced by Holland & Holland. James Sutherland (*Adventures of an Elephant Hunter*) used a pair of single-trigger Westley Richards .577s to bag 1,500 tuskers. Arthur Neumann (*Elephant Hunting in East Equatorial Africa*) and Maj. Anderson (*African Safaris*) both used the .577, and both are supposed to have bagged upwards of 1,500 elephants. George Rushby (*No More The Hunter*) and Peter Dawson, whose bags were a scant 1,000 elephants, both favored the .577.

Today's hunter does not buy a double rifle with the object of shooting a thousand elephants. There aren't enough elephants for that, and hunters were among the first to realize it. Today's hunter will be hard put to shoot a hundred rounds at game animals of all types during a lifetime. Nowadays, he who buys a double rifle buys it for the history, the elegance, and the romance it represents.

Anyone can buy a bolt-action .458 Winchester Magnum and lug it through the brush. But carry a double, any double, and you are walking in the company of Selous and Baker, of Hemingway and Ruark, of Hunter and "Pondoro" Taylor—the greats who hunted an Africa that existed once and, like the men, is gone forever.

The Custom Gunmaking Survey

Ron Frank

It was a cold, rainy day as I thumbed through my back issues of magazines searching for articles, pictures, anything having to do with custom firearms. I found an article that appeared in January 1975 concerning the individual preference of the custom gunmaker versus that of his client. This same survey had also been taken years before, in 1965. As a custom-gun fanatic, I thought it was time for a new survey of custom gunmakers to be taken. It would be interesting to see how custom gun preferences had changed, if at all, in the past 12 years.

Several months later I was in Las Vegas for the Third Annual Custom Gun Show, cosponsored by the American Custom Gunmakers Guild and the Firearms Engravers Guild of America. There, assembled under one roof, were some of the finest custom gunmakers and engravers in the world. Their work was an inspiration—those one-of-a-kind and limited editions fashioned by artisans whose skills are second to none.

I randomly asked gunmakers, members of the guild, if they would cooperate with the survey by filling out a questionnaire that paralleled the same information that was asked in the original two surveys. As expected, not all of those I approached were super-excited about the idea of completing a sheet of questions, nor did they appear overly enthusiastic when I requested the information no later than the next day. However, I was impressed by the humble and unselfish attitude of these fine craftsmen.

According to the information, what would you suppose the typical master gunmaker to be like? None of them is "typical," but of the 10 men who completed the questionnaire, the average age is 45 years, with 21 years' experience as a gunmaker. Oddly enough, the gunmakers surveyed in 1975 also averaged 21 years as makers of custom guns. Today's gunmakers average seven rifles a year with an average delivery time of 12 months. Twelve years ago our surveyed gunmakers av-

eraged 28 rifles per year and a delivery time of nearly 20 months per rifle. I'll let you reach your own conclusions on this.

Even if I were not surprised at the dissimilarity in rifle turnout and delivery time of 12 years ago compared to today, I was not surprised at the cost of the guns, which has nearly tripled. Twelve years ago the average cost for a completed custom job was in the $900 range. Today, according to the random survey, custom jobs ranged from $1,000 to $6,000, with an average close to $2,500.

I must emphasize that the trend today is toward specialization. Most of the 10 gunmakers surveyed this year are either stockmakers or metalsmiths. There are a few, however, who continue to manifest expertise in all facets of gunmaking, even to the extent of doing engraving and building oak/leather cases for their masterpieces. Thus, the cost estimate furnished by each man reflects either a specialized segment of the gun or, in some cases, the whole project of creating the rifle.

Under the "most expensive custom rifle made" category, answers ranged from $2,800 to $20,000—the latter being the combined efforts of stockmaker, metalsmith, engraver, and casemaker.

The trend in calibers ordered from these men held few surprises for me, but there are some changes worth noting. By awarding a "first" place listing three points, two points to "second" and one point to "third," **Table 1** shows how the trend today stacks up with 1975 and 1965.

Because of the nature of the survey, and the limited number of participants, this table certainly is not statistically valid. However, there are some points of interest that seem worthy of discussion.

The .280 Remington, a 7mm cartridge in the same class as the .270 Winchester, was introduced in 1957 and was not even listed on the 1965 chart. In 1975 it was listed sixth. Today it is first. The .280 Remington comes close to the 7mm Reming-

This article first appeared in American Rifleman

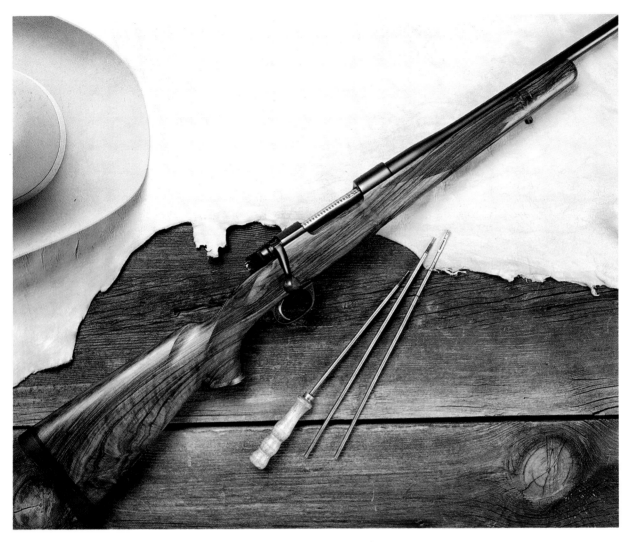

This FN Mauser, with classic English walnut stock from Kent Bowerly and metalwork by Pete Grisel, reflects contemporary gunmaking tastes. (Gary Alvis photo)

ton Magnum in performance, but with less recoil and a lot less powder burned. The .280 Remington deserves a top position on any list.

The .270 Winchester is still second from 12 years ago. It was dropped from first by the ever-popular 7mm Remington Magnum in '75—but only by a point. Undoubtedly the most flexible all-around big-game cartridge, the .30/06 is still third, following the same trend as the .270 of 12 and 22 years ago. That speaks well of their merits.

The .375 H&H moved from ninth in 1975 up to fourth today, while the time-proven 7×57mm has rated fifth for the past 22 years. The .338 Winchester Magnum made the chart for the first time, with the .243 Winchester returning to client popularity after an absence on the 1975 list. I was surprised that the 7mm Remington Magnum dropped from the top position of 12 years ago to

seventh position today, and that the .22/250 missed the 1987 list entirely.

Few surprises emerged among the preferred actions, the pre-'64 Model 70 Winchester is still the baron when it comes to client choice, with the Mauser (just barely) remaining as the gunsmiths' No. 1 pick. Out of all mentions for both the standard and the magnum actions, there were only a few votes for the Remington, Ruger, and single-shot Hagn; no one listed the Springfield, Weatherby, or any of the other possibilities. This was also the trend 12 years ago, as noted in the 1975 survey. With two points given for "first" and one point for "second," **Table 2** indicated preferred actions.

Though not noted in the tables, Douglas barrels were the overwhelming choice of both client and gunsmith. It should be of interest that Douglas

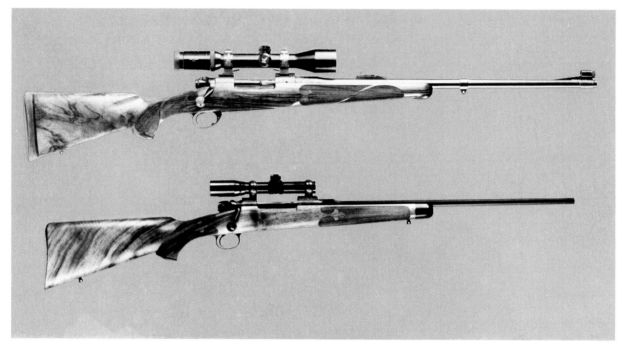

Top: Jere Eggleston chose California walnut for a Model 70 with metalwork performed by Herman Waldron. Bottom: Mauser with Model 70-style safety and octagon barrel by Charles Grace.

was listed as the first choice by clients 22 years ago and again 12 years ago. In regard to barrel length, 22-inch standard caliber barrels and 24-inch magnums are still the order of the day.

Stock wood choices held no surprises; English walnut was the first choice. I have placed English, French, and circassian, and their various California species, under the "English" category of wood since they all come from the same nut—*Juglans regia.*

I was delighted to see Bastogne walnut make the client and gunsmith preference list for the first time. This hybrid of Claro and English walnut deserves recognition.

Myrtle, mesquite, koa, rosewood, American black walnut, and others received very little attention in the custom ranks. In fact, some stockers refuse to work with any wood other than high-grade *Juglans regia.*

When it comes to hand checkering, the vote was very close. The clients prefer fleur-de-lis patterns, just as they did 12 years ago. Though not unanimous, the multi-point pattern was a whopping favorite among the gunmakers. Twelve years ago

TABLE 1: MOST POPULAR CALIBERS

	1987			1975			1965	
Rank	Cal.	Points	Cal.	Points	Cal.	Points
1	.280 Rem.	14	7mm Rem. Mag.	10	.270 Win.	15
2	.270 Win.	11	.270 Win.	9	.30/06	8
3	.30/06	8	.30/06	4	6mm Rem.	4
4	.375 H&H	7	6mm Rem.	4	.243 Win.	3
5	7 × 57 Mauser	6	7 × 57 Mauser	3	7 × 57 Mauser	2
6	.338 Win. Mag.	6	.280 Rem.	2	.222 Rem.	1
7	7mm Rem. Mag.	5	.25/06	2	.300 Win. Mag.	1
8	.243 Win.	2	.22/250 Rem.	1	.22/250 Rem.	1
9	.458 Win. Mag.	1	.375 H&H	1	—	—
10	.300 Win. Mag.	1	—	—	—	—

Three points were awarded for first place choices, two for second, and a single point for third.

TABLE 2: PREFERRED STANDARD-LENGTH ACTIONS

	Client Choice					Gunsmith Choice		
1987	*Points*	*1975*	*Points*		*1987*	*Points*	*1975*	*Points*
Model 70*	15	Model 70	9		Mauser	15	Mauser	9
Mauser	13	Mauser	6		Model 70	12	Model 70	7.5
Sako	2	Sako	3		Sako	1	Sako	1.5

PREFERRED MAGNUM-LENGTH ACTIONS

	Client Choice					Gunsmith Choice		
1987	*Points*	*1975*	*Points*		*1987*	*Points*	*1975*	*Points*
Model 70	15	Model 70	7		Model 70	15	Model 70	7.5
Mauser	6	Sako	4		Mauser	9	Mauser	2
Sako	4	Mauser	3		Sako	1	Sako	1.5
—	—	—	—		Remington	1	—	—

*Model 70s are pre- '64 Winchester

TABLE 3: PREFERRED STOCK WOOD

	Client Choice					Gunsmith Choice		
Now	*Points*	*1975*	*Points*		*Now*	*Points*	*1975*	*Percentage*
English	20	English	*		English	22	English	76%
Claro	4	Claro	*		Bastogne	4	Claro	10%
Bastogne	3	Maple	*		Claro	2	Maple	10%
Amer. Blk.	1							

*Points not available

Left: Engraving by Terry Wallace complements a Ruger No. 1 stocked by James Tucker. Metalwork is by Steve Heilmann. Right: Stocker Kent Bowerly found English walnut and fleur-de-lis checkering appropriate on a Gibbs-Farquaharson. Gunmakers' clients preferred the fleur-de-lis checkering patterns, according to both the current and previous surveys. However, gunmakers tend to like the multipoint pattern.

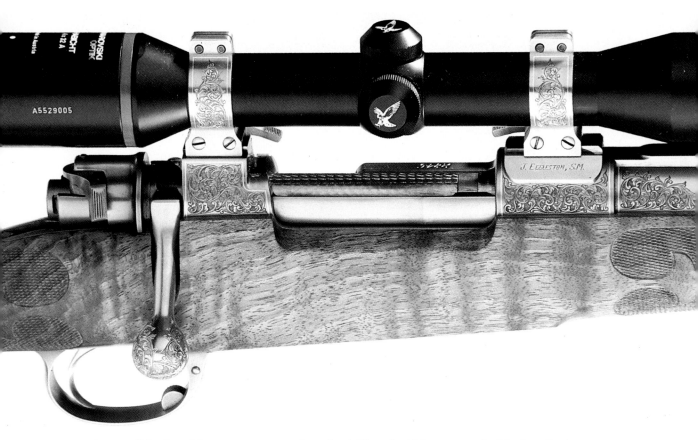

Austrian scroll by Tom Haynes graces one of a pair of Oberndorf Mausers stocked by Jere Eggleston.

100 percent of the surveyed gunsmiths said they personally preferred the traditional point pattern over fancier patterns. In regard to checkering size, both client and 'smith overwhelmingly picked 24-line-per-inch as their favorite, with the finer 26-line checkering running a distant second. Before completing this survey, I want to throw a few more "stats" at you. Nearly 25 percent of the custom gun clients desire some degree of hand engraving on their custom gun; approximately 75 percent insist on rust-blued metal rather than the standard hot dip caustic blue. When it comes to stock style, 98 percent prefer classic.

Although not all questions were answered by all the men involved in the survey, the replies make it apparent that tradition runs strong among custom gunners and craftsmen alike. Chances are the custom gunmaker survey of 1999 won't reveal many really drastic changes, either. Gunmaker fees excluded, of course.

Ron Frank of Ft. Worth, TX, is a full-time custom gunsmith and member of the American Custom Gunmakers Guild.

CUSTOM GUNMAKERS SURVEYED

John Bolliger, 1775 N. Elk Rd., Pocatello, ID 83204

Ken Bowerly, H.C.R. Box 1903, Camp Sherman, OR 97730

Larry Brace, 771 Blackfoot Ave., Eugene, OR 97404

Charles Coffin, 3719 Scarlet Ave., Odessa, TX 79762

Jere Eggleston, 400 Saluda Ave., Columbia, SC 29205

Bruce Farman, 2563 N.E. Wm. E. Sutton Rd., Bremerton, WA 98310

Charles Grace, 10144 Elk Lake Rd., Williamsburg, MI 49690

Steve Heilmann, 12985 McCourtney Rd., Grass Valley, CA 95945

Toby Leeds, 458 Western Ave., Fond Du Lac, WI 54935

James Tucker, 205 Trinity St., Woodland, CA 95695

PART TWO

RIFLES TODAY

Synthetic Stocks
Are Here to Stay

Jim Carmichel

SYNTHETIC STOCKS

I guess we've all kicked and screamed and protested long enough. Twenty years ago if someone had predicted that I would go afield with a "plastic" stock on my rifle I would have made unflattering comments about his ancestry. Even 10 years ago, by which time I was well attuned to the benefits of fiberglass stocks and used them in competitive shooting, I still couldn't see myself hunting game with one of the ugly things.

The reason I mention my past feelings about stocks made of synthetic materials is that the same opinions have been expressed by thousands of other hunters, maybe you included. In recent times however most of us have sensed an erosion of our prejudices against synthetic stocks, even to the point of seriously considering buying one of the things. Once this emotional hurdle has been cleared, the next big decisions are which brand of stock to buy, which rifle to use, and which calibers work best in synthetic stocks.

There was a time, not so long ago, when almost all synthetic stocks were custom fitted and fin-

ished by a handful of specialists. The only other available option was to buy an unfinished fiberglass stock and fit it yourself. I tried this a couple of times and can't truthfully say I enjoyed the experience. My previous do-it-yourself stockmaking efforts had been carving, sanding, and hand-rubbing wood stocks. This had always been pleasant because of the sweet smells of fine walnut and finishing oils. Fitting and finishing fiberglass stocks offered no such esthetic benefits because fiberglass resins will never smell like wood dust and spray paint will never be as sexy as linseed oil.

Today there are all sorts of ways to acquire a rifle with synthetic stocking. The quickest way is simply to buy a ready-made, over-the-counter rifle. Remington, Weatherby and Winchester as well as other name brand makers offer "put-of-the-box" rifles with stocks of fiberglass and other synthetic materials. Another source of these high-

This article first appeared in Outdoor Life

Carmichel has used this brightly colored synthetic stock in competition for the past few years, including the National Championships. The stock was made, fitted, and finished by Chet Brown, founder of Brown Precision. The rifle is a Remington Model–700 with medium-heavy barrel in .308 Winchester caliber. The scope is Bausch & Lomb, and the unusual-looking trigger assembly is a battery-powered mechanism by Frank Green that allows extremely light and uniform settings.

tech rifles is custom gunmakers specializing in synthetic stocks. These shops offer rifles already made up with synthetic stocks, or they will restock your rifle and add other custom touches such as lightening the metal parts. Your other option is to buy an unfinished stock and do the fitting and finishing yourself. Some of these unfinished fiberglass stocks are fairly difficult to finish, requiring specialized tools and plenty of previous experience. Others can be easily finished by first-time do-it-yourselfers. There are even completely finished synthetic stocks available that simply replace the original wood stock. All you need to fit this type is a screwdriver and a few minutes' time.

Before getting into specifics let's back up and think about what we're talking about. Synthetic stocks have been so universally praised that one gets the idea that they rank somewhere between sex and cheeseburgers on the all-time popularity list. While there is indeed much to recommend stocks of the various synthetic materials, they are not the answer to every hunter's prayers nor are they a universal cure-all that will unfailingly make great rifles out of mediocre ones.

The story of synthetic stocks goes back a lot further than most shooters suspect. If your definition of "synthetic" is anything that isn't wood, it can be argued that synthetic stocks have been around for centuries, though it wasn't until the 1800s that manmade synthetics became commonplace.

The first synthetic stock that most of us can re-

member was the much-despised plastic handles on the old Stevens Models–124 and 530M shotguns. These stocks were as ugly as a hungover coyote and much inclined to break. Everyone who owned one soon swore off "plastic" stocks.

During the late 1950s however Remington introduced a .22 Rimfire Autoloader that, in time, was to alter some of our prejudices against "plastic" stocks. Remington's rifle was the Nylon 66 and, as its name indicates, was largely constructed of a tough DuPont nylon. At first, shooters regarded it as just another "plastic" stock, and an ugly one at that, but in time the Nylon 66 earned a reputation for being nearly indestructible. But though the nylon stock gained respect for its toughness, it did not necessarily demonstrate that it improved accuracy. However, a couple of other historic forces were on a collision course that would, when they crashed together, forever alter the way we think about rifles.

One of these was the development of "fiberglass" bedding. The process of "bedding" a rifle in a matrix of chemical resins reinforced with particles of glass or metal or other materials is well known and widely used. Essentially what this glass bedding does is provide stable and uniform contact surfaces for the metal parts. In many instances, the accuracy of a rifle can be dramatically improved by glass bedding and within a few years of its development all serious target rifles were glass bedded as a matter of course.

The other major force that was chugging toward

its rendezvous with history was a funny little game called benchrest shooting. Benchrest was a strange sort of target shooting game because it was not necessary to hit the bull's-eye to win. The object was simply to make all the bullets go through a single hole. The game was also mighty strange because of the behemoth rifles used to shoot the tiny holes.

The rifles were so peculiar in fact that some of the game's wiser heads realized they were heading up a dead-end road. What good was a rifle that weighs 40 pounds? To get the benchrest game on a more practical track, additional rifle classifications were included in benchrest tournaments. One of these classifications, called Light Varmint Rifle, limited the rifle's total weight, including scope, to 10½ pounds. Another, the Heavy Varmint Class, restricted weight to 13½ pounds.

These new classes were immediately popular, and as rifles of this type were built their stocks became the focus of critical attention. Every ounce that could be removed from the weight of the stock could be reinvested in greater barrel mass where mass would yield better accuracy. Predictably, a lot of blind alleys were explored before someone hit on the logical solution to the problem. "Why not make the *whole* stock of fiberglass?" he reasoned. "We already know that fiberglass aids accuracy, so let's go all the way."

I'm not sure who actually built the first fiberglass stock, but the first I ever saw and used were made by an enterprising Californian named Chet Brown. As far as I'm concerned he invented the fiberglass stock and deserves most of the credit for winning public acceptance of synthetic stocks as they exist today. Happily, he is still very much around and able to see the effect he has had on today's—and tomorrow's—shooting.

Chet's early stocks were a hollow shell made of a few layers of fiberglass fabric held together with a resin compound. Since these stocks were, and are, essentially hollow (except for being filled with a cellular foam), they were exceedingly lightweight, weighing only a couple of pounds or so.

In addition to their light weight and great strength, fiberglass stocks were remarkably stable and untemperamental. A rifle-barreled action that shot well in a wooden stock would probably shoot even better in a fiberglass stock and continue doing so without your having to worry about warpage, zero shift, and the other problems associated with wooden stocks. Within a few years fiberglass stocks became a fact of life among benchrest shooters. This is so much so that it is almost fair to say that you don't win unless you use fiberglass. Nowadays fiberglass stocks are also widely used on other types of target rifles, especially in silhouette shooting where weight limitations are strictly enforced.

The language of shooting has a way of adopting certain words and phrases while ignoring other, sometimes more accurate, terms. An example is the word "fiberglass" which is almost universally applied to synthetic stocks and bedding compounds. The fact is that several different materials and techniques are now employed in the manufacture of synthetic stocks. For example, fibers of graphite or boron have been substituted for glass fibers in the making of even lighter and stronger stocks. Other stocks are made of a rigid, foamlike material while others are molded of space-age plastics. Still though, if the stock ain't wood, most of us call it fiberglass no matter what it really is.

Though target shooters were quick to appreciate the advantages of synthetic stocks, sport hunters were—and are—much harder nuts to crack. One of the main reasons that hunters would rather fight than switch is that they tend to love their guns and see them as objects of surpassing beauty. (A target shooter loves his rifle only when it

Below top is Remington Model–7 Custom KS Lightweight. Bottom is Remington Model–700 KS Mountain Rifle.

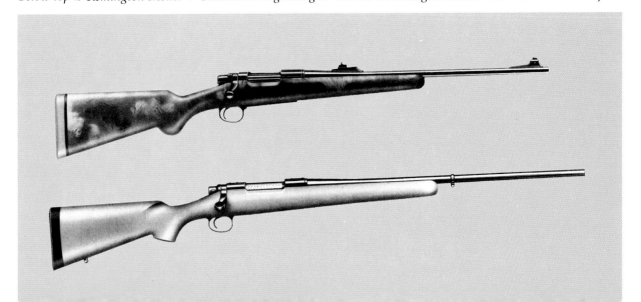

wins.) Much of the beauty a hunter sees in his rifle is in the rich glow and gentle warmth of its wooden stock. Caress a wood stock and it returns your love, but a fiberglass stock is a heartless thing, coldly mechanical and utterly incapable of passion.

But if a fiberglass stock is a heartless thing, so is a 9-pound wood-stocked rifle when you carry it up a steep mountain day after brutal day. A wooden stock can also be a heartbreaker when it is warped with rain and throws your bullet wide inches off the mark when you've worked hard for that one shot of a lifetime. That's why, about a decade ago, a few hunters began switching from wood to fiberglass.

At first the choice of hunting-style fiberglass stocks was a paltry selection of generally bad designs. As the number of manufacturers of synthetic stocks increased, however, there was steady improvement in both the selection and design of stocks available. Today there are designs available for just about every taste. If you like the spare lines of the classic or the Monte Carloed California look, or even a racy thumbhole job, there is something for you. Likewise, synthetic stocks are available for most popular rifles. Back at the beginning of the synthetic era, almost all fiberglass stocks fit only the Model–700 Remington action. Now they are made to fit just about all domestic makes and models of bolt-action rifles plus a few foreign models.

If you were to visit a major benchrest tournament, you would be astounded by the artistry exhibited in many of the synthetics. Most are brightly painted with splashy detail work that often originates, literally, in custom auto paint shops. Back when fiberglass stocks first appeared, no one seemed to know how they should look. At first the trend was to paint them ugly brown colors in what I suppose was an attempt to make them look more or less like wood. But all it did was make them look awful. Since they could never be made to look like wood, the trend was reversed with the fashion being to make them look totally *unlike* wood. That is still very much the trend today with many target shooters actively competing for recognition with elaborate paint jobs. Gorgeous hand-rubbed metalflake colors are often highlighted with airbrushed scenes ranging from the abstract to the outrageous. One long-range target rifle that was built for me by Chet Brown is finished in a metalflake blue that is easily recognized a quarter mile away. My silhouette rifle, also stocked by Brown, is painted a series of bright stripes. The vibrant color scheme serves a practical purpose by helping me easily locate the rifle during big tournaments when the racks are filled by dozens of otherwise similar rifles.

These eye-catchingly brilliant paint jobs have little appeal for hunters and may even explain why some hunters have shied away from synthetics. Over the past few years, however, some truly imaginative color schemes have been devised for hunting stocks that are both practical and attractive. Camouflage patterns are the most popular with the pattern sometimes continuing over the action and barrel and even the scope. Another popular finish for hunting rifles is a dull finish paint that dries to a slightly wrinkled texture, lending a nonslip feel somewhat like the checkering on wood stocks. Of course if you do your own paint job the only limitation is your imagination.

If you are considering a synthetic stock for yourself, you are surely wondering if it will be as good as you've heard. Or perhaps a better way to address this is to ask the question: "Is it possible to be disappointed with a synthetic stock?" The answer is—yes indeed. Disappointments with synthetic stocks are not especially uncommon. The most common reason for disappointment is poor or only mediocre accuracy. Also, some synthetic stock jobs do not significantly reduce a rifle's weight, if at all.

The occasional disappointments in accuracy with rifles having synthetic stocks remind me of an earlier era when "glass bedding" was hailed as a cure-all for accuracy ills. But even after expert glass bedding, some rifles refused to shoot any better than before. The reason was that stocking and bedding are only a couple of the myriad factors that affect accuracy. A bad barrel, poor threading, bum chambering, or uneven locking lugs can doom all hopes of accuracy.

So if you are considering having a synthetic stock fitted to your rifle in the hopes of improving accuracy you might be let down by the result. As a rule of thumb, if a rifle will consistently group five shots inside a 2-inch circle at 100 yards you can figure it has no serious accuracy defects and its accuracy will probably be improved by a *properly* fitted synthetic stock. If group sizes are over 3 inches at 100 yards with a good make bolt-action centerfire rifle, there is reason to suspect a problem that won't be cured by a new stock. So before investing in a restocking job, have the rifle checked for other problems. A good gunsmith can usually pinpoint them.

Hunters who have their rifles rebuilt so that they are extremely lightweight may also be disappointed with resultant accuracy. When actions are shaved and barrels turned down to pencil-thin profiles, there is often some loss of accuracy. I think it is unreasonable to expect a rifle weighing 6 pounds or less, with scope, to perform like a target rifle even when you are using the best action, barrel, and stocking. Some hunters who do not get the accuracy they expected from a lightweight, synthetic-stocked rifle fail to take into account that such rifles are often quite difficult to shoot well, especially from a benchrest. The best way to judge the performance of a hunting rifle with a synthetic stock is to note where the *first shot* hits. After all, stability and freedom from the effects of moisture, warpage, and temperature are the main selling points of synthetic stocks. So why not judge them with precisely these criteria? Here's how to do it.

Go out to the range and at 100 yards fire a single shot at a target. Save the target. Put the rifle in a soft case and then haul it around in the trunk of your car for a couple of days. Then go back to the range and fire one more shot at the original target. Now repeat the whole process three more times. At the end of a week if all your shots are inside a 2-inch circle you can figure the rifle is a real winner. Remember, the first shot is the one that counts. That's the shot you work for and pay for.

If you are considering a synthetic stock because you want to reduce the weight of your rifle, the first step is to remove the existing wood stock and see what it weighs. Next, using the addresses provided at the end of this article, write to the various synthetic stock manufacturers and ask for the *finished* weights of their stocks. Comparing these weights with that of your wood stock will tell you how much weight reduction to expect from the conversion if you use your barrel and action as they are.

If you want to further lighten your rig, a gunsmith can safely trim and chop the barrels of many existing rifles. Some of the specialists in fitting synthetic stocks are especially experienced in turning barrels and other weight reducing tricks. So when you inquire about having a new stock fitted, also check on the prices for this additional work. It may very well be worthwhile. As a general rule, the barrels on standard-size bolt-action rifles can stand to have about a half-pound of metal shaved away.

Here of late a few gunmakers have started offering rifles, and even shotguns, with stocks made of laminated layers of contrasting woods. These stocks have a striking appearance, made all the more so when the laminates form a camouflage pattern. It is my understanding that these stocks are impregnated with fancy chemicals that make them virtually waterproof and highly resistant to warpage and the other sins visited on stocks of wood.

Since these stocks have some of the favorable characteristics of synthetic stocks, and at the same time can be considered genuine wood, they have considerable appeal to shooters who aren't ready to make the change in one big leap. In my opinion, however, these laminated stocks are neither fish nor fowl and offer neither the beauty of wood or

Rifles shown here with synthetic stocks are from top: Shilen Heavy Varmint rifle; Remington Model 700 Silhouette rifle; Winchester Model 70; Winchester Model 70 target rifle; Ultra-Light Arms hunting rifle; Light Varmint Class benchrest rifle.

the performance of synthetics. I think they are serving only as a halfway house between wood and synthetics and will fade away within a few years, especially as synthetic stocks become more common and price-competitive.

At present, the biggest drawback to synthetic stocks is their rather high prices. Actually, they aren't all that costly, but the problem is that they don't *look* like they should cost very much. Much of the cost of synthetic stocks has been due to the hand fitting and finishing involved. Until recently every synthetic stock was custom fitted to the individual barreled action in much the same way that a gunsmith "glass beds" a wooden stock. This is followed by spray painting, rubbing, decorating and detailing.

Here's how the prices break down: An unfinished fiberglass stock from Brown Precision retails for $120. Their pre-finished stock, which is completely finished except for final bedding, sells for $299. A completely fitted and finished stock in your choice of color is $494 for a Remington rifle and $581 for most other types of bolt rifles. (The price difference owes to the additional fitting difficulties of Mauser-type actions.) By way of comparison, a replacement factory-made wooden stock for a Remington Model–700 BDL is $220 and a finished stock by a large-scale commercial and custom stockmaking firm starts at over $300.

I expect we'll be seeing more and more "drop-in" stocks of fiberglass and other synthetics. These come ready-made with the inletting and exterior surfaces finished plus recoil pads and sling swivel studs installed. All you do is take the barreled action out of your old stock and drop it in the new one. Tighten the screws, and you're ready to start shooting. I've tried a couple of these, one by Gale McMillan and the other by Ram-Line, and I suspect they represent a major new trend in synthetic stocks. The McMillan stock, which is neatly contoured and of fiberglass construction, is available for most popular brands and makes of bolt-action rifles and is priced from $225 to $250. The weight runs about 1¾ pounds. The Ram-Line stock is molded of an aerospace polymer plastic similar to

"Drop-in" synthetic stocks, such as this one, are available for several popular rifles.

Lexan and reinforced with strands of glass fibers. This is an exceptionally strong and dense material, with the stocks weighing about 2¼ pounds. The Ram-Line stocks, which are also available for an increasing number of bolt-action rifles, retails for $124.95.

Though these new drop-in stocks offer all the strength and stability of custom-fitted synthetic stocks, they may not be quite as accurate. The problem is not with the stocks, which are precisely inletted, but with the barreled actions. The receivers of bolt-action rifles are not always uniform and true, and when they are screwed tightly into a stock, some flexing or twisting may occur, which degrades accuracy. This will happen with drop-in synthetic stocks just as it does with factory-made wooden stocks. When such problem actions are "glass bedded" by an expert the bedding compound molds itself to the receiver's contours so that flexing and stressing are reduced or eliminated. This is one of the main reasons for the

accuracy of synthetic stocks. In order for a synthetic drop-in stock to reach its full accuracy potential, it may have to be "glassed" with a "wiper coat" of epoxy filler. This thin wiper coat is easily done by a gunsmith or experienced amateur and can improve accuracy dramatically because it fills in the gaps around an action and gives support where needed.

Despite the attractive options now available in synthetic stocks I think the day will come when nearly all such stocks will be standard items produced and fitted by the major gunmakers. After all, that is certainly the most convenient way to obtain a rifle with a stock of fiberglass or other synthetic material, and the arms makers aren't at all inclined to sit back and let someone else sell a product that they could be selling. I predict that competition among the major gunmakers will drive down the prices of their synthetic stocks until customers will have their choice of wooden or synthetic stocks at virtually the same prices. When that day arrives, and it isn't far off, synthetic stocks will truly have arrived.

Here's a list of manufacturers who offer synthetic stocks or finished rifles with synthetic stocks:

Brown Precision Co., P.O. Box 270W, 7786 Molinos Ave., Los Molinos, CA 96055
Fiberlite, P.O. Box 1027, Houston, TX 77011
Fiberpro, 3636 California St., San Diego, CA 92101
Game Haven Gunstocks, 13750 Shire Rd., Wolverine, MI 49799
Jim Garrett, Garrett Accur-Light Inc., 1414 B.E. Olive Ct., Fort Collins, CO 80524
H & S Precision, 112 N. Summit, Prescott, AZ 86302
Mannlicher Rifles, Gun South Inc., Box 6607, 7605 Eastwood Mall, Birmingham, AL 35210
MPI Stocks, P.O. Box 03266, 7011 N. Reno Ave., Portland, OR 97203
Mitchell Arms of California, 2101 East 4th St., Suite 201A, Santa Ana, CA 92705
Millet Industries, 16131 Gothard St., Huntington Beach, CA 92647
Gale McMillan Co., 21421 North 14th Ave., Phoenix, AZ 85027
Ram-Line, Inc., 406 Violet St., Golden, CO 80401
Remington Arms Co., 1007 Market St., Wilmington, DE 19898
SAKO Rifles, Stoeger Industries, 55 Ruta Court, S. Hackensack, NJ 07606
Six Enterprises, 6564 Hidden Creek Dr., San Jose, CA 95120
Shilen Rifles Inc., 305 Metro Park Blvd., P.O. Box 1300, Ennis, TX 75119
U.S. Repeating Arms Co., Box 30-300, New Haven, CT 06511 (Finished rifles with synthetic stocks)
Ultra Light Arms Co., P.O. Box 1270, Granville, WV 26534 (Finished rifles with synthetic stocks)
Weatherby's, 2781 E. Firestone Blvd., South Gate, CA 90280 (Finished rifles with synthetic stocks)

The Alaskan Rifle

Finn Aagaard

Alaskans often refer to their state as the "last frontier." While there are undoubtedly other areas that could claim the title with equal justice, Alaskan hunting conditions certainly differ enough from those in the "lower 48" to require special consideration for what rifles to take along on an expedition to that great land.

There are two main factors to take into account. The first is that Alaska is a harsh and ofttimes wet and cold country that is rough on equipment. Rifles and scopes must withstand getting thoroughly drenched from bashing through dripping alders, being tumbled into streams, sloshing around in the bilges of a boat, or from penetrating rain driven by 30 mph winds. They may have to ride in the hold of a Cessna together with a wet, salted bear hide, or be tied to the wing struts of a Super Cub. They will be rubbed against backpacks, dropped in the snow, jarred in the inevitable falls, dragged over rocks, and suffer neglect from hunters too bone-weary to think of anything but getting some hot food and crawling into their bags.

In Alaska rifles tend to be regarded as tools, like knives and hammers and chain saws, and they should be able to take similar treatment.

The other important factor is *Ursus arctos*, the same grizzly/brown bear that taught Lewis and Clark that eastern deer rifles might not always be entirely adequate for everything on this continent.

Overall, other Alaskan game animals do not require exceptionally powerful cartridges. Caribou, the most common game animal, is somewhat bigger than a deer, with bulls going 300 to 400 pounds live weight. But any good, long-range mule deer round, from the .270 Winchester and up, should be perfectly satisfactory for them. Moose, particularly Alaskan moose, are huge. They strike me as being comparatively easy to kill, though it often takes them a little while to realize it, and one does need enough penetration to get through a lot of hide and meat, and massive bones. But any thoroughgoing elk cartridge is fine

Clad in hip boots, the author cradles his .338 Winchester Magnum Model 700 Remington during a hunt along the Kejulick River in Alaska.

on moose also. Alaskan Dall sheep, Rocky Mountain goats, and blacktail deer require no more powerful cartridges than those suitable for the same species elsewhere.

The difference is that in much of Alaska, no matter how innocuous a quarry he is seeking, the hunter may encounter a brown or grizzly bear. In fact, I am told that during deer season on Kodiak Island the bears are beginning to come to the

This article first appeared in American Rifleman

sound of a shot to dispute possession of the kill with the successful hunter.

Even compared to the elephant, buffalo, and lions of my native Africa, these bears are impressive beasts. Together with polar bears, they are the largest terrestrial meat eaters, and until the coming of effectual firearms, they were pretty much the dominant animals hereabouts. They feared nothing, did as they pleased, and appropriated whatever they wanted. Every now and again they still act the same way.

Although both brown and grizzly bears are considered to be members of the same species, there is a distinct size differential between the salmon-fed coastal brown bears that can weigh well over 1,000 pounds and the smaller interior grizzlies that seldom exceed 750 pounds. It has been claimed, however, that the grizzlies are often even more aggressive than the brown bears.

Nevertheless, considering the number of encounters that must occur in Alaska every year, bear attacks are remarkably rare. Most bears (outside the national parks) run like rabbits the moment they become aware of a human anywhere in their vicinity. When I asked registered guide Phil Shoemaker how many people were killed by bears in Alaska every year, he replied that most years no one was killed, and that there were on average only three or four maulings a year. Still, bears may fight if a man, often quite inadvertently, appears to be threatening their cubs or trying to steal their food, and there is the occasional sorehead who is just mad at the world.

No one wants to be even a rare statistic of this sort; so sport hunters in Alaska tend to carry somewhat heavier artillery than the rest of us. Jim Laird, a friend of mine presently stationed at the Elmendorf Air Force Base near Anchorage, has used a left-hand .300 Weatherby Magnum for most of his hunting both here and in Germany for many years, and on an African hunt he took all his game but buffalo with it. Only in Alaska has he been chided for carrying too *light* a gun!

I spent some time talking to the salesmen in several gun stores in Anchorage, in an endeavor to learn what cartridges residents favored based on sales. The majority felt that while the .30/06 was still the leader, the .338 Winchester Magnum was becoming more popular all the time. They said it was perceived as offering very adequate stopping power for bears and as being a dandy moose cartridge, while at the same time it was not ridiculously overpowered for deer. To me, this makes good sense.

I gathered that the .375 H&H Magnum was well liked as a bear gun, while the .458 was mostly used by guides. One gun store owner said he sold a fair amount of .45/70 ammo, and that Marlin Model 1895 lever guns in that caliber enjoyed a good reputation as close-range bear stoppers. Both the Weatherby and Winchester .300 Magnums were popular, he reported, but he felt that there was less demand for the 7mm Remington Magnum than previously.

He remarked that of course there were still a lot of .30/30 Winchesters out there, and that many surplus military rifles chambered for such cartridges as the 7.65mm Argentinian, the 6.5mm Swedish and Japanese rounds, the 8×57mm, the .303 Lee Enfield, and all the rest were in use. Most of these, though, were in the hands of trappers and subsistence hunters.

Regarding ammunition, as a rule the demand was for the heaviest bullets available. His customers wanted 300-grain bullets in the .375, 220-grain (or 200-grain Nosler Partition) in .30 caliber, and 175 grains in the 7mm magnum. He said if a load with 300-grain bullets were available for the .338 Winchester Magnum, he could sell a lot of it.

Not a single person I discussed the matter with thought that a .44 Magnum revolver or any other belt gun offered the best defense against a bear attack. Without exception they said they would prefer to have a rifle in their hands during such a confrontation—any rifle—from the .30/30 up.

The point was made, though, that a .44 Magnum revolver is a lot handier when one is just fishing or backpacking. And the handgun is more likely to be on your person in an unexpected emergency, whereas all too often a rifle might be leaning against a tree some yards out of reach.

Other Alaskans claimed that trying to stop an enraged bear with any handgun was tantamount to committing suicide and that the best tactic was to play dead. Perhaps so, but I believe that I would opt for the handgun, though I would by all means try to avoid having to use it.

In any case, it seems that penetration is the most essential requirement in a handgun cartridge intended for use against bears. The only certain way to stop a bear in time at close quarters is to brain it or smash the spine, though I am told that breaking its shoulder generally puts it down and allows for follow-up shots. To ensure sufficient penetration, many .44 Magnum users like the Barnes load with the 300-grain bullet.

It will be interesting to see what sort of following the big Freedom Arms single-action .454 Casull revolver gains in Alaska. In power it approaches the normal .45/70 rifle load, but it is heavy and costs about twice as much as most .44 Magnum revolvers. Besides, most of us are more likely to place our shots in the right place with a rifle or carbine than with any handgun, even at quite close range.

In contrast to sport hunters, the Indian and Eskimo subsistence hunters often use what most of

Alaskan brown bear makes its way into a stream, while inset photo shows two practical bear rifles. The top one is the author's Remington Model 700 Classic in .338 Winchester Magnum. Below is guide Phil Shoemaker's Mauser-based .458 Winchester Magnum. Conditions in Alaska can be very rough on firearms. So the author puts a coat of paste wax on exposed metal surfaces to prevent rust. (Bear photo by Len Rue Jr.)

Shoemaker's rifle has a 2.5× Leupold in Redfield mounts. Pilkington lever releases scope quickly . . .

us would regard as totally inadequate cartridges. Some years ago gunsmith Roy Dunlap reported that a Model 70 .22 Hornet sent to him by an Indian hunter for rebarreling was accompanied by a list of its bag, which included moose and polar bears, in addition to numerous seals and caribou.

I learned that there is no longer much demand for the Hornet, but that the .222 Remington is extremely popular among the native hunters, with the .223 Remington not far behind and starting to overtake it. The .22/250 Remington apparently has a good following, while there is some revival of interest in the .220 Swift. The Remington "Accelerator" loads for the .30/30 and .30/06 also sell well, according to one Anchorage dealer.

The reason native hunters prefer these light calibers, I was told, is that they do not like much recoil. In addition, the ammunition is more portable and less expensive.

One should keep in mind that there is a considerable difference between subsistence hunting for food and sport hunting, especially trophy hunting. The subsistence hunter goes about it as an everyday job. He is unlikely to be excited and will usually get close and wait until he can place his shot exactly before he opens fire. He also generally knows there will be other opportunities, so he can afford to turn down the difficult shots that a trophy hunter would be tempted to try. If his beast runs off a way, he has the ability to track it up. And he has the knowledge and skill to avoid unfavorable confrontations with bears.

The stopping power of shotguns on bears seems controversial. Phil Shoemaker says that the Alaska Department of Fish & Game tested buckshot on bear skulls at 15 yards and found it woefully lacking in penetration. I expect that at 10 feet or so, before the pattern has opened much, it might be a different story. All the same, the consensus seems to be that slugs are better, though even they may lack penetration.

In the outhouse at his base camp near the Kejulik River, some 45 minutes by Super Cub south of King Salmon on the Alaskan Peninsula, Shoemaker keeps a single-barrel 12 gauge together with one round of No. 7½ shot and three rounds loaded with the Brenneke slugs. The shot cartridge is to drive off the bear, while the Brenneke slugs, which are credited with giving more reliable penetration than domestic rifled slugs, are the last resort should a bear be absolutely set on violating the occupant's privacy.

(Shoemaker's guiding area is superb bear country, by the way. We saw bears every day, several of them from his comfortable plywood cabin base camp. His address is: Phil Shoemaker, P.O. Box 876110, Wasilla, AK 99687.)

Shoemaker used to back up his bear hunting clients with a .30/06, using handloads with 200-grain Nosler Partition bullets. Then some years ago a wounded grizzly got away into the brush. They glassed the cover carefully from a vantage point and found a patch of brown that did not move for 30 minutes, and so they hoped they had a dead bear.

Shoemaker and his hunter went in, but found only melted snow and blood in an ambush position beside the trail. They followed the spoor slowly and cautiously, circling around all likely ambush sites, and moved the bear once, but did not see it. Now dark was coming on, so they hurried more. Shoemaker was peering into a little clearing when there was a hair-raising roar to his left, about 20 feet away and a little above him. As he turned to face it, the bear was already coming.

He wanted a brain shot, but the bear's head was moving about too erratically, so at the last moment he pointed the .30/06 at the bear's shoulder and fired. The bear came to an abrupt halt, with a dazed look in its eyes (possibly from the muzzle blast, it was close enough), then lunged forward again. Swerving aside, it collided with

. . . giving access to the handy pop-up rear sight.

a tree, which it attacked in apparent fury. Shoemaker poured two quick shots into it close behind the shoulder. The bear immediately came at him once more. The client stepped up and shot the bear with his .300 Winchester Magnum, whereupon it stopped, turned around, and fled. They eventually found it some 40 yards away, quite dead.

After this incident, Shoemaker acquired a .458 Winchester Magnum. He got an Interarms Mark X Mauser barreled action, lopped the barrel off to about 21 inches, and gave it a fiberglass stock which he cross-bolted behind the recoil shoulder. A Leupold 2.5× scope is fitted in Redfield SR (two-piece) mounts. One of the rear adjusting screws has been replaced with a Pilkington (Pilkington Gun Co., P.O. Box 1296, Muskogee, OK 74402) lever, which allows quick removal of the scope, while the other is epoxied in place so that the scope will retain its zero when replaced. The rifle has a sturdy front sight, and one of the very neat little folding aperture sights Redfield used to make is attached to the rear mount base.

All the metal work except moving parts has been painted with flat black Rustoleum rust-preventing paint, which apparently is quite durable, and is especially valuable in preventing rust from forming unseen on the metal hidden inside the stock. Aircraft "wing walk compound" has been applied to the pistol grip and fore-end of the stock in lieu of checkering and is very effective. Shoemaker daubs the stuff on anywhere he wants a nonslip surface, such as inside the bed of his pickup truck.

Shoemaker encased enough lead inside the fiberglass stock to give the rifle the balance he wanted and to raise its weight to about 9½ pounds with a full magazine. That is almost exactly what my own Winchester Model 70 .458 weighs, and in my opinion is about the optimum heft for a stopping rifle of this caliber.

I tried a few shots with Shoemaker's rifle, and I found it to be a nice-handling piece that was comfortable to shoot. I can't imagine anything much better for following up wounded bears in the alders. Shoemaker says he has just used it on half a dozen bears so far, and in every case they went down to the shot. He has yet to recover any of the 500-gauge soft-point bullets, even one which broke a bear's hip from the rear, raked all the way through, and exited from the chest.

This is not to say that one can expect to stop a bear by hitting it just anywhere with a .458—any such delusion could prove fatal. Whatever the shooter is using, proper placement of his shot is essential. A powerful stopping cartridge like the .458 gives one a trifle more leeway, but that is all.

I gathered that guides feel that 100 yards is about the ideal range on bears. But sometimes a long shot is justified, and occasionally it is necessary to attempt to stop a fleeing wounded bear at a considerable distance. For this work the .458 is somewhat handicapped by its steep trajectory curve; so the .375 H&H is still probably more popular as a backup gun. I do hear that one of the better-known guides on Kodiak carries a Holland's double-barreled .500 Nitro Express. I imagine it is a very comforting piece to have in one's hands when a thoroughly disgruntled bear must be winkled out of the thick stuff.

I had along a Remington Model 700 in the .338 Winchester Magnum. It had one of the New Six Enterprises "drop-in" synthetic stocks, and it was fitted with a Leupold Vari-X 1.5-5× scope that performed perfectly. I used a scope lens cover cut from an inner tube, and I put a strip of electrical insulating tape over the muzzle to keep out snow, mud, or freezing rain, as did Shoemaker and his guides. In addition we had a strip of spare tape wound around the barrel. There is of course no need to remove the tape before shooting, as it has not the slightest effect on velocity, accuracy or point of impact.

I gave all the external metal a coat of Johnson's paste wax before I left home. I deliberately did not wipe any moisture off the outside of the gun during the whole trip, nor did I apply any oil except a touch to the bolt. Not a speck of rust developed on the waxed metal; thus it seems that wax may offer longer-lasting protection than oil.

Alaska is a wonderful and absolutely fascinating wilderness country. It is also a hard and utterly ruthless land that suffers not fools or illusions and is capable of testing men and equipment to the uttermost. Alaska is no place for delicate elegance or fancy gimmicks; simple, rugged reliability, the ability to get the job done expeditiously, and the ability to withstand tough conditions are required of hunting rifles as well as the men who carry them. Take my word for it.

Light as a Feather

Jim Carmichel

At long last the truly lightweight big-game hunting rifle has arrived. At least I think it has. But gun writers were telling us about "lightweight" rifles a quarter-century ago so I guess our perception of weight is only relative.

For most of this century the lightweight big-game rifle was something of a myth, or at least a promise unfulfilled. Gunmakers have advertised "light" rifles for as long as I can remember but as often as not the difference between light and heavy has been only a few ounces. A classic example of this was a bolt-action rifle made for a brief time back in the 1930s. It came in a standard version with a 22-inch barrel and a "lightweight carbine" version with 20-inch barrel. The carbine's weight averaged only about 2 ounces less than the standard model yet the advertising copy would make one believe it was as light as a fluff of goose down.

During the 1950s Winchester introduced their Featherweight version of the famed Model–70 bolt rifle. The Featherweight was trimmer looking than the standard model, with a shorter and thinner barrel. An aluminum buttplate and triggerguard assembly replaced the steel parts used on the standard model. Hunters of the time supposed they had, at last, been blessed with an honest to goodness lightweight hunting rifle. But was this really the case?

In order to get a fair reckoning, I just now weighed four Featherweight Model–70s from the 1950s era and four standard Model–70s made about the same time. The Featherweights *averaged* nearly 2 pounds lighter (1 pound 14 ounces) than the standard models so I guess the folks at New Haven had indeed produced a lighter rifle. But was it truly a lightweight? The weights of the four Featherweights, all in standard hunting calibers, ranged from 6 pounds 10 ounces to 7 pounds 3 ounces for an *average* weight of 6 pounds 10 ounces. So I guess the question becomes Can a

This article first appeared in Outdoor Life

rifle of this weight, without scope or sling, be considered a lightweight?

Before we can answer this question, let's hold off for a moment and decide on other essential criteria for a hunting rifle.

The whole idea behind a lightweight rifle is of

course to lighten the load we carry afield. Brush hunters might point out that lightweight rifles have fast-handling qualities that make them desirable in hunting conditions where you have to aim and fire fast or not at all. In truth, however, the need for such fast-handling qualities has never been the motivating force behind the quest for lighter rifles. There is in fact a profound difference between the light, fast-firing carbine-type rifles we associate with woods hunting and the kind of rifle that you strap across your back and carry to the top of the mountain. Jack O'Connor termed them "Mountain Rifles" back in the 1950s and no one has come up with a better name. Jack was a sheep hunter so he knew what it was like to struggle up endless mountains with a rifle slung over his shoulder.

Mountain hunters often exist on the edge of exhaustion. Unnecessary weight that has to be carried up the mountain then back down again, be it only a pound—or a half pound—is the unforgivable sin. The agonies of the mountain, more

than all other factors combined, have been the inspiration of the truly lightweight rifle. Many is the time I have clung to the crest of an Alaskan peak, trying with all my might to wish away a few ounces from the body of my rifle.

Another criterion for the lightweight rifle is that it be chambered for a modern high-intensity cartridge capable of hitting and killing big game at considerable distances. Preferably this rifle should be a repeater. In other words, it has to be an accurate and powerful hunting rifle. This is why the development of lightweight rifles has dealt almost exclusively with bolt-action designs. Occasionally one sees single-shot rifles custom rebuilt into snazzy lightweights but these are mostly showpieces rather than honest hunting tackle.

The need for good accuracy has been something of a stumbling block in the development of lightweight rifles. Hitting a wild sheep or goat at several hundred yards calls for the best in rifles, ammo and marksmanship. In mountain hunting days of exhausting work can be rewarded by an opportunity to bag a trophy under do-or-die circumstances. That's why mountain rifles must have *better* accuracy than we normally expect from a typical hunting rifle.

The paradox of this demand for fine accuracy is that lightweight rifles tend to be less accurate than heavier ones. There was even a time, not so long ago, when light weight was considered a guarantee of poor accuracy. The lighter the rifle the poorer the accuracy. Thus, the developers of the modern lightweight rifle have also been very much concerned with ways of improving accuracy. After all, without the necessary accuracy refinements the development of extremely lightweight rifles would have been meaningless.

Now that we have pretty much decided what should be expected from a lightweight rifle, let's talk again about weight. Winchester, you'll recall, had more or less established the gun industry's standard for a lightweight rifle with their Featherweight Model–70, which averaged close to 7 pounds without sights. These Featherweights certainly must have felt light to veterans of World War II who had spent the war years toting an M–1 Garand weighing about 9½ pounds. Even the beloved '03 Springfield used in World War I weighed about 9 pounds.

A fascinating sidelight to the story of Winchester's first Model–70 Featherweights is that they were not a runaway success. Though they were sold in respectable numbers, many hunters still

Ultra Light rifle in .308 (top) is a featherweight at 4½ pounds, not including scope and mounts. Winchester Model 70 Winlite in .30/06 weighs 6¼ to 6½ pounds, again for the rifle only. (Deborah Denker photo)

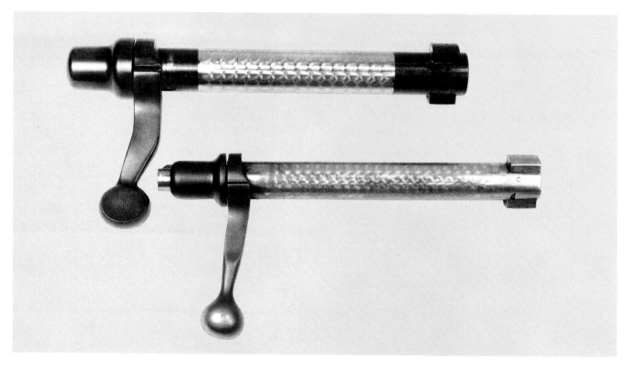

Ultra Light Arms Company keeps the weight of their rifles down by reductions in size of noncritical parts, such as the rifle bolt. Note the difference between the Remington M-700 bolt (top) and the Ultra Light bolt below it. The Ultra Light bolt has been trimmed down in all areas except the locking lugs.

preferred the heavier model. Probably the main reason for so many customers staying with the heavier Model–70 was the prevailing notion that heavier rifles "shoot better."

To be fair I must point out that Winchester's Featherweight Model–70 was not the first lightweight hunting rifle. A half-century earlier the Austrian firm of Mannlicher-Schoenauer had introduced an elegant bolt-action rifle that weighed a scant 6½ pounds. Other European gunmakers as well as domestic manufacturers had their turns at producing lightweight rifles as well. The reason the Model–70 Featherweight stands out as the bellwether lightweight is that it was actively advertised and promoted as such and that it represented a serious attempt to significantly reduce the weight of a previously existing model. Very likely the folks at Winchester felt they had done all that could be done. They certainly had reason to be pleased with what they had accomplished.

While this was going on, Jack O'Connor, who was then the Shooting Editor of *Outdoor Life* magazine, was growing older and wiser and thinking more seriously about his mountain rifles. About a hundred miles from where Jack lived was a talented gunmaker by the name of Al Bieson who was beginning to earn a reputation as one of the finest custom stockmakers and rifle builders this country has ever produced. Bieson was well tuned

to the concept of a mountain rifle and deftly translated O'Connor's requests into elegant creations that relentlessly redefined the prevailing limitations of weight and accuracy.

By the decade of the 1960s a mountain rifle weighing between 7 and 7½ pounds *with scope* was a reality. Considering that scopes of that era weighed upwards of a pound with rings and bases, we see that Bieson and a few other rifle builders were producing rifles with a base weight of about 6 pounds. The problem was that such rifles were custom-built affairs and therefore quite expensive. I once did a bit of price shopping and discovered that the price for one of these rigs went up about $100 for every ounce of weight reduction.

The skills of talented custom riflecrafters such as Al Bieson notwithstanding, there was a practical limit to how much weight could be removed. A wood stock can only be shaved and hollowed so much before it becomes critically weakened, and a barrel can be turned down only so far before it becomes unsafe. Besides, no matter how much the barrels and stocks were lightened, the action remained the major problem. Then, as now, the action most used as the basis for custom rifles was the basic Model–98 style Mauser or one of its many variations. An unaltered Mauser action will weigh about 2¼ pounds. Added to this is the trigger-guard assembly, which brings the total action weight to almost exactly 3 pounds. By trimming and skeletonizing the action and guard assembly it was possible to eliminate perhaps a quarter pound, but even so it seemed that rifles could never get lighter than 6 pounds or so.

Apparently the quest for the ultimate lightweight hunting rifle had come to the ultimate conclusion. But then something happened that forever changed the way we will think about rifles.

That something was the introduction of fiberglass stocks. Whereas the minimum weight of a wood stock was about 2 pounds, a fiberglass stock of similar size weighed only about 1½ pounds. So all at once there was a half-pound reduction in total weight. Not only were these new fiberglass stocks lighter, they were also remarkably strong and resistant to temperature and moisture and most of the other factors that have a bad influence on stocks of wood. This stability and warp resistance of fiberglass stocks not only yielded better accuracy but, of even greater importance, helped ensure resistance to zero shift. Wooden stocks, especially the slim stocks used on light rifles, sometimes tended to swell, shrink, or warp when exposed to the elements. When this happened it was a sure bet that the bullet's point of impact would be changed, sometimes by enough to miss the target. With a fiberglass stock, a hunter could stand in the rain for days and still be confident that his first shot would be on target.

Though the first fiberglass stocks were used on target rifles, hunters soon got tuned in to their advantages. That's not to say however that fiberglass stocks were an immediate hit in hunting circles. In fact there was, and still is, a good bit of resistance to stocks made of fiberglass and other synthetic materials. Wooden stocks are as sacred as motherhood and apple pie and many, possibly most, of the current generation of hunters simply won't forsake their cherished walnut stocks. Men who went to the mountain were the first to make the change to fiberglass stocks, and by the end of the 1970s hunters could choose from several styles and makers of fiberglass stocks.

Developments in firearms technology tend to stimulate further developments. The development of fiberglass stocks and the possibilities they offered had the effect of stimulating new and even better thinking about the possibility of making rifles lighter than anyone had ever dared imagine. First of all the old ways and old concepts of rifle building had to be tossed out. For example, it was realized that trying to figure out how to make existing actions lighter was a waste of time. A Mauser or Model–70 action can be lightened only so much. After that the action is still too heavy, so why bother in the first place?

One of the few existing actions considered light enough to work with was Remington's Model–700, which weighs slightly over 2 pounds in the short version and about 5 ounces more in the long version. The short Model–700 action is not only relatively light, it is also easy to bed in fiberglass

Quartet of today's factory produced lightweight rifles include from top: Remington's M-700 Mountain rifle; the Remington M-7; Winchester's M-70 Featherweight; and Ruger's M-77 International.

stocks. And its stiff, cylindrical form makes it one of the most accurate actions ever made. That's why the short Model–700 action has served as the basis of more super lightweight rifles than any other. By shaving ounces here and half ounces there, specialists in superlight rifles were able to drop the weight of some rifles below 5½ pounds (without sights). This in itself represented a new frontier in rifle building but at the same time the means of achieving such lightness were somewhat self-limiting. For example, the short Model–700 action will accommodate only medium-length cartridges such as the .308 Win., .284 Win. and 7mm/08 Remington. In order to build a rifle in, say, .30/06, .280 Rem. or 7mm Rem. Mag., it was necessary to use a longer action with a corresponding increase in weight. So, once again it seemed that the final weight limits had been achieved.

This is where a pleasant-mannered West Virginian named Melvin Forbes stepped in. Melvin recognized that if rifles were to ever be lighter than 5½ pounds it would be necessary to use actions specifically designed and built for the purpose. So he set about building what was to become known as the Ultra Light Action. At first look the Ultra Light appears to be a Model–700, but on closer inspection one discovers that the major components are considerably trimmer than the Remington. In designing his action Forbes made practical use of a seldom noted fact about the strength of rifle actions. That fact being that much of the mass and bulk of almost all rifle actions contribute virtually nothing to their strength. By centering strength where it is actually needed, in the locking area and barrel attachment, one can radically reduce the rest of the mechanism with nothing lost except weight. This design concept makes it possible to build full-length actions with relatively little increase in weight. Thus Forbes can offer his Ultra Light rifles in all standard calibers and even some Magnums without serious penalty of increased weight. The model numbers of Forbes' three action sizes, the Models 20, 24, and 28, also signify their actual weight in ounces.

An interesting bonus of Forbes' Ultra Light action is that it allows him to put weight back into areas where it will do some good. For instance, the barrels on his rifles are surprisingly plump and long enough to ensure that there is no serious loss of bullet velocity. By adding bulk, and therefore stiffness, to his barrels, Forbes made his Ultra Light rifles deliver surprisingly good accuracy. An Ultra Light rifle in 7mm/08 caliber that I bench-tested grouped the first three shots inside an inch at 100 yards. The weight of that rifle *including a 3–9× scope*, was a scant 5 pounds, 4 ounces!

The lightest rifle made by Ultra Light Arms is an open-sighted woods rifle in .358 Winchester caliber weighing 4¼ pounds! Among their heavier rifles is a .338 magnum weighing 6¼ pounds, with scope.

You've probably been wondering about the recoil of these super-light rifles, and with good reason. Make no mistake, a 6-pound rifle in a magnum caliber can kick like thunder. In fact, some hunters might even find them unshootable. That's why Forbes fits a highly effective muzzle break to his magnum-class rifles. This device, which operates by using the gas pressure at the muzzle to counteract recoil, works so well that a 7mm Remington Magnum seems to have virtually no recoil at all.

Forbes' Ultra Light Arms Company is by no means the only firm making lightweight rifles. The reason his rifles are the lightest at present is his action. Conceivably, another ambitious riflemaker will come up with a design that makes even lighter rifles possible. Possibly, the major arms companies will bring their resources and technical expertise to bear in developing even lighter rifles. The technical "spillover" from designing extremely light sporting rifles might very well lend itself to military applications.

The major arms makers have already tested the market for lightweight rifles with a number of interesting models. Remington's Model Seven, introduced a few years ago, weighs 6¼ pounds with a wooden stock. Remington introduced a Kevlar reinforced fiberglass stock for the Model Seven that drops the weight to 5¼ pounds. Remington also offers their Model–700 rifle with a fiberglass stock, for a weight reduction of about 1 pound. Ruger's Ultra Light and International versions of their Model–77 bolt rifle are both in the 6-pound range while at the same time avoiding the squeezed down and starved look of many lightweights. The same can be said for Remington's Model–700 Mountain Rifle and Winchester's (USRAC) Model–70 Featherweight. Both of these rifles were obviously designed with as much emphasis on stylish good looks as keeping their weight to a minimum. Interestingly, Winchester's Model–70 Lightweight Carbine, at 6 pounds, is a half pound lighter than their Featherweight Model–70.

How much lighter can rifles go? Will new technologies make a 4-pound rifle a reality? Already actions are being made of titanium, a super-light but strong metal. And fiberglass stocks are giving way to even stronger but lighter stocks reinforced with fibers of graphite and boron. Scope makers are also experimenting with space-age plastics that have excellent optical qualities but only half the weight of traditional glass lens. Putting these ideas together, it is not at all outrageous to predict a scoped rifle weighing less than 5 pounds.

Jack O'Connor would have been amazed.

Made in Japan

Jim Carmichel

Zen and the art of Japanese gunmaking: Employees in Japanese gun factories work with a cultural serenity missing in Western plants. And the quality of the guns they produce gives you serenity in the field at a reasonable price. Here an SKB craftsman eyeballs the final finish on a shotgun barrel. Although computer-controlled work has a firm foothold here, an amazing amount of work is done by craftsmen who reduce metal to finished dimensions—from memory, rather than from production jigs or models.

D o you know the difference between a fish and a naked lady?
I think I discovered the difference a few months ago when I journeyed to Japan to visit SKB, since 1855, one of the world's most venerable sporting arms makers. As I will reveal shortly, the difference between a fish and a pretty woman in her altogether goes a long way toward explaining the difference between guns made in Japan and those made in the world's other gunmaking centers. It also explains the almost universal acceptance of Japanese-made shotguns and rifles by American shooters and hunters. The same sportsmen, only a generation ago, would never have considered owning a gun marked "Made in Japan."

This reversal of attitude is all the more remarkable when you consider the almost total contempt the world held for Japanese products—especially guns—during the years immediately following World War II. Our first impressions of Japanese guns were based almost entirely on souvenir military rifles brought home by GI's who had served in the Pacific Theater. These bolt-action rifles were the 6.5 mm (6.5 × 50) and 7.7 (7.7 × 58) caliber Arisakas, and some of them were as rough as a homemade wagon axle. Those made after 1943 were so crudely finished that the actions appeared to be rough sand castings, giving rise to the widespread but erroneous notion that Japanese guns were made of "cast iron." Anyone who held to this belief hadn't seen any of the beautifully finished pre-war 6.5 Arisaka rifles, named after Colonel Nariake Arisaka. I once owned one of these that was as well fitted and finished as any military arm I've ever seen, including turn-of-the-century Mausers.

Following the war a widespread rumor had it that the souvenir Arisaka rifles were unsafe to fire. But a series of "blow-up" tests proved that the

This article first appeared in Outdoor Life

Japanese rifle was actually stronger than our '03 Springfield, the M–98 Mauser, and even the 1917 Enfield. More recently a few of the world's high-tech gunmakers have been crowing about their development of a space-age radiused groove rifling which, upon inspection, proves to be nothing other than the same rifling system used in the old Arisaka rifles. The point of this thumbnail history is that the Japanese gun industry is much older, and certainly more sophisticated, than is generally realized. In many ways it is a continuation of the Samurai sword-making tradition—the most elegant arms-making process ever conceived.

Modern Japanese sporting arms made their first tentative appearance on American soil during the late 1950s. The first of these I saw were over/under shotguns bearing the trademark Miroku and were distributed by an importer in Washington state. They were very similar to the vaunted Browning Superposed shotguns but, with a 1959 retail price of about $215.00, cost about a third less than the lowest-grade Browning. The time for Japanese guns, however, had not quite arrived because Spanish doubles were the fashionable item among price-conscious sportsmen, and high-quality guns from other European makers were still affordable. American gunmakers were also buzzing with exciting new designs, and at that time the concept of the over/under shotgun, the design milieu in which the Japanese would ultimately excel, had not yet captured the fancy of American wing-shooters. At that time the Japanese still had many hurdles to jump because "Made in Japan" was still synonymous with shoddy quality. Except for a few good cameras, Japanese optics were still third rate, the Sony electronics colossus was still only a gleam in Mr. Morita's eye, and a Japanese auto on an American highway was as unthinkable as eating raw fish.

Landmark successes are often the result of lucky timing and the merger of unforeseen events. This has never been truer than the combination of forces that led to an unprecedented boom in shotgun shooting during the '60s. Spurred by a generous economy, "leisure pursuits" was the byword of the era. Thousands upon thousands of wage earners now found such high-hat socializing as trap or skeep shooting within their grasp. Reloading your own shotshells not only saved money but was lots of fun too and meant you could shoot twice as much. And a drive out to the gun club was a great time for the whole family. Blue-collar shooting leagues on the order of bowling leagues were formed, and it seemed that everybody wanted to buy a shotgun.

Serious shooters quickly learned two things: It takes a good gun to win and the gun to win with was an over and under. But over/unders could be costly, even out of the 1963 buying reach of newly

affluent industrial workers. That's the year the firm of Charles Daly took over distribution of the Miroku shotguns. Charles Daly had imported German-made shotguns before the war and had a reputation for good quality. The Daly name on a shotgun sounded more appealing to American ears than Miroku which was too, well, too Japanese. But there was certainly no doubting the appeal of the Charles Daly price tag.

That same year, with the introduction of their Model–101 over/under, Winchester became the first major arms maker to give its name to a Japanese gun. The price tag was $249, and the gun featured a ventilated rib, a single selective trigger, automatic ejectors, hand engraving and, like the Charles Daly-Miroku, it looked a hell of a lot like a Browning Superposed. This similarity caused many shooters to speculate that there was but one big gun factory in Japan, making Browning look-alikes under a variety of labels.

This rumor ended with the arrival, also in the early 1960s, of the SKB shotguns which were totally different from other Japanese guns in design and appearance. The SKB-made guns, which were distributed in the U.S. by Ithaca from '66 to '76, also differed from other Japanese makes by maintaining SKB as their primary identity.

The Japanese firearms industry, like gunmaking in other industrialized nations, is an interesting blend of high-tech high production equipment and old-fashioned "hands-on" craftsmanship. This SKB worker is operating a computer-controlled machine that turns shotgun barrel blanks to finished contour.

When Browning gave their name to a line of Japanese-made shotguns in the early '70s and Roy Weatherby moved his manufacturing operations there as well, the remaining prejudices all but evaporated. Even gun buyers who still harbored prejudices against Japanese products were forced to concede that Japanese gunmaking was a force to be reckoned with and that respect for their products had been fairly earned. Thus, in only a handful of years our attitudes toward Japanese guns had done a complete about-face.

One of the principal reasons for the Japanese success is well worth considering because it reflects a smart manufacturing strategy. Thumbing through your collection of old gun catalogs, you'll discover that the Japanese have never attempted to compete at the low end of the gun market. Instead, they have concentrated on the upscale segment of the market where quality, as much as price, is a determining sales factor. Early in the game they homed-in on the Belgian-made Browning shotguns as the standard of quality they should strive for. How close they have come to this goal is the subject of some debate, but the Japanese can certainly claim that they have never made a cheap sporting arm—nor a bad one.

In terms of craftsmanship Japanese guns have been a continuous puzzle to me because the two areas of handwork in which I would have expected them to excel, checkering and engraving, have been the most consistently disappointing. It has only been during the past five years or so that the checkering on even their top-of-the-line models approached what I would call acceptable quality and even now is nowhere as good as their skill at fitting metal. This is not to say that Japanese checkering is bad, but it doesn't compare well when judged the way the Japanese themselves want to be judged. I suspect that part of the problem may be with foreign importers who have had neither the inclination nor knowledge to show Japanese gunmakers what good checkering really is and how it should be done.

The same is probably the case with Japanese engraving. It covers, and to some degree it decorates, but seldom is it art. I get the notion that Japanese gun engravers often have to copy designs presented as rough sketches or fuzzy photographs and are seldom given the opportunity to show what they can really do. As with any art, if an engraver is to become really good, he has to see good engraving. I expect Japanese engravers seldom, if ever, have an opportunity to compare their work with the world's best, much less benefit from topflight instruction.

Sometimes though they have an opportunity to get it all together in one truly excellent package. Probably the best examples of this are the Parker Reproduction side-by-sides. This is the gun that

Close fit of wood and metal, characteristic of SKB shotguns, is the result of careful handwork. The delicate work of final stock shaping and fitting is done entirely by hand, though craftsmen are able to do the job nearly as fast as production machinery.

should erase anyone's doubts about the Japanese ability to make fine guns.

An interesting difference between Japan's gunmakers and other segments of Japanese industry is their apparent preference for being suppliers to the world shooting trade without trying to establish either strong name recognition or a distinct international visibility. Whereas such major firms as Sony and Honda spend millions of dollars each year promoting their names, Japanese gunmakers would seem to want their products to be known by the names that appear on them. Such names as Browning, Weatherby, Winchester, Parker, Mossberg, Charles Daly and others. Perhaps the Japanese feel they learned a valuable lesson when Miroku shotguns sold better when they were renamed Charles Daly. The one big exception to this rule is SKB, which carries the strongest name recognition of any Japanese maker, but even this identity is hidden when they make shotguns bearing the Weatherby signature.

For the record, here are the big names in Japanese gunmaking: SKB makes shotguns bearing their own name and the Weatherby shotguns. Howa makes Weatherby rifles and Mossberg rifles and shotguns. Olin-Kodensha makes Winchester shotguns (*not* the Winchesters made by U.S. Repeating Arms Co., which are U.S.-made) and the Parker Reproductions. Miroku makes the Japanese Brownings.

An American flag was flying over the SKB plant on the days Ernie Simmons III, Tom Nichols, and I were there. Ernie is the honcho at Simmons Enterprises, the importer of SKB guns and Nichols is a major SKB dealer. The factory is situated in a pretty village with a name that is utterly unpronounceable with an American tongue. Neat rice paddies edge the town and beyond are densely wooded mountains. This looks like a good place to live and work, especially since it is a good two hours' drive from Tokyo's bustle.

The SKB parking lot was well filled with new-looking autos and in a corner of the compound was the executive putting green. (Golf is Japan's latest religion, with millions of devoted followers.) Inside the main offices there were neat rows of street shoes, left there by the staff who, in Japanese custom, wore the traditional slippers. These dainty little slippers apparently aren't made in Tennessee farm boy sizes so I accepted our host's greetings in sock feet.

The president of SKB is Jiro Miura, a compact but powerfully built man of middle age who, I was to learn, is one of Japan's top Olympic class shotgunners. He is very much the Japanese industrialist, leaving no doubt that he was the guy in charge of everything. He was obviously very proud of his shotguns, and I quickly gathered that he would rather be in the factory than in the office.

Gun factories tend to be very much alike. Some are new and some are old, but the screech and chatter of gunmaking machinery is the same worldwide. The steaming dungeons where gunmetal is blued don't differ much from upstate New York to the Black Forest of Germany, and the perfume of walnut dust is as seductive in Japan as it is in New Haven.

When you tour a gun plant, your hosts like to show you the big stuff, the floor-shaking machines that have computers for brains and chew truckloads of steel into baskets of gun parts. But computer-controlled gunmaking machines all speak the same language and if given half a chance they'd be making identical guns. That's why I always look *behind* the big machines to see who is pushing the buttons. I want to see the faces and hands and workbenches that give a particular gun its distinctive personality. That's right, there's no doubt about it, a gun has a personality. Haven't you noticed how one gun can sing to you while another of almost identical design and function is as devoid of character as a handful of wet sawdust?

I didn't have to look far to find some of the rea-

This worker feeds billets to a milling machine to make shotgun receivers. Here again, the operation depends on the machinist's skill—there are no automatic computer controls, and no jigs or patterns. But at SKB the finished product is a receiver that fits other associated components with precision.

sons that Japanese guns are what they are. By modern production standards, an amazing number of operations were being performed on small, manually controlled milling machines and drill presses. Even more amazing were the machine operators who reduced metal to finished dimensions without the aid of blueprints, jigs, or production models. Working entirely from memory a craftsman at a milling machine would produce a part that would fit perfectly with another part made by another craftsman in another part of the factory. Not only did the parts fit, but also they were produced with a speed that rivals modern high-production machinery. There seemed to be a symbiosis between a worker and his milling machine. The machine was his friend, the older the better. The workers never seemed to hurry but neither did they slow down. I got the idea that they could continue working indefinitely—and be quite content to do so.

As I wandered from machine to machine, from workbench to workbench, I became increasingly aware that there was a fundamental philosophical difference between the Japanese gunmaker and the craftsmen in other gun factories I've visited. But for a long while I couldn't quite put my finger on the difference. Then it hit me. *Fish and flowers!*

The typical workbench decoration, be it in the hallowed halls of Holland & Holland or the rustic shops at Remington, is a pinup calendar or a picture of a very nude lady torn from a naughty magazine. But not in a Japanese gun factory. Their pinups are pictures of fish and pictures of flowers. There was my answer, the key to the mindset of the Japanese worker; a self-induced serenity that converts dull, mind-numbing labor into a perpetual image of self-fulfillment. Call it Zen and the art of gunmaking.

While we watched a barrelmaking operation, a worker passed by with a cart heavily loaded with barrel blanks. A wheel fell into a crack in the floor, upsetting the cart and causing a great clatter. The worker was horrified! No damage had been done, but the worker's sin was spoiling the serenity of the workplace. His first reaction was to cover his face with his hands and stand before us in shame. Then, discovering he had offended no one in our party, he gathered the scattered barrels like a squirrel grabbing nuts, bowing over and over before disappearing.

As a gun nears completion it is handled with increasing respect. Each gun is regarded as an artistic expression and therefore worthy of the respect due any form of good art. Especially artful is the Japanese way of working with wood. In this they have excelled for centuries and even their woodworking tools have achieved artistic status. The chisels and gauges used by the stock fitters are so beautifully sharpened and polished, with delicately turned and carved handles, that they are a pleasure to use. (It's the Zen concept again—perfect tool plus perfect state of mind equals perfect product.)

There was no question that the guy in charge of staining the stocks considered himself an artist—and with good reason. Rather than spraying or wiping on a coat of ordinary walnut stain, he sat at a workbench covered with many pots of

Checkering Japanese-style is done with a clumsy hand tool, and this may account for rather disappointing checkering characteristic of Japanese stocks. The tool's large ring has cutting teeth; the ring must be rotated to bring a new set of sharp teeth into place.

different hued stains. Each stock was thoughtfully considered and a stain was brushed on that was *just right* for that particular piece of wood. Occasionally he blended stains to achieve what he considered the perfect color match for a butt and forearm set. I watched him for a long while, but I don't think he was ever aware of my presence, so total was his concentration that nothing encroached on his serenity. Zen.

For years I've wondered why the checkering on Japanese guns is so inconsistent with the craftsmanship apparent in the fitting of metal to metal and metal to wood. I took one look at their checkering shop and the reasons were clear. To begin with, the tools the women used were absolutely impossible. The cutting edges were on the outside edge of a steel hoop some 5 inches in diameter. As the cutting teeth dull the hoop is rotated in the handle, exposing sharp teeth. From the cost and maintenance standpoints such a tool may be somewhat efficient, but there's no way such a gadget can produce high-quality checkering. If an electric checkering tool were introduced to Japanese gunmaking the results would be something to see. But, on the other hand the buzzing of an electric tool might disrupt the serenity. Who knows?

There is not much hunting in Japan and gun ownership is limited. A shotgun owner may do some gamebird hunting, but more likely he enjoys international-style trap or skeet at one of the country's beautifully manicured shooting clubs. Rifle ownership is restricted and handguns are virtually unseen except for nonshooting replicas, which delight Japanese collectors. Even though a worker in a Japanese gun factory is probably not a gun owner or hunter, he feels a close kinship to those who are and considers himself a partner with whoever buys a gun he has helped build. Frequently I was asked by the workers if I owned a SKB shotgun and, if so, did I enjoy shooting it. When I replied that I owned *two* SKB shotguns they were wide-eyed with wonder, and when I told them how many birds I had bagged with each they would break into spasms of joy, bowing and grinning with unrestrained delight. I suspect that if I had told them that I also occasionally miss a target they would have succumbed to despair. They seem to have the idea that if a target is missed with an SKB shotgun they are as much at blame as the shooter.

That attitude pretty well sums up Japanese gunmaking. If a gun is not good, then it is very, very bad. And bad is a disgrace. A gun is like a Samurai sword: It must be beautiful to behold but ultimately its purpose is not for looks but for use. And only when it is used is its worth validated. That is when the spirits of the steel, the craftsman, and the warrior become united. Zen.

PART THREE

SHOTGUN CORNER

Sporting Clays:
The New Shotgun Challenge

Robert W. Hunnicutt

It seems the fate of all sports to become ever more abstract, complex, and expensive. As they do, they are separated from everyday experience.

The simple desire to see who can go faster evolves into Formula 1 auto or unlimited hydroplane racing. A fall afternoon's entertainment for college boys grows into a multibillion-dollar industry with its own labor union. Matching a pair of sailing boats takes on the engineering proportions and nationalistic overtones of a moon shot.

The shooting sports are not immune from this. Fortunately, there is a countervailing tendency. As a sport matures, as the hardcore aficionados drive the expense and dedication required beyond the means of the many, people find new ways to bring back the simple pleasure and spontaneity that is the true reason for sport.

The process is underway in the shotgun sports.

Almost everyone agrees that skeet and trapshooting have reached something of an evolutionary dead end. They are sports that mean a lot

to their devotees, but require money and time that intimidate the would-be shooter and eventually burn out all but the most dedicated competitor. Research has shown that the average skeet shooter stays with the game about four years—the average trapshooter keeps at it about seven years.

Obviously, thousands give up the shotgun sports every year, and thousands more never get started in competitive shooting, preferring to restrict themselves to hunting or the occasional round of "recreational" skeet or trap.

It is ironic that a possible solution has come from Britain, a land where gun ownership is constantly endangered and where shooting has been imagined a perquisite of the landed gentry.

Sporting clays has been contested in Britain since the 1920s, and on the European continent under names like *parcours de chasse* for decades. It has just recently begun to see explosive growth in the United Kingdom as a favored activity of the

This article first appeared in American Rifleman

Imported from Britain, the new shotgun sport is adding to the thrill of competition for American scattergunners. And it has drawn big-time corporate sponsorship. At the Glenlivet Scotch Sporting Challenge shown here, Seagram's, Rolls-Royce, and many other corporations were represented.

resurgent Thatcher-era middle class, a class that perhaps longs to recapture some of the atmosphere of aristocratic country life.

Sporting clays provides some of the action and excitement of hunting, but at a price the middle-income sport can afford. The purpose of the game is to recreate the kind of shots found in traditional British hunting (or "shooting" as the Britisher calls it—what we call deer hunting is "stalking").

As good ideas will, this one has spread to the United States, and there are now several dozen places to shoot sporting clays, with more being built every day.

The secret of sporting's appeal is that no two layouts are exactly alike. A sporting field uses the natural landscape as an integral part of its design, and the game species native to the area as the inspiration for the shooting problems it presents.

This gives it an immediacy and a relevance to the hunter, and it gives the local shooter an advantage over the visitor—it's hard to imagine the development of a class of touring professionals in sporting competition who scoop up the prizes everywhere, as some top trapshooters do.

Creating an authentic field atmosphere requires space, cover and considerable labor. While trap and skeet shots are taken basically in one general direction at relatively low angles, sporting shots are taken in all directions, at angles ranging from below the horizon to straight overhead. This means safety and impact zones must be planned with great care. Walking paths and spectator areas must be protected from shotfall.

Natural cover is one of the features that give the game its appeal. Targets are thrown between trees, from the top of hills and down hollows. Each target should give the shooter a new problem in seeing, lead estimation, and timing.

Sporting layouts require considerable labor, both in their construction and in match operation. A sporting layout cannot be run by a couple of listless trap boys, as some operators have found. Getting plenty of well-motivated labor is a major part of the tournament sponsor's problem.

Though some sporting layouts in this country utilize electrical traps, many, and most of them in Britain, use hand-cocked and -loaded traps that require full-time attention from a trap boy or "trapper" as the British say.

While the labor requirement is large, so is the flexibility provided by hand (often called "foot") traps. They can be placed almost anywhere and can be adjusted quickly to throw targets in almost any direction. A good sporting tournament sponsor changes his layout often to present new challenges to the shooters, and this is a cinch with hand traps.

The economy of hand traps is important to small or remote clubs. For the price of a pair of electrical machines, a club could buy 100 Trius, Outer's, or Hoppe's traps or several dozen of the European sporting traps like the Farey or Laporte.

While every sporting layout has a "personality" of its own, certain shots have become traditional and are found on almost every course.

The target American shooters will find most familiar is the walk-up. A typical walk-up requires the shooter to fire six times, in pairs, reloading between each pair. He starts at the head of a track 10 yards or so long and walks forward. The trapper may release targets at will, though a specified time, usually five seconds, is provided for reloading. Targets are thrown generally at low elevation and straight ahead to imitate the flight of quail or other flushing species. The Fairfield Shooting Grounds near Chestertown, Maryland, adds a special fillip to its walk-up—a "covey rise" with six targets rising at once from hand traps. If a shooter is lucky enough to break two or more targets with one shot, they count; but such "flock shooting" usually has the same result it has in the hunting field—a miss.

"Pigeon" is a designation usually applied to a very long crossing shot. At the Beretta World Sporting Championships in 1987, a Norwegian

Rabbit targets in sporting clays are rolled down a track of rubber or soft grass. They tend to bounce unpredictably, just as the real-life rodents do. The targets are H-shaped in cross-section.

member of my squad took 60 paces to cover the distance from the shooting stand to the crossing point of one pigeon target. These targets test the shooter's ability to calculate lead and to follow through on shots that seem impossibly long.

Springing teal targets attempt to duplicate the jump of surprised ducks. Hand traps are mounted sidewise or at extreme angles to throw targets almost straight up. Teal targets can be quite easy at close ranges, fiendishly difficult when the distance is long. The Atlantic Coast Gun Club near Wardensville, West Virginia, had a pair of teal targets set at about 40 yards range across a pond. They defeated everyone except one shooter who discovered he could hit them reliably—by figuring lead from the *bottom* of his over/under's muzzles.

Partridge targets are incomers, traditionally taken over the crest of a hill or treeline. They are fast and low, and often require the shooter to take one shot directly in front of the stand and the second at an angle.

Rabbits are very confusing for the first-time shooter. They are thrown by a trap mounted perpendicular to the ground. The trap throws the target onto a track made of rubber matting or close-mown grass, where it rolls and bounces its way to a limit point, usually a bale of hay. Any irregularity in the surface will cause the target to bounce unpredictably. Many a good shot has dropped a point when a rabbit target jumped into the air just as the shot charge arrived.

In Britain, special rabbit targets are used, but in this country many range operators find that international skeet and trap targets work well if the track is kept clean and free of target fragments.

Probably the most vexing target in sporting for the average American shooter is the high pheasant. It should be recalled that in Britain, pheasants are driven toward the hunters by a line of beaters. The birds climb rapidly and cross the line of shooters at high altitudes at their top speed.

The British use targets thrown from high towers to duplicate the pheasant's flight, and some of them can be frighteningly impressive.

I was lucky enough to get some professional instruction on pheasant technique at the Holland & Holland Shooting School outside London. There, instructor Andrew Perkins drilled me on the fine points of shooting targets from the 100-foot tower. I shot and shot, and each time his analysis was the same—"missed behind." Finally, I gave it three or four times the lead I thought possible, and the hits started coming. I thought I had pheasants doped out—until I visited another British club that had erected a 70-foot tower atop a 70-foot hill.

Big towers are still rare in this country, though some have been built and others are on the way. More common is a pheasant shot from a hillside. The Atlantic Coast club has one thrown from a clifflike hill; the shooter stands on the edge of a little stream below. This provides the effect of a 100-foot tower without the expense.

The shooting stand itself is a distinctive feature of British-style sporting shooting. It is intended both to ensure the safety of spectators and to limit

The sporting stand is designed to prevent firing in unsafe directions and to limit the shooter's options in taking any given shot.

the shooter's options in taking the shot. Stands at the Apsley Shooting Grounds, site of the 1987 Beretta World Sporting Championships, for example, were sturdy frame structures covered with strips of slab lumber. Only one shooter at a time could stand inside, and openings were made so the gun could be pointed only in a safe direction. Competitors and spectators could walk by on paths below gun level.

Initially, it was a little unnerving to pass by these little buildings with shotguns going off directly overhead. But they were designed with such care that there was no real possibility of accident. Almost as important, the shooter was isolated from the press of more than 600 competitors and hundreds of spectators. Once inside, all that could be seen was the spot in the sky where the target was to be broken.

Now most sporting stands aren't so elaborate, many being made of light lumber and chicken wire, but the principles remain the same—to limit the shooter's options and, far more importantly, to protect competitors, spectators, and trappers from an errant shot.

A sporting course usually incorporates 10 stands at which 10 targets are fired on for a round of 100 targets. Some have more—the Beretta World shoot featured 15 stands and 120 targets—and many others, especially new clubs in this country, have fewer.

In the United States, clubs generally follow trap and skeet practice and group shooters in squads of five. These then pass from stand to stand, in order, and arrive at the end of the course together. In Britain, a more free-form system is used. Each shooter is issued a scorecard that he carries from stand to stand. He can get together with friends in a squad, or he can wander along alone. He can shoot the stands in any order, so long as he finishes by a given time, often 5 P.M.

On arriving at the stand, the shooter presents his scorecard to the referee and takes his place in line to shoot. He can observe the targets as other shooters fire on them. If he is the first to arrive at the stand, he can view the targets, though not from the shooting station itself.

The referee marks the shooter's scorecard, and marks his score on a master list that forms a record of every shooter's score on that stand. He initials the scorecard and hands it back to the shooter, who then may proceed to the next station.

This system seems a bit undisciplined to those of us used to the regimentation of trap and skeet shooting, but it works very well, and it allows large crowds to use a facility without endless backups. Despite the large attendance at the Beretta World shoot, I found that my turn always seemed to come a lot sooner than I preferred!

Once the shooter takes his place on the shooting

station, he may load and call for the target. The butt of the shotgun must be visible beneath the armpit when the call is made. In practice, this leads to a lot of different interpretations. Continental Europeans I've shot with tend to adopt the international skeet position, with the toe of the buttstock at hip level. Some Britishers and Americans, on the other hand, stretch the "beneath the armpit" rule to its utmost minimum limit.

The target then is released after a delay of as much as three seconds. The release may be done by the trapper himself, by a release in the hand of the referee, or by a signal from referee to trapper. At the Apsley grounds, this was accomplished by using old-fashioned battery-powered doorbells. All that was required was a button, some lamp cord, a lantern battery and the bell. Most U.S. ranges require the trapper to hear the call and release the target, so a loud, sharp call from the shooter is required to cut through the noise of firing.

Targets may be released in a number of ways. Singles can be fired on with a one-shot limit or, as in international trapshooting, with two shots.

Doubles come in many varieties. Silmultaneous doubles are just like trap and skeet doubles—both targets are thrown at once. Generally speaking, if both are broken with one shot, both are counted dead. Following doubles are thrown one after another, with a predetermined delay between. This is generally enough to prevent shooting both with one shot.

Report doubles start with one target; when it is fired on, the trapper releases the second target. "Fur and feather" is a combination of a rabbit target and an aerial target.

A combination popular at hunting-oriented clubs is a double with a "hen" or "poison" target. Shooting the designated target (usually a white night skeet clay) costs the hapless shooter a penalty point or points.

While doubles in Europe are scored as in international skeet—that is, proof doubles are required if one target is broken by the thrower—U.S. rules allow the first target to be scored dead or lost.

One of the interesting parts of sporting competition is the use of several different types of clay targets. The most common target type is the standard 108.5mm target used in trap and skeet competition, though many clubs like the international target because it better resists breaking.

The "midi" target is 90mm in diameter in comparison to the 110 of the international clay. It is heavy, despite its small size, and carries a great distance. The midi isn't always immediately recognizable, and that can cause lead errors if the shooter thinks he's firing on the standard target.

I encountered a clever use of the midi at a shoot

Hand traps allow the course designer almost infinite flexibility in duplicating the flight of gamebirds. This installation is for "springing teal."

where it was used for a pair of "partridge" targets. The traps were placed well back from the brow of a hill, and tossed the clays low and fast over the shooter's head. The deceptive speed and "carry" of the midis made them tougher-than-expected targets.

The "mini" target is 60mm in diameter, and it is easily recognizable when thrown. It is easy enough to hit in open air, but it is difficult when thrown in dense undergrowth.

The battue target is similar in diameter to the standard target, but it is only only about ⅜ of an inch high. It requires a special trap arm and a large impact area because unlike standard targets that impact softly, it bores into the ground on impact. Shooters often refer to battues as "flying razor blades."

Rabbit targets are used only for rabbit stands, and have a very heavy rim for easy rolling.

While trap and skeet targets generally are painted or have painted domes, sporting targets are more often all-black, since many shots are taken against the open sky. When all-black clay targets are taken at low angles beneath the tree line, they can be, just as gamebirds are, very hard to see.

Guns for sporting competition can be of any type. One successful Maryland shooter uses a 30-inch barreled Browning BPS pump gun with full choke.

More often, though, the sporting shooter uses an over/under shotgun. The superposed has even caught on big in that side-by-side citadel, Britain. A gun wholesaler there told me he could sell all the Beretta stackbarrels (and autoloaders) he wanted, but was stuck with dozens of Spanish side-by-sides.

Barrel length and choke are still topics of controversy and experimentation, especially now that choke tubes are becoming universal. Chokes may be changed between stations, and some shooters busily spin their spanners at any opportunity. One suspects an electric choke tube tool will come on the market any day!

The best British shooters, though, seem to have arrived at the conclusion that improved cylinder will handle any sporting target, and a 30-inch barreled gun with improved cylinder tubes is becoming something of a standard.

I became a believer in the virtues of improved cylinder chokes when firing that 60-yard crossing shot at the Beretta World shoot. The gun was a Beretta 682 with improved cylinder and improved modified tubes. I broke five of eight, three with the more open choke, two with the tighter.

Some will find a 30-inch barreled gun a little imposing, but the extra weight and sight radius come in handy. My own gun is a Krieghoff Model 32 with 30-inch Briley-tubed barrels, a field-type buttstock and forend. And my Krieghoff has a Bear Trap recoil reducer.

Tipping the scales at just 3 ounces less than 9 pounds, and measuring almost 4 feet long, it would seem at first blush that such an arm would be a handful in simulated field shooting. But recoil is damped to near-imperceptibility, and the weight up front keeps the gun moving for a smooth follow-through.

Beretta has jumped solidly on the sporting bandwagon with a series of guns in its 682, 686 and 687 lines. The 682SP Sporting is an excellent choice, especially for the shooter who wants to use a sporting gun for skeet or field shooting. Guns like the Browning Citori Invector and choke-tubed Ruger Red Label have the advantage of a very thick-walled barrel construction for recoil reduction and barrel "hang" that makes them good moderately priced choices.

European shooters are partial to the Winchester Model 101, especially a version that has the same receiver style as the U.S. American Flyer pigeon gun. The Weatherby Athena or its equivalent in the SKB line would be good choices.

Were I looking for a moderately priced replacement for my Krieghoff, I'd try the Valmet 412ST, a reasonably priced arm with good length and heft, choke tubes, and an excellent trigger, priced at less than $1,200.

While over/unders are favored by the experienced competition shooters who are getting into sporting, there's certainly no law against other action types. While in Britain, I bumped into an old acquaintance, world clay pigeon record-holder Dan Carlisle, an active sporting shooter. He was using a Beretta Model 302 autoloader with good results, and a Beretta representative told me that the self-loader is finally racking up deservedly big sales in the United Kingdom.

Meeting the challenge of sporting clays (below, from top to bottom): Weatherby Athena with 30-inch barrel; Krieghoff Model 32 with 30-inch barrel; Beretta 682SP with 28-inch barrel.

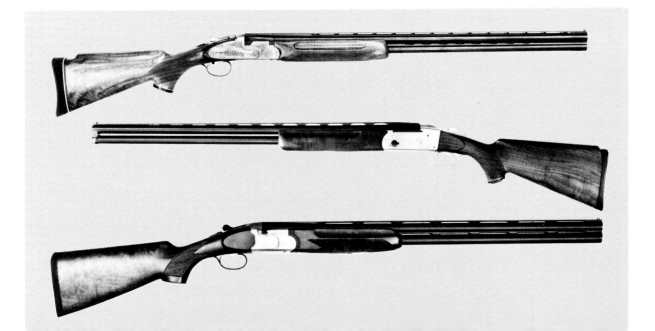

Certainly the Remington Model 1100 would be a perfectly adequate sporting gun, especially with the new Rem Choke-tubed barrel. I've seen a smattering of other autoloaders, Benelli, Browning, Winchester, and others, and if you have one and are used to it, feel free to try it.

Side-by-side doubles were *de rigeur* in the early days of British sporting competition but have been almost entirely supplanted by the superposed. I saw a few used while shooting in England, and some were shot well, but their users were regarded as lovable eccentrics. They shouldn't be underestimated, however; one acquaintance of mine has consistently scored best with a 16-gauge Parker of 1930s vintage.

It is possible to shoot sporting with a pump gun, and some do it well. But unless you're really wedded to that trusty Model 12 or 870, I'd suggest a double gun or autoloader.

While high trap stocks have become popular for both trap and skeet, they won't do for sporting. Those high overhead shots on "pheasants" require a stock with a little drop, or keeping the head glued to the comb becomes an almost impossible task.

A group almost as determined as the choke tube-spinners is the ammo-changers. You can spot them by the four or five different boxes they're carrying. Any ammuniton with a shot charge of 1⅛ ounces or less and No. 7½ or smaller shot is legal, and I suspect some sporting shooters are determined to try them all, especially the expensive high-velocity stuff with copper or nickel-plated shot.

I wouldn't want to discourage anyone, especially since equipment experimenting is the mainstay of the industry, but 2¾-dram shells with No. 8 shot will cover 99 percent of the shots you'll ever encounter in sporting competition. Keep in mind that you'll often be shooting at the underside of targets, with much more area exposed than in trap or skeet.

I like Dan Arms, 2¾-dram No. 8 loads for sporting, because the price is right in this area, but Federal's Extra-Lite, Remington's Premier, and Winchester's Super-Lite are all good choices. Those who don't mind the cost and the punishment level favor heavier stuff like Dan Arms' copper-plated Max Trap or nickel-plated trap loads from Fiocchi or Rottweil.

Federal is first into the fray with a specially marked sporting shell. It has remarked its T122 load, a paper-hulled, fiber-wadded round intended for international skeet use, and added a No. 8 loading to the existing No. 9. The T122 gives emphatic breaks, but using it will remind you why plastic wads were such a revelation in the 1960s— barrel leading is heavy and recoil quite sharp.

In England, Eley ammunition seemed to be the choice, though some shooters favored Maionchi, Cheddite, and other Continental brands. The Holland & Holland school provided some private-branded 2½-inch shells made with Fiocchi components. They were delightfully mild and broke targets with sufficient authority for almost any taste.

Little other equipment is needed for sporting. Hearing protection is a must, as it is everywhere, and eye protection is even more essential than in

Sporting Clays Clubs. The following is a partial listing of clubs that conduct sporting competition. Since the sport is growing at a very rapid pace, it should in no way be considered exhaustive. Clubs that have recently opened sporting courses should contact "A Place To Shoot," *American Rifleman*, 470 Spring Park Pl., Suite 1000, Herndon, VA 22070.

California
  Carlisle Shotgun Sports, Norco
  Pachmayr Hunt School, Monrovia
  Sacramento Sporting Clays, Sacramento
Colorado
  Buck Point Club, Glenwood Springs
  Glenarm Sporting Clays, Montrose
Delaware
  Ommelanden Range, New Castle
Florida
  Osceola Farms, W. Palm Beach
Georgia
  Forest City Gun Club, Savannah
Iowa
  N. Iowa Sporting Clays Club, St. Ansgar
Maryland
  Beretta Gun Club, Glenn Dale
  Fairfield Shooting Grounds, Chestertown
  Hopkins Game Farm, Kennedyville
Minnesota
  Minnesota Horse & Hunt Club, Prior Lake
Mississippi
  Wilderness West, Jackson
Montana
  Mallards Rest Sporting Clays, Billings
New Hampsire
  SKAT Upland Game Preserve, New Ipswich
New York
  Mashomack Fish & Game Preserve, Pine Plains
  Rochester Brooks Sporting Clays Association, Rush
Texas
  Champion Lakes Gun Club, Houston
  Cypress Valley Preserve, Austin
  Dallas Gun Club, Lewisville
  Highland Bend Shooting School, Fulshear
  La Paloma Sporting Club, San Antonio
  National Gun Club, San Antonio
  Spanish Dagger Hunting Resort, Uvalde
  Upland Bird Country, Corsicana
West Virginia
  Atlantic Coast Gun Club, Wardensville

Hand traps placed in large trees allow high-flying target presentations. This one is up about 40 feet.

other shotgun sports, what with lots of incoming targets. The leafy environs of most sporting layouts require somewhat lighter tints than common in skeet and trapshooting—I have found Decot's Bronze No. ½ work well for all but the most dismal days.

An essential accessory is a bag of some sort to carry ammunition. The British favor a leather shell bag somewhere between a big purse and a fishing creel in size. I have found that an Eddie Bauer day backpack is just about right for carrying the six boxes of shells required at the Atlantic Coast Gun Club, with room for choke tubes or a little snack.

Sporting shooting is somewhat diverse in its governance. On the European continent, FITASC—the *Federation Internationale de Tir aux Armes Sportif de Chasse*—sets the rules. FITASC, which also governs pigeon and universal trap shooting, sponsors what is probably the toughest version of the sport, requiring an international skeet-style starting position and allowing 1¼-ounce loadings. FITASC shooting has lots of battue, mini and midi targets, and is for the real sporting enthusiast.

In Britain the sport is governed by the Clay Pi-geon Shooting Association, whose rules are closest to U.S. sporting practice.

In this country, a pair of organizations are vying for the loyalty of sporting shooters. The U.S. Sporting Clays Association, with most of its leadership drawn from the south Texas hotbed of the sport, was first out of the blocks. But the National Skeet Shooting Association has started its own program and held a large sporting shoot in conjunction with its 1987 World Shoot. Both organizations are aggressively promoting their programs in an effort to spread the sport from its present enclaves in Texas and on the coasts.

An excellent way to get a better picture of sporting is to see the Holland & Holland video, "Sporting Clays Shooting," available from Blacksmith. While it won't instantly make you a sporting champ, it provides an excellent picture of how the game is shot in Britain. It would be a superb choice for someone looking for ideas on range setup.

Two excellent books on the subject are *"A Manual of Clayshooting,"* by Chris Cradock, and *"Clay Pigeon Marksmanship"* by Percy Stanbury and G.L. Carlisle.

The U.S. Sporting Clays Association has range plans available and also is conducting training courses around the country in a effort to develop a cadre of qualified instructors.

Sporting clays is an exciting development that many hope will become the equivalent of silhouette shooting—a sport that will bring in new blood and reinvigorate competitors who've grown tired of existing games. If there's a range in your area, give it a try. If not, get a few foot traps, some targets and some shells, and make your own sporting layout. Once you try it, you'll have to come back for more.

Sources

Books:
David & Charles, Inc., N. Pomfret, VT
Rules and range plans:
National Skeet Shooting Ass'n, P.O. Box 68007, San Antonio, TX 78268
U.S. Sporting Clays Ass'n, 50 Briar Hollow, Suite 490 East, Houston, TX 77027
Targets and traps:
Farey, SKAT Shooting Preserve, P.O. Box 137, New Ipswich, NH 03071
Laporte, 1170 Route de Nice, 06600 Antibes, France
Trius, Box 25, Cleves, OH 45002
Hoppe's, Penguin Industries, Inc., Airport Industrial Mall, Coatesville, PA 19320
Outer's Laboratories, Inc., Rt. 2, Box 37, Onalaska, WI 54650
Video:
Blacksmith Corp., P.O. Box 424, Southport, CT 06490

Super-Fox:
The Waterfowling Legend

Michael McIntosh

It's impossible to know now just whose idea it was. For a while, it seemed that everyone but Gandhi and Calvin Coolidge claimed to have had a hand in inventing the Super-Fox.

Ironically, the one man who had nothing at all to do with the finest waterfowl gun of its day was Ansley Fox himself. He was out of the gun business altogether by then, busy building automobiles.

Actually, the Super-Fox was the product of several minds, all focused on the remarkably complicated problems involved in getting a shotgun reliably to deliver a high percentage of its shot to roughly the same place at any distance much beyond 40 yards. It also was the product of technologies unknown before and of splendid talents brought together at precisely the right time.

By the end of World War I, the search for a truly long-range shotgun had been underway for nearly two generations. Often it was more a process of discovery than of solution, as each new advance uncovered more problems. Choke-boring had been an almost universal practice since the turn of the century, but gunmakers were learning that there is more critical territory in a shotgun barrel than the few inches taken up by choke.

They began to understand that the relationship between chamber and bore, and even the bore itself, influenced the behavior of a shot charge in important ways. Exactly how these influences came to bear and exactly what to do about them loomed as questions yet unanswered.

Cartridges, too, came in for a share of attention. By then, the limitations endemic to the older generation of shotshells were becoming clearer. Smokeless powders, still relatively new, showed unexplored possibilities.

Smaller-gauge guns were showing potential unthought of only a few years before. Eightbores had been legislated out of existence, and the 10-gauge was a moribund graybeard of a gun, tottering along on failing legs.

In those days, the standard 10-gauge load carried a maximum 1¼ ounces of shot, and the 12-gauge already had proven itself capable of digesting at least that much in a lighter, better-handling gun. The trick was to make it so at distances useful to the wildfowler, for the once-vast flocks of waterfowl were nearly gone. What chances the average gunner got at game came more and more often at the ragged edge of his shotgun's reach or beyond.

Onto the stage thus set, enter E.M. Sweeley and Maj. Charles Askins, Sr. Sweeley was a lawyer in Twin Falls, Idaho, a University of Michigan football star from the days of Coach Harry Fielding Yost, and a shotgunner keenly interested in ballistics. He also was an intelligent, hardheaded experimenter determined to find some answers to the old problems of extending the shotgun's range. Maj. Askins was the best-known and most authoritative gun writer in the country, a superb game shot, and also preoccupied with learning why a shotgun behaves the way it does.

One of Sweeley's more fruitful notions was that overboring would improve a gun barrel's performance. It wasn't an original idea, but Sweeley demonstrated to his own and Maj. Askins' satisfaction that it worked, using a gun reportedly custom bored by Ithaca. He experimented with ammunition as well, at one point using thin, flexible copper over-powder wads that he believed would promote tighter patterns.

Perhaps they did, but a real breakthrough in shotshell design was already on the way. By 1920, John Olin, owner of the Western Cartridge Co., was nearing the end of a project that would have a profound effect upon shotgunning worldwide.

This article first appeared in American Rifleman

A pair of fine Super-Foxes share company with two classic Canada goose decoys carved about 1923 by Charles Birch of Willis Wharf, Virginia. The guns include a standard HE Grade 12-gauge (left) and the finest known Super-Fox, the XE Grade. This special-order XE gun has barrels bored by Burt Becker.

This is the line engraving on the XE Grade Super-Fox.

For several reasons, a shot swarm traveling through the air spreads in length as well as diameter. Some stringing seems to be inevitable, but from even the best shells of those days, pellets at the tail end of the swarm might lag 30 feet or more behind those at the front.

Olin correctly saw such extreme stringing as a major weakness in shotgun performance even at relatively close ranges, and he also recognized it as a problem caused mainly by deformed pellets. His solution was to use harder shot and to develop a progressive-burning powder that pushed rather than blasted the pellets down the bore.

Maj. Askins did a great deal of field-test work with Olin's experimental shells, and as he, Sweeley, and the Western ballisticians studied what they were learning, it became clear that a combination of specially designed barrels and Western's remarkable new shotshells was the key they'd all been looking for.

There remained only the task of finding a gunmaker to wrap all the pieces together. In that, there was only one logical choice. A.H. Fox Gun Co. already was deeply interested in Olin's project—and employed the best barrel man in the country, besides. In June, 1922, Maj. Askins headed for Philadelphia to meet with Fox factory officials and with Burt Becker.

Becker was a gunsmith in the best European tradition. He was an engineer, a machinist, a barrelmaker, a stockmaker, and an engraver—all at a time when specialization was the order of the day. He worked for Parker in the 1890s and reportedly built the guns Parker exhibited in the Columbian Exposition at Chicago in 1893.

Similarly, he is said to have built the Remington doubles displayed at St. Louis in the 1904 Louisiana Purchase Exposition. By the end of World War I, Becker was in Philadelphia, working as a master gunsmith and doing custom work at A.H. Fox.

For all his talents, Becker's particular gift was for boring barrels. Of the guns that John Olin had used to test his new cartridges, the best was a Becker-bored Fox 12-gauge with barrels carefully overbored ahead of 3-inch chambers. In 1921, Olin sent the gun and eight unmarked boxes of shells to an old friend in Memphis, asking that he try them on ducks and geese and report back with an opinion. With that, Olin delivered Burt Becker, and eventually the Super-Fox, into the hands of history.

Nash Buckingham was not yet the most famous sporting writer in America, but he was well on the way. He was, though, certainly the finest long-range wingshot of the last generation to know firsthand a truly enormous wealth of American game. He was just the man to test the limits of any gun and ammunition.

Buckingham was so impressed by the performance of Olin's gun and shells that he immediately abandoned his 34-inch Parker and whatever cartridges he'd been using. By the time Maj. Askins arrived in Philadelphia, Buckingham had a Becker-bored Fox of his own, and Olin's shells were beginning to appear in sporting goods stores around the Midwest, marketed under the trade name Super-X.

Fox had assigned Becker and a small design staff the task of developing a gun that would realize all the potential the new ammunition had to offer. Through the summer of 1922, Becker and Maj. Askins bored and tested gun after gun, refining both the design and the manufacturing techniques. By October, the Super-Fox was ready for delivery to the trade.

Fox announced the gun with a full-page ad in the January 1923 issue of *The Sporting Goods Dealer*, billing it, with modesty that Ansley Fox would certainly have approved, as "the outstanding shot-gun achievement of the past twenty years." The text declares the Super-Fox proven to kill single ducks "with the greatest certainty at sixty yards, perfectly capable of killing singles up to seventy yards, with ability to take birds out of flocks at much longer range." The copywriter, whoever he was, earned his pay, despite his tacit encouragement of flock-shooting. In an excess of enthusiasm it would later regret, the Fox Co. guaranteed that every Super-Fox would deliver minimum patterns of 80 percent.

Behind the hype was a gun that for the most part would do exactly what they said it would.

Though Fox assigned the gun status as the HE Grade, the Super-Fox actually is a separate model. It is mechanically identical to other Fox guns and made from the same materials, but it is significantly different in execution. The frame is massive, built to 10-gauge scale and, as with the barrels, milled from Fox's own formula of high-chromium steel, trade named Chromox.

A Super-Fox could weigh as much as 9¾ pounds. Only 30- or 32-inch barrels were available; if the buyer wished, they would be bored and honed for a specific load or shot size.

Ejectors and double triggers came as standard equipment, with the excellent Fox-Kautzky single trigger available as an option. All other Fox options could be had as well—vent rib, beavertail fore-end, rubber recoil pad, skeleton steel buttplate, and Lyman ivory bead sights.

The guns were stoutly stocked with fairly plain, straight-grain English walnut and made to standard dimensions of 14⅛-inch pull, 1⅝-inch drop at the comb and 2⅝-inch at the heel. Grips could be straight-hand, half-hand, or full-pistol, all at the same price. Fancier wood and custom dimensions were available upon request. There is some evidence that William Naracom, head stockmaker at the Fox factory, personally fitted and shaped all Super-Fox wood.

The standard Super-Fox is a plain gun, treated only to simple line engraving around the contours of the color-case hardened frame. The pattern is almost identical to that of the standard A Grade Fox of about 1910.

Twenty-gauge Super-Foxes are not mentioned in Fox catalogs or price lists until about 1925, but factory records indicate that they were available from the start. The earliest to show up so far is No. 202900, shipped from the factory Dec. 14, 1922. The 20-bore Supers are built on standard 12-gauge frames and can weigh as much as 8¼ pounds. Like the big-bores, they came with 30-inch or 32-inch barrels, which are proportionately even thicker-walled than the 12s.

In 1923, when it first appeared in the factory price lists, the Super-Fox cost $100, $25 more than the A Grade and only $15 less than the much more elaborately engraved C Grade Fox double.

Super-Fox shown below was a gun for the experienced and fit shotgunner. It had 32-inch barrels and weighed in at about 9 pounds, thanks in part to its massive frame built to 10-gauge scale.

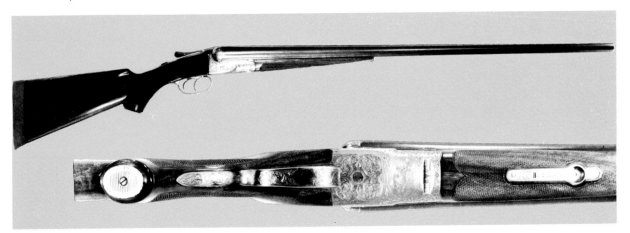

The buyer got plenty of gun for his money. What the Super-Fox lacked in cosmetic appeal was more than made up by the meticulous craftsmanship of its fit and finish and by its startling performance. The heart of that came from the special wizardry of Burt Becker.

Getting a breechloading gun to pattern as efficiently as a muzzleloader was a problem for gunmakers at the turn of the century. It must have seemed though the improved firepower and convenience of the self-contained cartridge had come at the expense of good performance.

The problem is that the inside diameter of the shell case should be the same size as the bore, which in turn means that the chamber must be larger than bore size. It took gunmakers a while to discover that the forcing cone—the tapered section of barrel between the chamber and the bore—is a critical point.

Short, steep-angled cones batter the shot charge as it passes from the case to the bore, deforming the pellets on the outside of the column and bashing the inner ones together. Once free of the muzzle, these misshapened pellets either fly wide of the main swarm or lag far behind, contributing

nothing to pattern efficiency. Muzzleloaders don't have that problem because they have neither chamber nor cones.

Becker clearly understood the advantages of keeping a gun barrel free from abrupt changes in diameter, and his solution involves a threefold approach. First, Super-Fox chambers are bored to extremely close tolerances, and most will not accept a shell that is even slightly oversize. There also is a bit more taper in Super-Fox chambers than in the average gun.

Becker's forcing cones are unusually long and obliquely angled, so that shot columns are eased rather than squeezed into the bores. Finally, to reduce the difference between chamber and bore diameters even further, Becker overbored the barrels. A 12-gauge Super-Fox actually has 11-gauge bores, and the 20s are similarly treated.

Becker gave his bores a high polish to reduce leading and to minimize the inevitable abrasion between the barrel walls and the outer layer of shot pellets. At the time, 30 years before ammunition makers began wrapping shot columns with protective plastic collars, polishing was about all a gunmaker could do.

The Super-Fox (right) is built on a 10-ga. frame with a heavy overbored barrel, giving a far more massive look than the standard Fox shotgun. With 32'' barrels, weight could approach 10 lbs. The bores were oversize, but chambers were tight.

Much of Super-Fox's muzzle-heavy feel came from its extra thick barrels, revealed here by the muzzles.

Becker's choke cones are bored on the same principle as his forcing cones—long and gradually tapering. Super-Fox chokes are of parallel configuration, with the cones set back a few inches and a straight, untapered section of bore for an inch or two at the muzzles.

The same attention that went into making Super-Fox barrels efficient also went into making them strong. For one thing, 12-gauge barrels struck for a 10-gauge frame naturally will have unusually thick walls. Moreover, all tubes were proved twice, first in the rough with an English proof load of 7½ drams of black powder behind a 1⅞ ounces of shot, and again as finished barrels with a 1¼-ounce shot charge and enough smokeless powder to generate about 14,000 pounds of pressure.

Because it was built specifically with Olin's new Super-X ammunition in mind, the standard Super-Fox was chambered for 2¾-inch shells—unlike most other Foxes made in Philadelphia, which were chambered at 2⅝-inch. Three-inch chambers were available in the Super-Fox upon request.

Fox for some reason didn't normally mark chamber length on its guns; apparently, you were just supposed to know. Once in a while, a Fox will turn up with a chamber-length stamping, but most of these appear to have been added sometime after the gun actually was built. Foxes built after 1930 more often were stamped, but occasionally they weren't, even then.

It's wise to check the chamber length of any Philadelphia Fox before you shoot it, but pay special attention to a Super-Fox. The tight, tapered chambers are almost impossible to measure accurately with the typical drop-in gauge, and factory-bored 3-inch Super-Fox chambers can appear to be 2¾-inches or even less.

As yet another misleading feature, many Super-Foxes have a stamping on the barrel flats that reads "Barrels Not Guaranteed—See Tab." This refers to the ill-advised guarantee of minimum 80 percent full-choke patterns that Fox tossed around during the first few months of the Super-Fox's life. Some very early guns are stamped "Barrels Guaranteed—See Tag."

Whoever came up with the whole idea of guarantees and stampings and tags apparently didn't know that a shotgun can be as fickle as a high school beauty queen, or at least failed to realize that the factory had no control at all over the shells that might be stuffed into one of its guns. Even though Fox hedged its bet by qualifying the guarantee with such phrases as "with the proper loads" or "with shells recommended," it no doubt had to replace or at least rework some guns that didn't perform as promised.

At any rate, the "Barrels Not Guaranteed" mark first appeared on Super-Foxes as early as 1924 and probably was applied to all of them built thereafter. Presumably, a hang-tag of some sort was attached at the factory, explaining the stamp's meaning, but such things inevitably get tossed away. Anyone buying the gun secondhand would have no way of knowing that the stamp refers to pattern density, not barrel quality.

As often as not, these days, you're apt to see a Super-Fox with the word "Not" obliterated—obviously done by some bozo who wanted to sell the gun and who figured nobody would notice if he chiseled off a word here and there.

Guaranteed or not, a Super-Fox shotgun on a diet of Super-X cartridges was—and still is—a formidable tool for any wildfowler. Edward C. Crossman, a well-known gun writer and firearms editor of both *The Sporting Goods Dealer* and *National Sportsman*, pattern-tested a Super-Fox shortly after the guns appeared on the market. He found much to praise in the gun's design and workmanship and, after some field experience as well, concluded that he was "inclined to think the Western and gun making people are pretty much correct in their claims of eighty yard range."

The Super-Fox soon caught the attention of other gunmakers, and within a couple of years, Ithaca, L.C. Smith, and Parker all went a-courting in the wildfowler's market. None took the pains that Fox did to create a long-range gun from scratch. In 1924, Ithaca simply lengthened its 10-gauge chambers from 2¾- to 2⅞-inches and called the results the Super 10.

The same year, L. C. Smith brought out its Long Range Wild Fowl Gun, which for the most part was a standard 12-gauge with 3-inch chambers and a reinforced splinter between the barrels behind the fore-end lug. Parker in 1925 offered a 12-gauge waterfowl gun built on a No. 3 frame and

"Barrels not guaranteed" is a rollmarking that has caused confusion through the years. It refers to shot pattern percentage, not the barrel quality.

fitted with 34-inch barrels chambered for 3-inch shells.

Crossman compared the Super-Fox and the Smith Wild Fowl in yet another series of pattern tests. The Smith performed well enough, but Crossman, who generally seemed more comfortable doling out criticism than praise, was moved to write, "I should characterize this 2¾-inch Beckerized Fox as the best shooting twelve-bore I have ever tried, and the most useful."

High praise, indeed, but the best was yet to come. In 1926, Nash Buckingham contacted Fox sales manager Adolph Roll and commissioned a 12-gauge Super-Fox waterfowl gun for work on what Nash liked to call "the tall ones." He specified that the barrels were to be bored by Burt Becker, which was easily accommodated, since Becker bored or at least supervised the boring of all Super-Foxes. This time, though, the results would make Becker the undisputed guru of long-range shooters. The gun itself would become the most famous shotgun ever built in America.

Becker built the gun himself, from start to finish. It was Fox No. 31108, with 32-inch barrels chambered for 3-inch shells and regulated for Buckingham's favorite Super-X load of 4 drams of powder and 1⅜ ounces of No. 4 coppered shot. It had a straight stock, which both Buckingham and Becker preferred, a rubber recoil pad and, at Nash's order, no safety. The finished gun weighed just under 10 pounds, and when it left Philadelphia both barrels would put 90 percent of the shot charge into a 30-inch circle at 40 yards.

Becker engraved Buckingham's name on the left barrel and probably put his own name on the gun

as well. But soon it had a name of its own: "Bo Whoop," named by writer Harold Sheldon after the characteristic hollow roar of the big gun's report. It is of such stuff that legends are made.

Buckingham was so pleased with the gun that he did everything but canonize Burt Becker. Soon, all of the gunners in the little coterie that gathered around Buckingham had Becker-bored Super-Foxes of their own.

Nash and "Bo Whoop" were virtually inseparable, both in literature and in fact, for more than 20 years, until the gun was lost in a careless accident near Clarendon, Arkansas, on Dec. 1, 1948. Despite a search that actually included roadblocks and radio announcements, "Bo Whoop," was never seen again.

There was a second "Bo Whoop," built in 1950. Becker was retired by then, and there is good evidence that he bored the barrels and subcontracted the rest of the work. Nash used the gun until 1968 and then sold it to his old friend Dr. Andrews of Memphis. It still exists.

From the beginning, the Super-Fox could be ordered with high-grade engraving and figured wood. The remaining factory records have so far revealed only four guns so bespoke. The first, built in 1924, is a 9-pound, 4-ounce 12-gauge with 30-inch barrels and pistol-grip stock. The order specifies dark, figured wood and B Grade engraving—a curious choice since Fox had discontinued the B Grade six years before. Perhaps someone wanted a Super-Fox to match an old favorite gun that he already owned.

Another high-grade Super left the factory in February 1926, another 30-inch 12-gauge. This one was ordered with C Grade engraving and X Grade wood made to standard dimensions with a half-hand grip. It weighs just under 9 pounds.

The finest Super of all was completed in June, 1925, a 9-pound 12-gauge with 32-inch barrels, ordered with X Grade engraving and dark, X Grade wood for both butt and fore-end. Both barrels were bored full choke, regulated for No. 4 shot; chambers originally were 2¾ inches rebored to 3 inches sometime later. It had double triggers, ivory bead sights, a Silvers recoil pad and a pistol-grip stock. Whoever ordered it wanted the finest.

He also bought it to use. The old gun has seen service on the Carolina coast, in the Texas Gulf, at Buckingham's old Beaver Dam Club—for by some chance, in the late 1950s, it ended up in the possession of one of Nash's acquaintances. He queried Buckingham on the Becker connection, and Nash's reply, a paean to St. Becker, concludes, "You are exceedingly fortunate to have such a fine weapon by so fine a master of his trade." Of course, the current owner naturally feels much the same way.

In 1928, Nash himself ordered a high-grade

Like all Philadelphia-made Fox guns produced after World War I, Super-Foxes had barrels made of high-chromium content steel the firm referred to as Chromox. The formula resulted in durable barrels.

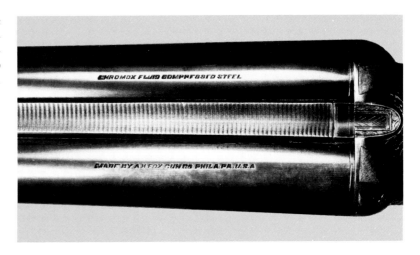

Super in 20-gauge, probably for his shooting chum Hal Bowen. The order specified C Grade engraving and checkering, a high-combed stock with cheekpiece, and two sets of barrels. One set is 30 inches long, choked improved-modified and full, the other 28 inches with both tubes choked improved cylinder. Nash mentions the gun again and again in his stories, usually as "the big 20-gauge."

One curious footnote to the high-grade Super-Foxes: Even though the standard engraving patterns of B, C, and X grade Foxes include some engraving on the barrels, there is no barrel engraving on any of the factory-made high-grade Supers. ("Bo Whoop II" has some, but Fox was long out of business by 1950.)

The economic holocaust of 1929 brought the already-faltering Fox Gun Co. to its knees. Savage Arms bought out the gun business that year and moved the operation to its plant at Utica, N.Y. Burt Becker chose to remain in Philadelphia, at his shop on Gratz Street in the Germantown section of the city. He continued to bore Super-Fox barrels and to do other custom work on Fox guns as long as Foxes were built.

Though the Super-Fox appears in every Savage Fox catalog from the first in 1930 to the last in 1942, it seems unlikely that many of them actually were built during the Depression. The great droughts of the early '30s devastated North American waterfowl populations to the point where even the few who could afford a Super-Fox couldn't find much opportunity to use it. Savage discontinued the 20-gauge version, which never had sold very well anyway, in 1931.

Still, there was an inventory of Super-Fox parts taking up warehouse space, and in 1934 Savage announced the Fox Sterlingworth Wildfowl Grade—a 12-gauge of about 9 pounds heft, fitted with ejectors and 30- or 32-inch barrels chambered for either 2¾- or 3-inch shells. It was, in fact, the Super-Fox without the standard HE Grade engraving, stocked in plain American walnut. Everything else was the same, down to the finger-lever fore-end latch, which the standard Sterlingworth never had.

Obviously, Savage hoped to clear out the Super-Fox parts and make a bit of money at the same time, but it wasn't much of a bargain. At $62.50 in 1934, the Wildfowl cost $23 more than the standard Sterlingworth and only $9.50 less than the HE Grade.

As the Depression dragged on, the Wildfowl found a few takers but only a very few. It does not appear in the catalogs after 1940.

Even in its best years, from 1923 through about 1928, the Super-Fox was simply too specialized an item to sell in great numbers. Though it was available for 20 years, total production probably was no more than about 300 guns, nearly all of them in 12-gauge. Factory sources indicate about 55 Supers built in 20-bore.

Judging from the ones I've seen, and in talking with the most advanced Fox collectors, Super-Fox guns with 30-inch and 32-inch barrels seem to exist in about equal numbers. Records suggest a majority bored with 2¾-inch chambers, though many apparently were later rebored to 3 inches.

A completely original, mint-condition Super-Fox will fetch a good price on the current collectors' market, but don't hold your breath 'til you find one. They were guns meant to be used, often under conditions that are as hostile to guns as they are attractive to ducks. Even with careful attention, it's not easy to make a 9-pound double shotgun that handles gracefully, and some of the Super-Foxes have all of the snappy dynamics of a bridge timber. Others, though, are simply astonishing, both in hand and on target—just as they were meant to be.

PART FOUR

HANDGUNS

Handguns and Cartridges for Long-range Varminting

Bob Milek

Handgunning game at long range is a relatively new shooting sport. It wasn't until after 1963, when Remington introduced the XP-100 bolt-action pistol in .221 Fire Ball chambering, that we had the wherewithal to make long-range game shooting a viable sport. Sure, there was some long-range shooting done prior to this, but both the handguns then available and the cartridges for which they were chambered lacked the accuracy and punch required to consistently kill game at long range. No, it wasn't until the advent of the specialty pistols—bolt actions, break-open, and falling blocks—that long-range handgun hunting came into its own.

In the world of long-range handgun hunting, one sport stands alone—varmint shooting. Taking varmints at long range is to handgun hunting what dry fly fishing is to angling—the ultimate refinement of the art. Besides requiring considerable skill on the part of the shooter, the equipment used—from the pistol itself right on through the bullets—must be state of the art. Varmints come in a variety of sizes; thus there can be some differences in the equipment used. Regardless of the size of the varmint though, you'll be shooting at very long range—100 yards to well beyond 300 yards—at targets that are small, elusive, and in some instances pretty tenacious.

What does it take, then, to successfully hunt varmints at long range with a handgun? Well, let's begin by first looking at the cartridges. As I see it, cartridge selection comes first because until you know for sure which cartridge you want, you can't decide on the handgun itself. Any cartridge for long-range varmint shooting must meet a few stringent prerequisites. First, it must be capable of generating velocities high enough to produce a flat trajectory so that the shooter isn't doing a lot of guessing at long range. Second, bullets must be available for it that will go to pieces on contact with small, thin-skinned animals at the reduced downrange velocities common to handgun cartridges. Third, the cartridge must possess inherent accuracy. I'll be the first to agree that much

This article first appeared in Guns & Ammo

Inset photo: Ron Reiber of Hornady used his custom XP–100 Remington to anchor this chuck at over 300 yards. Right: I do some test firing.

of the accuracy experienced with a specialty pistol has to do with the handgun itself, but it's a fact that some cartridges just aren't capable of the accuracy required.

The varmint hunter needn't waste time even considering any of our straight-wall pistol cartridges. They won't meet any of the prerequisites. This is the reason that we have so many wildcat chamberings in the specialty pistols—to get cartridges that will perform. Today, though, I think we actually have three classes of cartridges for which specialty handguns are chambered. Commercial cartridges are those for which you can purchase factory-loaded ammunition and are represented by such offerings as the .221 Fire Ball, .222 Remington, and .223 Remington. Then we have what I call semi-wildcats. These are cartridges for which the specialty guns are commercially chambered, but for which factory-loaded ammunition isn't available. In some instances you may be able to buy formed, unprimed brass—for example, the 7mm Bench Rest Remington—while in other instances you will have to make the brass—the 6mm T/CU and 7mm T/CU. I feel that cartridges like the 6mm/.223, 6mm Bullberry, and 6.5mm JDJ also fall into this category because Contender barrels chambered for them are available from custom barrel makers, and all you do is order one in and snap the barrel onto your receiver. Then we have what are really wildcats—cartridges for which you'll have to deal with a gunsmith and have him make you up a special

barrel for your pistol. In many instances you may even have to foot the cost of the reamers to get the job done. Then, too, special form dies are usually required for true wildcat cartridges and these in themselves are very expensive.

I've always felt that we were losing members in the long-range handgunning ranks because not everyone was willing to invest the dollars and time required to shoot a wildcat, yet we kept pushing nothing but the wildcats at the shooting public. I hammered long and hard on this subject to Remington, the result finally being the introduction of the XP-100 Varmint Special in .223 Remington chambering and marketing of formed 7mm Bench Rest Remington brass. Both the .223 and the 7mm Bench Rest are superb long-range varmint cartridges and shooters are no longer having to fool with wildcatting if they don't want to. Likewise, by making formed 7mm Bench Rest brass available, Remington took all the work out of bringing the cases down to two more very popular wildcats: .22 Bench Rest and 6mm Bench Rest.

What are the best calibers for long-range varmint hunting with a handgun? In my experience nothing larger than .30 caliber will work, and by far the best results are obtained with the .22s, 6mms, .25s, 6.5mms and 7mms. The reasons for this are twofold. First, in all of these calibers, there are relatively lightweight bullets available that have thin jackets yet have ballistic coefficients good enough to ensure good downrange velocity

Two of the many choices among handguns for long-range varminting: (top photo) Pachmayr's Dominator in 7mm Bench Rest Remington is attached to an M–S Safari Arms frame, topped with a Redfield 4× scope; (bottom photo) Thompson/Center Contender in 6mm with a special Bulberry barrel.

retention. When you get to the big bore light-weights, even in .30 caliber, the bullets are almost as large in diameter as they are long. This results in a poor ballistic coefficient, fast velocity loss, and thus poor trajectory and poor bullet performance at long range. My personal preference is the .223 Remington and several 6mm wildcats. The little .223 is a great performer under normal conditions, but when the wind gets to whooping it up as it so often does here in Wyoming, the 6mms have a decided edge. Another thing in favor of both .22 and 6mm is that in both calibers there is a large selection of bullets that perform well on small varmints.

What is the minimum muzzle velocity that a specialty pistol cartridge must generate to be classed as a good long-range varmint cartridge? This is difficult because so much depends on caliber and the particular bullet being used. I'll go out on a limb though and say that in .22 caliber the minimum muzzle velocity with a 50-grain bullet is 2,800 fps (feet per second). For 6mm it's 2,700 fps with a 70-grain bullet, while for .25 caliber it's 2,600 with a 75-grain bullet. In 6.5mm it's 2,500 fps for an 87-grain bullet and 2,400 fps in 7mm with a 100-grain bullet. Remember, if the varmint is worth hunting, he deserves to be killed quickly with one well-placed shot. At velocities below those indicated, you'll have to limit your maximum range to 200 yards to be sure of quick kills.

Once you've chosen a cartridge for varmint

shooting at long range, it's time to pick the pistol to shoot it in. Just as with cartridges, specialty pistols have come a long way in the past few years. Bolt action, break-open tip-up action, falling block—all are available chambered for some excellent varmint cartridges. Each has its own good and bad features; so the choice is yours alone. You'll usually find that the bolt guns shade the others just a hair in the accuracy category, due mostly to the rigidity of the action itself. On the other hand, break-open guns like the Thompson/Center Contender and falling blocks like the M.O.A. Maximum have interchangeable barrels, greatly reducing your investment if you intend to get into two or more calibers. When the proper cartridge is chosen, all of them are extremely accurate.

I do recommend that any pistol you choose for long-range varmint shooting have a barrel between 14 and 15 inches long. This isn't because the longer barrel is more accurate than one 10 inches long, but rather because the cartridges best suited for the work are most efficient in the longer barrels. Since it's desirable to wring the most velocity possible from the load, use the longer barrels. However, I have a thing about pistol barrels that exceed 15 inches in length.

How accurate must a pistol be to qualify for long-range varmint shooting? Again, this is difficult to pin down, but I have one rule that serves me well. If it won't hold five shots in 1 inch or less at 100 yards—from a benchrest, of course—

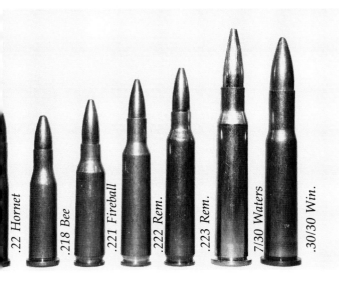

Left: A few of the commercial cartridges for specialty pistols. The Hornet and Bee should be confined to a maximum of 100 yards. At right are my favorite cartridges for long-range shooting. The .223 Remington is great except in high winds, where the 6mm's show an edge.

Wildcat calibers shown on the left require a custom barrel. For semi-wildcats on the right, there are no commercial manufacturers, but Thompson/Center does make chambered barrels for these calibers.

I won't hunt with it. Now this may sound a bit unreasonable considering that most sporting rifles won't shoot this well, but believe me, good specialty pistols will! With the exception of a couple of heavy-barreled varmint rifles in my cabinet, I don't own rifles that will shoot with the best of my long-range specialty pistols.

To achieve such accuracy with a pistol, you need three things—a good trigger, an excellent long eye relief pistol scope, and carefully tailored loads. When all three of these are combined, the specialty pistol becomes an amazingly accurate piece.

Not all factory-issue triggers can be adjusted

I demonstrate one of my favorite field rests for long-range handgun shooting. This one can be put together quickly, using a combination of daypack and hat set atop a handy rock.

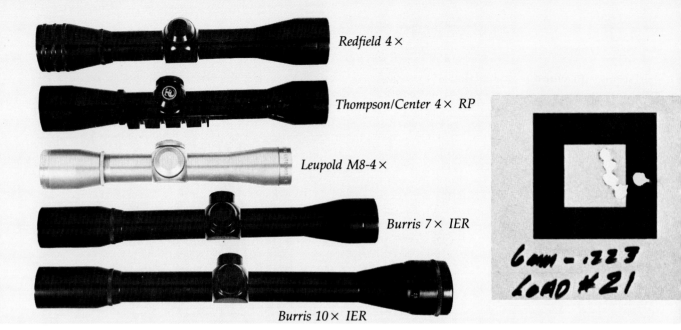

Above left are five pistol scopes used by varmint hunters. The 4 × models are better for inexperienced shooters. The 7 × and 10 × are for advanced shooters. The 1-inch group at right indicates the accuracy necessary for a pistol to be used for long-range varminting.

Top: New Herrett custom-stocked Remington XP-100 in .223 chambering. This Herrett package features a Timney adjustable trigger. Bottom: The Kimber Predator is another long-range handgun.

safely without having some work done on them. All I can suggest is that you try making the adjustments as directed by the manufacturer and if you aren't satisfied, have a good gunsmith work the trigger over. The manufacturers of specialty pistols are aware of the fact that the shooters buying their products insist on good triggers, and they're giving them to us.

It should go without saying that a scope is a must on any handgun intended for long-range varmint shooting. The only question is, what magnification is best? Use all the power you can handle easily. The field of view of pistol scopes is quite small as compared to rifle scopes of equal power, and this poses a serious problem to some shooters. I recommend that if you're just getting started or will be taking shots at a moving target such as a coyote, use a 4× scope. When you can handle this easily, try more magnification for small, stationary targets. My favorite varmint scope is the 7× Burris IER. The field of view with this one is only 6.5 feet at 100 yards, but if you're used to shooting a pistol scope, you'll have no trouble picking up your target quickly. The Burris 10× IER is the ultimate, but also the most difficult to shoot. Placement of your eye, both as to eye relief and in relation to the optical center of the scope, is critical. If it isn't perfect, you can't see a thing. Then, too, the field of view is only 4 feet at 100 yards. You have to have a lot of experience with pistol scopes to locate a prairie dog in that small field.

Varmint shooters are handloaders. To begin with, you couldn't afford to buy the amount of ammunition that it's possible to shoot up on a good day. It isn't unusual to go through 400 or 500 rounds of ammo per session on prairie dogs or rock chucks. More important, though, only by handloading can you tailor a load that gives not only the best possible accuracy from your pistol, but which uses a bullet that performs as it should on the game being taken. For example, consider factory loads for the .223 Remington, a superb varmint cartridge. Factory ammo is loaded with 55-grain bullets that leave a 14-inch pistol barrel at about 2,800 fps. This is relatively impressive from a pistol, but those bullets are designed for use at appreciably higher velocities in rifles. Hit a prairie dog or chuck with one of these at 200 to 250 yards and you'll punch a hole through him, but expansion will be minimal and quick kills aren't a sure thing. But, handload a 50-grain quick-expanding bullet like the Hornady SX, Nosler Expander, or Sierra Medium-Velocity Blitz to around 3,000 fps and you'll vaporize a prairie dog at 200 yards. I've found that it often takes a lot of testing to find just the right combination of bullet, powder, and primer to wring the best accuracy from my pistols, but once I find a good load, I know I can trust it to do the job.

Now, all of the right equipment and the best possible handloads are all for naught if, when you get into the field, you can't get locked into a rock-solid shooting position. I don't know how many times I've watched beginners at the game bang away at tiny distant targets from shaky positions. Needless to say, they're not too successful. A scoped long-range varmint pistol should be fired from a rest—period! Shooting from any other position is an exercise in futility. It's not difficult to get a field rest that's as solid as your shooting bench, but it takes a little planning and imagination. I've tried any number of innovative field rests intended to give the varmint shooter a solid shooting surface. Most of them work relatively well, but they all have one major drawback—they're either bulky, heavy, or both.

Sandbags set atop rocks or other natural objects provide me with my favorite handgun rest. However, because these bags have to be carried in the field, they aren't filled with sand. Instead, I fill empty lead shot bags with grain. It's light, yet compacts nicely when I use the bags as a rest. I can pack several of these in a day pack without being weighted down.

Some shooters like to use the Harris Bipod attached to a sling swivel on the forearm of their pistol. I've never had a lot of luck with the bipod, but this is just me, not the product. One of the best long-range handgunners I've ever shot with—Ron Reiber of Hornady Manufacturing—is a faithful user of the bipod. Most pistols aren't furnished with a swivel stud that the bipod can be attached to, but installing one is no big job.

When all else fails or I'm in a hurry, I fall back on two faithful aids for acquiring a fast, steady shooting position—a day pack, my hat, or both in combination. I can whip my hat off, flop it atop a rock or tree, scrunch it up a little and have an instant firm but soft rest for my pistol. Granted, I've practiced using the hat for years so that it comes mighty easy to me, but there's nothing faster. However, for a really good rest, I'll lay the day pack on the rock or tree and place my hat atop the pack. Sometimes, depending upon how full the pack is, it makes a perfect rest by itself.

I'm sure that by now many of you have decided that successful long-range varmint shooting with a handgun is nothing more than choosing the right cartridge and pistol. The uninitiated are fond of saying that I'm not shooting a handgun but, rather, a short-barreled rifle. Where accuracy and ballistics are concerned, this may be true, but believe me, there's a whole lot of difference between hitting a chuck at 300 yards with a varmint rifle and pulling off the same shot with a specialty pistol. When you take away the shoulder stock, you introduce more problems than you'd ever believe. The gun is no longer locked to your carcass via the shoulder stock, so even from the steadiest of positions the slightest movement ruins your long-range accuracy. No, there's a lot more to successful long-range varmint shooting with a pistol than just selecting the proper equipment. Success requires practice, practice, and more practice—and maybe just a little bit of luck.

.22 Handguns

Jan Libourel

A sad fact of life is that most people who enter the sport of handgunning go about it
in the wrong way. Entranced with notions
of defending himself from the forces of evil, the
beginner buys himself a double-action "wonder-
nine," a .357 Magnum, a .45 auto, a .38 snubby
or whatnot—almost anything except the handgun
he *should* start out with, this being, of course, a
good target-grade .22 rimfire.

Now, anyone who reads this magazine regularly knows that I have nothing against 9mms,
.45s, .357s et al.—I like 'em all and shoot them a
lot. However, they are not the best guns for
learning the fundamentals of handgun marksmanship. Muzzle blast and recoil can be intimi-
dating to the tyro. Although most quality out-of-
the-box revolvers have good trigger actions, the
pulls on many service-grade autoloaders are pretty
coarse. Unless they are already handloading for
rifles, few if any first-time handgun buyers are
going to buy full handloading outfits at the same
time they acquire their handgun. This means that
much range practice will be an expensive proposition for all except the very well-to-do.

The point of all of this is that you are much
better off if your first handgun is a good-quality
.22 rimfire. Ammunition will be far less expensive
than factory centerfire ammo or even any commercial reloads I've ever priced, and this means
that you'll be able to do a lot more practicing with
a .22 than with any other handgun. Recoil and
blast are close to nonexistent with a .22 handgun
of any size, and consequently you can devote your
attention to the fundamentals of stance, grip,
trigger squeeze, and sight picture without the
distractions attendant on a gun that is somewhat
abusive to shoot.

Moreover, a .22 is just plain pleasant and fun
to shoot. You can fire your .22 for hours without

This article first appeared in Guns & Ammo

developing a sore or lacerated hand or suffering from the fatigue caused by violent muzzle blasts repeated again and again and again! Good .22s are also usually extremely accurate with ammo they like; they'll give the beginner all he (or she) can hold for and then some, which is a nice confidence builder.

Although I fear this may be getting repetitive to longtime readers, I don't know of a better handgun for the beginner to start out with than the Smith & Wesson Model 17 K-22 Masterpiece. This gun has all the positive safety features of a quality double-action revolver. (Although every handgun must be handled with extreme care and vigilance at all times, the modern double-action revolver is, most would agree, the most idiot-proof of repeating firearms.) These revolvers are usually very accurate, and if the trigger action

For the beginner or expert, any of these .22 handguns should give fine service: (1) Smith & Wesson Model 17 K-22 Masterpiece; (2) Smith & Wesson Model 63 22/32 Kit Gun (stainless); (3) Ruger New Model Stainless Super single Six; (4) Pre-WWII Colt Woodsman; (5) Manurhin PP Sport; (6) Ruger Mark II Government Target Model; (7) Smith & Wesson Model 41 (Herrett's Trainer stocks); (8) High Standard Trophy (Pachmayr grips); (9) Colt Ace conversion unit mounted on an Essex frame assembly.

Single-action revolvers such as the Ruger Single-Sixes seem to just beg to be taken plinking. Three single-sixes shown here are: (top) Ruger's newest single-action, the Bisley Single-Six; (center) the author's S&W M–34 Kit Gun customized with Herrett's Shooting Star stocks and a Flaig's trigger shoe; (bottom) the Ruger New Model Single-Six, a modern handgun classic.

doesn't happen to be first rate as it comes from the box, any pistolsmith worthy of his stones can soon correct that situation. This is a top-quality handgun and one that will always remain a prized possession, no matter how many other handguns the owner subsequently acquires. The S&W Model 17 is available with 4-, 6-, and 8⅜-inch barrels. (Formerly the 4-inch version was called the Model 18.) I think the 6-inch version is the best for the beginner's gun; the 4-inch, however, will do just fine and may be a little handier afield; the 8⅜-inchers have always struck me as a little unwieldy, and I suspect this effect may be magnified for the novice.

If the price of the Model 17 strikes the newcomer as a little steep, a very acceptable lower-priced alternative might well be the Taurus Model 96. This Brazilian-made revolver is very similar to the Smith K-22. Although I don't have any experience with this specific model, other Taurus revolvers of recent manufacture have impressed me as being very good guns indeed and top values for the money. Another full-sized .22 double-action revolver is the Dan Wesson, and this revolver's unique interchangeable barrel feature may well appeal to prospective handgun buyers.

If the shooter has very small hands, or if he or she wants to tote the revolver long hours afield as a hiker's companion or hunter's backup, the Smith & Wesson .22/32 Kit Gun in either its blued

(Model 34) and stainless (Model 63) versions is a charming little revolver. Its lack of weight and smaller frame size make it less well suited for mastering handgun marksmanship, but it is nonetheless a very appealing rimfire six-gun. Charter Arms makes the Pathfinder, which is very

Most common .22-caliber rimfire rounds are (left to right) the Short, Long, and Long Rifle. The .22 Long Rifle is the most popular of them.

Simplicity and safety of a double-action revolver make it ideal for novices learning to shoot a handgun. The author considers the Smith & Wesson K–22 Masterpiece to be the best .22 handgun for beginners. His K-22 (shown below, center) wears a set of Herrett's Tropper custom stocks. Ease of loading and unloading double-action revolvers like this S&W Model 63 (below right) is a safety plus.

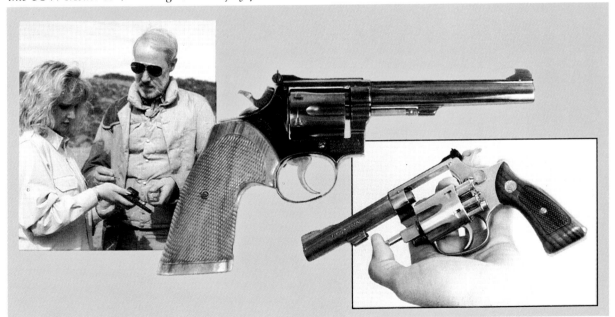

Ruger .22 autos (above left) are now available in stainless steel. These pistols can be superbly accurate, yet modestly priced, making them a good choice for the beginning competitor. Target versions of the Ruger Standard Model (above right) are great for both match and less formal shooting.

similar in its characteristics to the Smith Kit Gun, and I gather that Taurus is coming out with a nine-shot target-sighted small-frame .22 revolver in the immediate future.

Sad to say, the number of good .22 double-action revolvers seems to be dwindling. The Harrington & Richardsons are gone. Ruger, for whatever reasons, has never made a DA .22 revolver. Colt used to make some very nice .22 revolvers, but they are all things of the past. In the post–World War II epoch these included the Officer's Models, the Trooper Mark III, and the Diamondback. If you can find any of these three on the used-gun market at attractive prices, they should serve you well.

Many shooters are entranced by the glamour and romance of the old West, and nothing appeals to them quite so much as a single-action revolver. The Peacemaker-styled single-action is, in my opinion, somewhat less suitable for the beginner than a double-action of comparable quality. First and foremost, it is not as easy to inspect to see if it is loaded as the swing-out cylinder of the double action. Trigger pulls are often less refined, and the heavy hammer fall of the single action is distracting to many. Nonetheless, there are some very nice single actions out there that will serve the beginner well. The Rugers are the leading guns in this field. The buyer has a choice of the New Model Single Six or the Bisley variant thereof. The latter would be my personal choice unless I wanted to keep weight down. These Rugers are high-quality revolvers and usually are extremely satisfactory. There are also some very attractive looking single-action .22 revolvers made abroad

by firms like Uberti of Italy and brought into this country by several importers. Some of these are true, full-size replicas of the legendary Colt Peacemaker, and others are scaled-down guns that rather resemble the Rugers. Again, I have almost no personal experience with most of these guns, but they are handsome and appear to be well made. Less expensive plinker-grade .22 single-actions are offered by FIE at very reasonable prices.

A self-loading pistol requires more vigilant handling than a revolver, generally speaking, and this is especially true if the auto pistol has a concealed hammer or striker. Unfortunately, the latter is true of almost all the best-grade .22 auto pistols, and so I can only recommend them as training guns for beginners with extreme reservations. This is especially true if the pistol is to be used off-range for plinking or other casual, unsupervised informal shooting. Nonetheless, there are some very fine .22 auto pistols on the market.

If you are serious about entering match competition, it's probably wisest to start out with the pistol you will be using in formal matches. The two standouts here are the Smith & Wesson Model 41 and the Ruger Mark II Target Models. Both these pistols are extremely fine performers that will be well suited for the most demanding competition. The Smith & Wesson is a better finished pistol, usually has a somewhat nicer trigger action, and is far easier to fieldstrip and reassemble. In the Ruger's favor is the fact that it costs much less.

Sad to say, these two pistols are about the only two American-made .22 pistols really suitable for serious competitive shooting. The High Standard firm is now defunct, but they made some wonderful .22 autos in their day, and if you can get a nice Victor, Trophy Military, 10-×, or whatever, on the used gun market at a good price, you won't regret it.

There are some other .22 auto pistol options worth looking at. AMT makes their Lightning, which is more or less a copy of the Ruger auto in stainless steel. Browning makes the Buck Mark and the Challenger III. These are more in the category of high-grade field pistols and plinkers than true match pistols, but Browning does offer a Silhouette version of the Buck Mark for the increasingly popular rimfire silhouette matches that features a large wooden fore-end. The fixed-sighted Ruger Standard Model is also in the field/plinking class, and the same would apply to such pistols as the new Smith & Wesson Model 422, the Navy Arms Luger, and assorted imports that are often "grown-up" versions of the same firms' pocket pistols. Any of these pistols will give much shooting pleasure, although I think the most satisfactory results will be obtained with a top-quality match-grade pistol with fully adjustable sights.

At the other extreme are the very highly refined European .22 match target pistols made by outfits like Hammerli, FAS, Unique, and Walther in .22 Long Rifle for International Standard Pistol and in .22 Short for the International Rapid Fire game. These pistols are wonderful instruments for the serious competitor, but they are too expensive and sophisticated for the first-time handgun buyer. Most people serious about target shooting get a grounding in our native bull's-eye shooting before going on to International competition.

The .22 is unquestionably the best gun for getting started in shooting and also entering match competition. However, only a fraction of gun owners participate in serious competitive shooting. Nevertheless, even for those who have no intention of entering a bull's-eye match in their lives, a .22 can give enormous amounts of pleasure. With its inexpensive ammo, mild report, and nonexistent recoil, the .22 is the greatest fun gun in the world.

At one time the sport of plinking—informal shooting at makeshift targets—was far more accessible than it is today. Increasing urbanization has devoured many areas where a generation ago a youthful (or young-at-heart) shooter could line up a row of cans against a dirt bank and bowl them over with his trusty .22 rimfire. Even shooting in the open spaces and public lands that are reasonably near our great cities is often severely circumscribed by law—a sad legacy of inconsiderate "gun slobs" who disgrace the shooting sport for the rest of us.

Ready-made targets like the Quikset (below left) or tiny silhouettes (center) make durable targets for informal shooting. The .22 is used at the highest levels of handgun competition. The Olympics has included the Free Pistol match, which uses highly specialized single-shot .22 Long Rifle pistols.

If you are fortunate enough to be able to indulge in this delightful old pastime, you have a wealth of suitable targets available such as were undreamed of in the days of my youth. Cans are the classic plinking targets. (*Never* use bottles or other glass objects!) Strange to say, I have never much cared for cans as targets. I don't like packing trash into shooting areas, and I don't like packing shot-up trash out. I also find the modern aluminum beverage can a pretty unsatisfactory target. These cans are so light that bullets often pass clear through them without knocking them over. If they get somewhat shot up, bullets will often go right through the holes without giving any evidence of a well-placed shot.

The shooter has also an array of other improvised target choices. He can use such entertaining standbys as Necco wafers and animal crackers (although if you can hit a Necco wafer at any kind of range with a handgun, you're an *awfully* good shot). Today, however, there are many attractive and durable ready-made "fun" targets available. I have a set of miniature silhouettes for rimfire rifle shooting, and these make very good handgun targets at modest ranges. Other devices I have tried include the Qwik-set target from Motsey's Enterprises (again, you have to be very good to connect on these little plates with a handgun), the Seligman Duelling Tree, and a rebounding man silhouette from Targetmasters. There are a variety of other targets of this type. About the only drawback to these iron and steel targets is that they are heavy and not suitable for packing considerable distances into the backcountry . . . which

Specialized auto pistols in .22 Short like this Walther GSP (top left) are used for International Rapid Fire matches. Browning makes a special Varmint version of their Buck Mark .22 auto (upper right) that is designed for scope mounting. High Standard .22 automatics (center and bottom left) are out of production but are still available used, and are very fine performers.

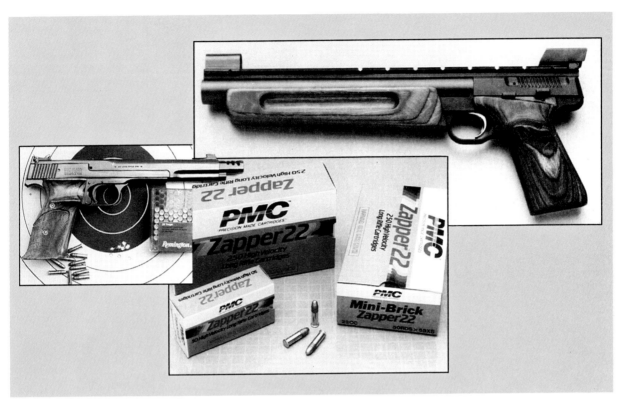

Smith & Wesson Model 41 (left center) has from its introduction been one of the finest American-made .22 caliber target guns. Another variant of the Browning Buck Mark is this pistol (right) designed for metallic silhouette target shooting. The .22 Long Rifle is world standard. The Zappers from PMC (bottom) were manufactured in Korea.

may be necessary if you wish to have a place to plink legally and safely these days.

Actually, your imagination can pretty well be your guide in selecting entertaining plinking targets. For example, I recently saw some molded rubber toy dinosaurs of the type offered by the Imperial Toy Company of Los Angeles used as plinking targets. The lightweight dinosaurs leaped and bounced spectacularly when hit, but sustained surprisingly little damage from repeated hits from a .22 pistol. These critters are priced three for $11 at my local emporium, and I can hardly imagine a more entertaining plinking target, especially for youngsters. In any event, wherever you plink and whatever you plink at, be sure to use a safe backstop and strictly observe all rules of gun safety. In an informal, relaxed, playful atmosphere like this, it's awfully easy to become lax about safety. You don't want a pleasant outing to turn into a tragedy because someone got careless.

When it comes to selecting ammo for your .22, about the only advice I can give is to buy as large an assortment of loads as you can and select the one which gives best accuracy and (in a self-loader) functioning. When you do find your best load, try to buy up as much ammunition from that specific lot as you can afford. Beyond that, what governs the preferences of .22 rimfires is largely a mystery to me.

As a general thing, expensive, match-grade ammo will prove to be more consistently accurate in a variety of firearms than cheap "loss leader" loads, but then I have seen many instances in which the cheap stuff actually produced tighter groups from certain guns than high-grade match ammo! Trial and error is really the only way to find out. If you are diffident about your shooting ability, try to enlist the help of the best handgun shot you know in accuracy testing your pistol.

The .22 Long Rifle cartridge and the guns that chamber it comprise a vast subject indeed, and I have barely scratched the surface. The use of the .22 as a small-game cartridge, the role of ultra-velocity loads, the .22 as a defense cartridge (something I don't much recommend), and many other aspects of the remarkable rimfire are all deserving of articles in and of themselves. Suffice to say, whether you're just learning to shoot, simply concerned with having fun in the back 40, or going for an Olympic gold medal in International Slow Fire, if you're serious, you need a .22 handgun, and probably more than one!

The .44 Magnum: Still the King?

Jan Libourel

Throughout the years of my youth and young manhood, the words ".44 Magnum" were most often spoken in tones of awe, respect and even fear. After all, it represented the upper limits of handgun power. Only the hardiest and most skilled were supposed to be able to master the terrifying piece of machinery that was the .44 Magnum revolver, and the violence of its recoil was likely to teach your right hand terrible things!

Today, the .44 Magnum has lost something of its mystique. In the 1970s and the early years of this decade, we saw the rise of the single-shot specialty pistols chambered for cartridges that made the mighty .44 look like a weakling in comparison. Handgun buffs of a traditionalist bent might console themselves that these contraptions were actually "sawed-off rifles" and that the .44 was still the king of the "real" handguns. However, the last few years have seen the coming of the "super .45" revolvers, most notably the long-awaited .454 Casull Magnum from Freedom Arms. The .454 can deliver twice the energy of the .44 Magnum, and the Freedom Arms revolver that chambers it is scarcely larger than a Ruger Super Blackhawk. Thus, almost the last vestiges of the .44's claim to the power championship are gone. Still, revolvers like the Freedom Arms Casull are very expensive, limited production items, and guns like the John Linebaugh conversions are custom, one-of-a-kind items. This means that the .44 Magnum is still the most powerful cartridge for which repeating handguns are widely available at prices the average hobbyist can readily afford.

The .44 Magnum was announced at the very end of 1955. By the glacial standards of firearms developments in this century, it is still regarded as a rather recent and "modern" handgun car-

This article first appeared in Guns & Ammo

tridge. Its origins, however, go all the way back to the early days of the metallic cartridge era. Smith & Wesson's first centerfire revolver cartridge was a .44 caliber round that was little more than a centerfire version of the rimfire .44 Henry. It used a heel-based, outside-lubricated bullet that was the same diameter as the outside of the case walls, just like today's .22 long rifle cartridges. This cartridge was known as the .44 Smith & Wesson American or .44/100. Soon after the introduction of this cartridge ca. 1869–70 and the large Smith & Wesson revolver that chambered it, the Russian government became very interested

Popularity of the .44 Magnum has brought into being a variety of fine handguns and rifles chambered for it. Above is an assortment of some of the top handguns. Clockwise from left: Ruger Super Blackhawk (old model); Smith & Wesson Model 29 with Hogue custom grips; Desert Eagle; Ruger Redhawk; Dan Wesson. Though the cartridge was designed for revolvers, light carbines (inset, lower right) have also been chambered for the .44 because of its power level. The close-range effectiveness of the .44 from one of these carbines has often been compared favorably with that of the .30/30.

Remington
240-grain LSWC

Federal
240-grain JHP

Hornady/Fron
240-grain LSV

Varieties of the famed .44 Magnum, by Remington, Federal, and Hornady.

in the Smith & Wesson gun and ultimately placed huge orders with the Massachussetts firm. The Russians were less enamored with the .44 S&W American cartridge, however, and developed in collaboration with Smith & Wesson a new .44 cartridge. In contrast to the .44 American with its heel-based bullet, it used a plain-base bullet; the walls of the cartridge case surrounded the bearing surface of the bullet, and the chamber was counterbored to accommodate the fatter case. In other words, it was just like all modern revolver cartridges (except .22s). This cartridge was known as the .44 Smith & Wesson Russian, and it was the direct ancestor of the .44 Special and Magnum.

The .44 Russian was somewhat more powerful than the .44 American, and it was superbly accurate. In its heyday, it was universally regarded as the most accurate of the big-bore six-gun cartridges, and it was used to set many marksmanship records in the late 19th century. Although not as popular as such cartridges as the .44/40 or .45 Colt, the .44 Russian saw considerable use on the frontier in Smith revolvers, and it was the choice of several foreign governments.

In 1907, Smith & Wesson brought out the firm's first large-frame revolver of their modern "hand-ejector" design. This was the famous Triple-Lock, which took its name from the fact that in addition to the usual fore-and-aft lockup of Smith revolvers, it had a third locking lug that engaged a notch in the yoke cut-out of the frame. With the Triple-Lock a new, elongated version of the .44 Russian was introduced. This new cartridge was known as the .44 Smith & Wesson Special. This cartridge, unlike the long-defunct Russian, is still very much with us today. Various reasons have been cited for its introduction, most of which are somewhat lacking in plausibility. For example, some histo-

rians have claimed that the Special case was made longer than the Russian to hold more black powder. This seems somewhat surprising in view of the fact that smokeless powders were well established in revolver cartridges well before 1907. An alternative explanation is that the smokeless powders of this era were bulkier than black, hence the elongated case. Again, this is questionable. Both Bullseye and Unique were in widespread usage by this time, and both leave plenty of air space in the Special case.

The .44 Special was reputed to have all the accuracy of its Russian predecessor, but it offered scarcely any ballistic gain over the shorter cartridge. It still acquired a considerable following, especially among knowledgeable handgun enthusiasts. Most of Smith & Wesson's peacetime

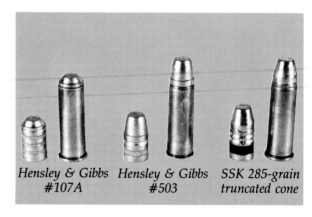

Hensley & Gibbs   Hensley & Gibbs   SSK 285-grain
#107A   #503   truncated cone

Cast bullets the author used for his loading work. He prefers plain-base cast bullets for all his .44 Magnum loads. The H&G 107A is his favorite for moderate loads, the H&G #503 for the heavier loads.

IMI/Samson
240-grain JHP

PMC
240-grain LSWC

Winchester
240-grain LSWC

More varieties of the .44 Magnum, by IMI, PMC, and Winchester.

large-frame revolver production was in .44 Special, and Colt chambered a modest number of New Services and Single Action Armies for this round.

By the late 1920s, a number of men had experimented with loading the .44 Special to higher pressures and ballistics than the somewhat feeble factory loads. By far the most famous of these was a young Montana cowpuncher by the name of Elmer Keith. Keith had begun his experimentation with heavy six-gun loads with the .45 Colt, but after blowing up several revolvers, he switched to the .44 Special with its thicker cylinder walls, and for some 30 years thereafter he proclaimed it the queen of handgun cartridges. Much of his early handloading work was done with the old Number 80 powder, but with the coming of Her-

cules 2400 in the 1930s, he switched to that powder, and it remained his favorite for the .44 Special and Magnum for the rest of his life. Around this period, he also developed the famous semi-wadcutter bullets of his design. The classic .44-caliber Keith bullet is the Lyman 429421. Hensley & Gibbs makes a virtually identical bullet of Keith design as the #503, and just about everybody else—RCBS, Redding–Saeco, NEI, Lee, and others—makes a Keith-style .44 mold in the 240- to 250-grain weight range.

Throughout the 1930s, the 1940s, and into the 1950s, Keith and like-minded individuals called for an extra-heavy factory loading of the .44 Special that corresponded to their heavy handloads. In fact, by the late 1940s, there was an informal organization of .44 Special buffs known as the .44

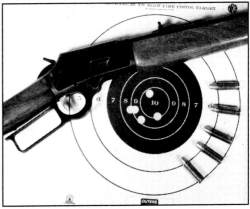

Continued popularity of the .44 Magnum has caused a number of rifles such as the Marlin 1894 shown here to be chambered for it. With H&G #503 bullet and 23.5 grains of 296, the author's 1894 Marlin printed this impressive 1.5-inch group (right) at 50 yards. He finds tales of cast-bullet inaccuracy to be for the most part invalid.

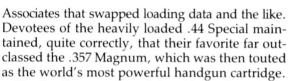

The gas-operated Desert Eagle's recoil is mild. A second case has cleared the ejection port (left) as the first flies over the shooter's head. This gun also groups well (right) from the bench with Black Hills Shooter's Supply 240-grain JHP. The single flier may be due to this gun's creepy trigger pull.

Associates that swapped loading data and the like. Devotees of the heavily loaded .44 Special maintained, quite correctly, that their favorite far outclassed the .357 Magnum, which was then touted as the world's most powerful handgun cartridge.

Finally, the pressure of the .44 fans bore fruit. Ammunition makers had been afraid of what a high-pressure load might do to the old Triple-Lock, and so they followed the same procedure that they had in the development of the .357 Magnum, lengthening the .44 Special case so that it could not be chambered in older revolvers and loading the new .44 Magnum round to much higher pressures. (Caution: It is sometimes possible for .44 Magnum handloads with a heavy roll crimp to be chambered and fired in a .44 Special, and this could be quite dangerous. Be on the alert for this if you own revolvers in both calibers.)

The .44 Magnum was a joint development of Smith & Wesson and Remington. The original .44 Magnum cartridge used a 240-grain lead gas-check semiwadcutter bullet that reportedly stepped out at a vigorous 1,570 fps (feet per second). This is far in excess of anything obtainable with today's loads. Although I didn't have access to a chronograph 20 years ago, my distinct impression is that the .44 Magnum factory ammo of that era was loaded a good bit hotter than present-day factory loads.

The first .44 Magnum revolver was, of course, the big Smith & Wesson that we know as the Model 29. With minor modifications, this revolver has remained in production to this day. Almost as soon as the .44 Magnum was announced at the end of 1955, the always enterprising Bill Ruger produced a slightly scaled-up version of his highly successful Blackhawk single action and got it on the dealers' shelves almost before Smith & Wes-

sons began arriving in any quantity. These old model, flat-top Blackhawks have enjoyed an almost cultic following in recent years—a fact I find somewhat puzzling since the only one I ever fired was a vicious knuckle rapper. Similar complaints prompted Ruger to bring out a new single action, the Super Blackhawk, a few years later. This revolver differed in having a larger all-steel grip frame, a squared triggerguard, an unfluted cylinder, a wide trigger and a lower hammer spur. I bought a Ruger Blackhawk 20 years ago. For most of that time it was my only .44 Magnum revolver. There is really nothing that I can fault about this superb six-gun. Just recently, Ruger started offering a New Model version of the plain Blackhawk in .44 Magnum with a 5½-inch barrel to please those who want a slightly lighter, more compact revolver than the Super.

For many years, the Smith Model 29 and the Ruger Super Blackhawk stood as the two "prestige" .44 Magnums, although there were a variety of imports like the Hawes, the Dakota, and others, some of which were actually quite good single actions. For much of the same period, the Smith 29s were all but unavailable except at scalpers' prices, first because of scarcities caused by the Vietnam War, and then because of the enormous demand created by the highly popular "Dirty Harry" movies starring Clint Eastwood, who, in the role of San Francisco Police Detective Harry Callahan, toted a 6½-inch 29 in a shoulder holster.

Within the last decade, two new high-grade .44 Magnum revolvers established themselves on the scene. The Ruger Redhawk is a big, burly double-action revolver of original design. It is immensely strong and usually very accurate. It is a special favorite of handgun hunters and experimental handloaders who wish to push the .44 Magnum

Ruger's Redhawk (top) is one of the most popular and sturdy .44 Magnums. The older Super Blackhawk (bottom right) is a favorite of the author. It made this 0.8-inch group at 25 yards.

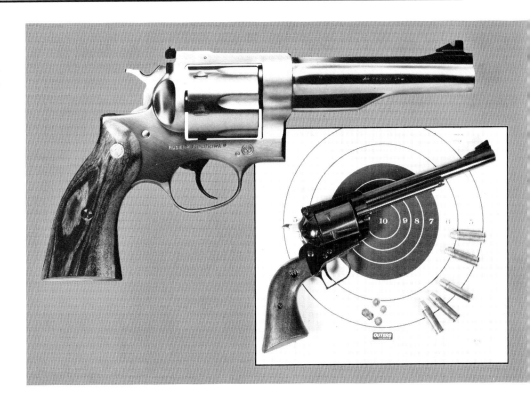

to its very limits of pressure and power. Another huge double action is the Dan Wesson .44 Magnum. This revolver is the overwhelming choice of metallic silhouette competitors, usually with an 8-inch barrel. Other recent .44 Magnum options have included the now-defunct Interarms Virginian Dragoon single action, the Abilene, the Seville, imported DAs from Astra and Llama, and probably some others that I have overlooked. Freedom Arms is now offering the magnificent Casull Magnum revolver in .44 Magnum, although why anyone would choose this revolver in .44 Magnum in preference to the .454 Casull Magnum remains a minor mystery to me. Just about all the popular .44 Magnum revolvers from Smith & Wesson, Ruger, and Dan Wesson are available in either blued or stainless steel.

Last year, we even saw the introduction of the

Ruger Bisley Blackhawk (top) has an excellent grip. The Llama (center) and Astra (bottom) are imported. Spanish double-action .44 Magnums appear to be nicely made.

first commercially successful .44 Magnum auto pistol. This is the Desert Eagle—a gas-operated, rotary-bolt single-action design made in Israel. I fired one of the first ones in the country, and a shooting session with another one at a recent outing confirmed the impression left by the first—that it is beautifully made, reliable, and very accurate. My only criticisms of this fascinating pistol are that it is awfully big and heavy and that the trigger pulls are not the best.

In addition to its role as a handgun cartridge, quite a few rifles have been chambered for the .44 Magnum round. Nearly all of these have been, predictably, lightweight carbines. Usually these have been lever-action carbines like the Marlin Model 1894, the Browning B-92 and the Winchester 94, but other .44 Magnums have included bolt actions (Remington 788) and autoloaders (Ruger). The now discontinued, little tubular-magazine Ruger self-loader was, if memory serves, the first long gun of note that chambered the .44 Magnum.

Well, the .44 Mag is obviously popular. Some critics have said that the primary purpose of the .44 Magnum was as a *macho* thing—to bolster insecure masculine egos. Leaving aside whatever symbolic or psychological significance it may or may not possess, what uses does the .44 Magnum have on today's shooting scene? In the realm of sporting competition, it is clearly the favorite cartridge for the revolver class of IHMSA silhouette competition, usually from Dan Wesson revolvers. It also sees some use in bowling pin matches of the extended table variety. The favored loads for such shooting usually involve a 240-grain bullet traveling about 1,000 fps.

As a defense cartridge against human attack, the .44 Magnum has its drawbacks. Most of the handguns that chamber it are awfully big and heavy for continuous wear. The Smith & Wesson Model 29 is certainly the most graceful of the DA .44s, and good double-action work is difficult with it in any but rather large male hands. Fine guns though they are, only a real Goliath could wield a Redhawk or a Dan Wesson effectively in fast DA fire. The full-charge .44 Magnum loads are rather too violent for best control in combat-style shooting, and the dangers of overpenetration in settled areas would be horrendous. Loaded down to a more controllable level, the .44 Magnum becomes quite an effective antipersonnel round, although the guns that handle it remain bulky.

As to the stopping effectiveness of the .44 Magnum in actual gunfights, it's good, but not as good as you might think. According to the statistical compilations of Sgt. Evan Marshall of the Detroit PD, most full-power .44 Mag loads deliver one-shot stops in actual shootouts with solid body or head hits about 70 to 72 percent of the time. The very best stopper is the Winchester Silvertip, which is a slightly reduced load—a 200-grain hollow-point at 1,299 fps from a 4-incher. This is a

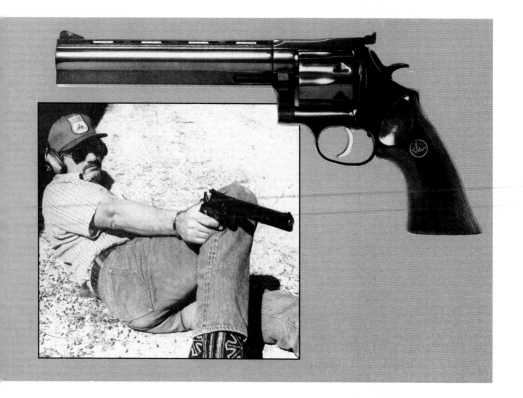

The massive Dan Wesson .44 revolvers are the favorites among silhouette competitors for the revolver class. The shooting in these matches is usually done from a supine or "Creedmoor" position.

75-percent stopper. To put matters in perspective, the .45 ACP and 9mm Parabellum in their most effective commercial loadings are 68-percent stoppers. The medium-power "combat" loads for the .44 (a 240-grain lead semiwadcutter at 950 fps) are 65-percent stoppers—about the same as the top +P .38 Special factory loads.

Nonetheless, according to Marshall, the .44 Magnum has a surprisingly large following in law enforcement circles. Probably because of this, we have seen quite a spate of .44 Magnums in belly gun configuration, with stubby 2½- or 3-inch barrels and rounded butts. Many of these have been custom guns, almost invariably Smith 29s and 629s, although I have even seen a Redhawk so chopped! Smith & Wesson has made several limited production runs of factory-standard guns of similar configuration. There is also the melodramatically named Astra "Terminator" .44 Magnum. I, for one, have never seen much sense in trying to make a hideout gun out of any large-frame revolver, although I guess some qualified people like them. I have always liked Evan Marshall's quip that such guns "provide an illusion of concealability."

One area of personal defense where the .44 Magnum has been the premier choice until quite recently has been as a sidearm for protection from large, potentially dangerous animals like bears. Just about any handgun is pretty feeble protection against an enraged grizzly, but many outdoorsmen like to pack a .44 Magnum as bear insurance, either because it is impractical for them to be constantly armed with a rifle or because they like to carry a revolver as a backup to their rifle. This is one area where I think the .44 Magnum will lose ground fast to the .454 Casull and other "Super .45" revolvers. I have been told by the people at Freedom Arms that more .454s go to Alaska than any other state, and I can easily understand why. If I *had* to rely on a handgun for protection against possible bear attacks (and I'd rather not), the only reason I can think of for preferring a .44 to a .454 Casull would be because I couldn't afford the latter gun!

The coming of the .44 Magnum took big-game hunting with a handgun out of the "stunt" category and turned it into a respected, recognized sport. One of the early pioneers of this game was Robert E. Petersen, who bagged such huge animals as polar and Alaskan brown bear and moose with a 6½-inch nickeled Smith 29. The consensus of most experienced handgun hunters these days seems to be that the .44 Magnum is quite an effective caliber for deer and smaller animals (e.g., javelina) at relatively short ranges—under 75 yards. For somewhat tougher animals like large wild pigs and black bear, opinion varies: some hold that the .44 Magnum is quite suitable for

Robert E. Peterson helped pioneer hunting with the .44 Magnum and bagged this giant polar bear to boot.

these animals *if* the ranges are appropriately short, *if* a bullet giving suitable penetration is used, and *if* the hunter can place his shot well. There are other hunters and guides of considerable experience, however, who regard the .44 Magnum as sub-marginal for such animals under any circumstances, period. Almost every large game animal, even elephant, has at one time or another been taken with a .44 Magnum, but I think most would agree that its use on dangerous game or animals weighing much over 400 pounds or thereabouts still falls into the stunt category.

To round out our look at the .44 Magnum today, I tried out a representative assortment of .44 Magnum factory loads and commercial reloads as well as some handloads of my own. To get some idea of comparative velocities from different barrel lengths, I tried Pro Load's 240-grain jacketed hollow-points in four different firearms. From a Marlin 1894 carbine with a 20-inch barrel, average instrumental velocity was 1,704 fps. From a 7½-inch Ruger Super Blackhawk, it was 1,347 fps, and from a 6-inch Smith Model 29, it was 1,372 fps. I was surprised that from a 6-inch Desert Eagle autoloader the average velocity was only 1,257 fps. I had rather expected this pistol to turn in velocities noticeably higher than the revolvers, but evidently operating its massive bolt and slide uses up a fair amount of the propulsive force of the powder gases.

All the other loads in our admittedly very incomplete sampling were chronographed from the Ruger (which I found a lot more pleasant to shoot with heavy loads than the Smith) and are shown in the accompanying chart. Top accuracy was turned in by the Pro Load 240-grain lead semi-wadcutters, which grouped just over an inch from the Ruger at 25 yards. Runners up in the accuracy class were the Federal 180-grain JHPs and their 220-grain silhouette bullets, which turned in groups under 1½ inches. I should stress that .44 Magnums are very temperamental and individualistic about what they will group well with, and because a factory load or handload groups well from my gun doesn't mean it will do so from yours.

I also tried five handloads. In recent years, I have come to rely on cast bullets for most of my handgun shooting. This is not to say that companies like Sierra, Speer, and Hornady don't turn out excellent bullets. I have the greatest respect for the products of all three companies, and for some specialized uses their products are doubtless better choices than cast bullets, but for most shooting I find that cast bullets are much easier on forcing cones and barrels and give markedly higher velocities with identical powder charges. Three of the cast bullet loads were proven favorites of mine, two others I tried for the first time.

My favorite light load for the .44 Magnum uses the Hensley & Gibbs #107A full wadcutter bullet (weighing 248 grains from the alloy I was using) and 5.5 grains of W–231. This has been very ac-

curate from both my Smith and my Ruger, grouping about 1½ inches at 25 yards from either gun. Velocity from my 6-inch Model 29 was 812 fps.

Three of the remaining loads used the Hensley & Gibbs #503 bullet. This is the classic Elmer Keith design, for all purposes identical to the better-known Lyman #429421, weighing about 250 grains. The first of these is a favorite of many shooters as an intermediate-level .44 Magnum load and uses 8.5 grains of Unique powder. Velocity was 949 fps from the Smith and 1,180 from the Marlin rifle. Groups at 25 yards averaged about 2 inches from either revolver, and at 50 yards the carbine printed similar size groups.

The next load used the H&G #503 bullet and 21 grains of Hercules 2400 powder. This is a slightly attenuated version of the classic Elmer Keith load, which used the same bullet and 22 grains of 2400. Velocities ran 1,356 fps from the Ruger and 1,739 from the Marlin. This was the most accurate load, factory or handload, in both revolvers. From the Ruger it was sensational, with groups running as small as 0.8 inch at 25 yards. Groups from the Smith were larger, but still good, averaging 1½ inches. I recall conversing with Elmer Keith about reloading the .44 Magnum. "I worked quite a bit with other powders like H-110," Elmer said, "but I always went back to good, old 2400." Elmer evidently knew what he was talking about . . . as he usually did.

The .44 Magnum was first chambered in the big Smith later known as the Model 29. The author's (left and center) wears a Hogue Monogrip. With the H&G #107A wadcutter bullet and 5.5 grains of W-231, it will print 1½-inch groups like this one. Elmer Keith (right) paved the way for the .44 Magnum with his heavy .44 Special handloads.

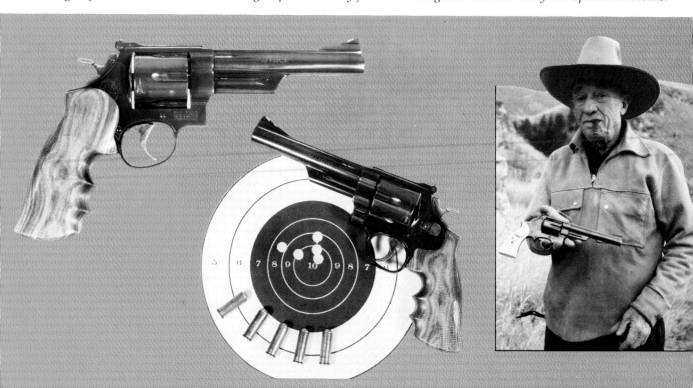

.44 MAGNUM VELOCITIES

Manufacturer	Bullet Weight & Type	Velocity (fps)
Federal	180-grain JHP	1,584
Federal	220-grain MCP	1,264
Federal	240-grain JHP	1,285
Winchester	240-grain LSWC	1,289
Black Hills Shooter's Supply	240-grain JHP	1,300
Black Hills Shooter's Supply	240-grain LSWC	1,020
Pro Load	240-grain JHP	1,347
Pro Load	240-grain LSWC	1,115
Accuracy	240-grain LSWC	1,175

WARNING: *The above loads should be approached with caution and responsible reloading methods strictly adhered to. Neither the author nor the publisher assumes any responsibility for persons using this reloading data.*

All velocities are instrumental velocities at 15 feet from a 7½-inch-barreled Ruger Super Blackhawk. Legend: JHP = jacketed hollow point; LSWC = lead semi-wadcutter; MCP = metal case profiled bullet.

Although I have always been extremely satisfied with 2400 for top loads in the .44 Magnum, many shooters these days like W–296, and so I tried a load of 23.5 grains of W–296 with the same H&G #503 bullet. I had thought that it would equal or surpass the 2400 load, but this was not the case. Velocity from the Ruger was a mere 1,206 fps and groups ran about 2 inches. This load was much more effective from the Marlin carbine, with velocities averaging 1,670 fps. It was also the most accurate I had tried from the Marlin, printing a 1½-inch group at 50 yards, which is probably about as well as I can shoot a lightweight, open-sighted carbine of this type. (I have left the factory open sights on this rifle because I bought it primarily for use in Western-style competitions, which mandate the use of such sights, just in case you're wondering.) I had heard from various gunshop commando types that Marlin rifles with Micro-groove rifling would not group with cast bullets, but evidently mine never got the word!

Finally, these days a number of handloading experimenters are working with extra-heavy bullets (about 300 grains) and heavy charges of H–110, W–296 or W–680. From strong revolvers like the Redhawk, the more daring are achieving velocities up to 1,500 fps and more with 300 grainers. The Freedom Arms .44 Magnum revolver would seem ideal for such experiments. I thought I might try one extra-heavy bullet load, and so I used a 285-grain truncated cone bullet designed by J.D. Jones. Molds are available through his SSK

Industries (Dept. GAH, Rt. 1, Della Dr., Bloomingdale, OH 43910). This bullet features two crimp grooves, one for use with shorter-cylindered guns like the Super Blackhawk, the other for longer-cylindered revolvers like the Redhawk. This bullet was cast by Penny's Hand & Machine Casting (Dept. GAH, P.O. Box 314, Topanga, CA 90290); all others used in this story I cast myself. With a load of 21.5 grains of W–296, velocity was 1,214 fps from the Ruger and 1,562 from the Marlin. Accuracy was especially good from the Ruger, with groups running about an inch at 25 yards. These extra-heavy bullets obviously have excellent potential, but I'm not going to play with top-end loads of this type until reliable, pressure-tested data is available. There were no signs of excessive pressure in the relatively cautious loads I tried.

Although I have largely forsaken jacketed bullets in this caliber in favor of cast bullets, I did a fair amount of shooting with them in my pre-casting days. Rather curiously, I always achieved best accuracy with relatively light bullets and Unique powder. My all-time favorite is the Hornady 200-grain JHP and 13 grains of Unique, followed by the Sierra 180-grain JHC and 13.5 of Unique. These are slightly below max, the Hornady load traveling a little over 1,300 fps, the Sierra about 50 fps faster. Both were extremely accurate.

These days, though, I am satisfied with a bullet that just cuts a big, full-caliber hole and drives deep, straight and true. For comparison purposes at my latest outing, I fired three loads into a line-up of four blocks of duct-sealing compound, each about 2½ inches thick. The Federal 180-grain JHP penetrated into the second block and disintegrated. The same firm's 240-grain JHP penetrated a little deeper, and the mushroomed bullet was an inch in diameter. By way of contrast, the cast H&G #503 slug backed by 21 grains of 2400 plowed straight through all four blocks and kept right on going, cutting a nice, even .44 caliber hole all the way. I, for one, would prefer to forgo expansion in favor of deep, consistent penetration like this, especially when you have plenty of bullet diameter to begin with.

The .44 Magnum may have lost some of its mystique and glamour to the giant specialty pistols and the .454 Casull, but it is still a powerful and highly useful cartridge. Although .44 Magnum handguns can be fastidious about what will group well with, the cartridge can be handloaded with good accuracy over a wide range of power levels—from mild practice loads to all the power most shooters will ever want in a one-hand gun. I'm sure I'm not alone in suggesting that if there could only be one big-bore revolver cartridge, we would probably be best served by making it the .44 Magnum.

PART FIVE

SHOOTING

Triggers and Trigger Control

Jim Carmichel

I probably shouldn't tell this on myself, but I have a recurring nightmare. With variations, the scene is a dusty street in an old western town and I'm having a showdown with an ugly galoot who has come to our fair community to rob, rape, and pillage. He grins at me with yellow teeth, spits on the sidewalk (which is against the law—and he knows it), then grabs for his gun. I react like lightning, clearing leather and thumbing the hammer back in a spare particle of an instant. Now I've got the drop on the hated invader. With the touch of a trigger I'll shoot the gun out of his hand and our town will again be a safe place to raise children and where pretty ladies can walk the streets unmolested. So I pull the trigger.

Nothing happens.

I pull harder this time. And nothing happens again.

"Curses," I exclaim, "My six shooter has a hard trigger."

This time I give the trigger a violent jerk and, reluctantly, my faithful revolver goes off, damn-near hitting me in the foot. By now the ugly galoot is laughing like a drunken hyena and wanders off into the town to do what he came to do. Variations on the same dream involve encounters with rampaging Indians, charging elephants, and unrea-

sonable husbands. Invariably I am done-in because of triggers with a heavy pull. Alas, such are the dreams of gun writers.

In real life I've also had plenty of problems with reluctant triggers but haven't we all. The importance of trigger pull in the way we hit or with rifle, pistol or shotgun cannot be overstated. Ask any shooting champion to number the essential ingredients of marksmanship and, invariably, good trigger control will be high on the list. Without good trigger control we can't hit what we shoot at, and we can't have good control if we have a bad trigger. This is a simple fact of shooting.

Of course there is a rather large gray area between "good" and "bad" triggers, and I'd say that about three-quarters of all guns fall into this in-between category. The remaining 25 percent of all guns have either very good or very bad triggers.

Before we get too deep into good and bad triggers—and all those in between—I'd better discuss "trigger control" and its importance to good shooting.

Let's say you're on the edge of a high-country

This article first appeared in Outdoor Life

meadow and you're zeroed in on a gang of elk about 200 yards distant. You're in a hunter's sitting position with the rifle sling tight behind your elbow. You try to settle the sight on a big bull's chest, but with the excitement and all, the crosshairs are jumping all over the animal and even the empty space around him. You try to steady your aim, but the crosshairs take a wild leap every time your heart pumps. There are short moments however when the crosshairs become reasonably steady, still enough for you to fire a shot with good certainty of hitting the target. But the trick is being able to pull the trigger precisely at this optimum instant, and doing so without otherwise spoiling your aim. *That* is good trigger control.

Of course good control comes with practice and experience, but the trigger mechanism is also vitally important to good shooting because as trigger quality declines there is a corresponding decline in the probability of your being able to "break" or get off the shot exactly when you want to.

For example, one of the elements of trigger quality is weight of pull, the pressure you must apply to the trigger to release the sear. Generally speaking, as the pull weight of a trigger is increased, trigger control becomes correspondingly more difficult. Also, as weight of pull goes up, you find it more and more difficult to fire a shot without disturbing your aim. This is because the muscle effort you apply to the trigger tends to move the whole gun, thereby pulling your aim off target.

Just about everyone who served in the military will remember the small arms instructor screaming that the triggers on rifles and pistols should be "squeezed." Actually, I think those old-time instructors told us to "squeeze" only because that's what they'd been taught to say. In truth, the squeezing technique is a very poor form of trigger control because it induces excessive muscle tremor and thereby degrades the steadiness of your aim and hold.

You've also heard that when you squeeze a trigger the "right" way the shot will surprise you when it breaks. The notion behind this theory is that if you pull the trigger gradually but steadily the shot will break at a random point in time in which you have only marginal control. The idea being that the bullet will probably hit closer to the target than if you try to anticipate the shot and possibly jerk the trigger. Of course almost any technique is preferable to jerking the trigger, which virtually guarantees a miss, but being surprised when the shot is fired is only the lesser of the two evils.

If you are going to be a truly good marksman, you must be able to precisely determine when your gun will fire. That is the only way you can take advantage of those brief moments of opti-

Best placement of finger on trigger for most shooters is to position it so that centerline of the trigger lies under the root of the fingernail.

mum hold and aim. And this sort of control takes us right back to trigger quality.

Putting two and two together, a shooter will conclude that if a heavy pull interferes with trigger control then the obvious solution is a lighter pull. But alas, a lighter pull solves only part of the problem. In fact, if a trigger is too light it can cause some new problems that we can do without.

For several centuries past, it was not uncommon for fine hunting and target rifles to be equipped with double-set triggers. This system, also commonly called a "hair" trigger, is operated by pulling a trigger that "sets" the mechanism so that it will be fired by only a light touch on the firing trigger. Ordinarily a set trigger will fire with only a few ounces of pressure, but some mechanisms can be adjusted to such a light letoff that the weight of the trigger itself will fire the rifle if the muzzle is elevated.

Double-set triggers are pretty much out of style these days, except on muzzleloading rifles where they are still useful as well as traditional, and on some European-made rifles. Even target and benchrest shooters have almost entirely abandoned set triggers. The reason being that simpler triggers have been developed that offer the advantages of set triggers without the disadvantages—of which there are several. For example, Remington offers a 2-ounce pull trigger for their 40–X bench rifles and several independent makers also market similar triggers for other makes of rifles.

But don't go running out to buy one of these fancy triggers for your rifle before you are sure what you're doing. Chances are that a lightweight trigger isn't going to help your hunting marksmanship. And anyway, there's a good chance that the trigger on your rifle, pistol, or shotgun can be adjusted or refined so that you will have the best possible control.

All things considered, the most ideal trigger pull for a big-game hunting rifle is about 3 pounds. This means that the sear releases, firing the rifle, when 3 pounds of rearward pressure is applied to the trigger. Three pounds sounds like a lot of pull, but is in fact moderately light. The reason a 3-pound, or thereabouts, pull is ideal for a big-game rifle is that it is light enough to allow precise control but is at the same time heavy enough to give a firm enough trigger feel to prevent accidental firing. I've witnessed a number of occasions when a hunter inadvertently applied too much pressure to a light trigger and fired before he was ready. It's relatively easy to deal with a light trigger when you're practicing at the range on a balmy day, but when your fingers are numb with cold or you're excited by a trophy buck, your finger might blunder into the trigger, causing you to fire before your aim is perfect.

You can easily check a trigger's weight of pull with small scales that hook to the trigger and indicate the weight required to release the sear. A simple deadweight arrangement can also be used. If you are particularly interested in firearms performance or like to do a bit of gunsmithing, a trigger scale is a useful accessory. It doesn't cost much.

If you were to weigh the trigger pulls on a variety of today's sporting rifles and shotguns you'd discover that the average weight is 5 pounds or

Double-set triggers are not as popular as they once were except on muzzleloading rifles such as this Thompson/Center Hawken caplock. Also referred to as "hair triggers," the double-set trigger mechanism is operated by pulling the rear trigger to a "cocked" position. The rifle is then fired by lightly touching the front trigger.

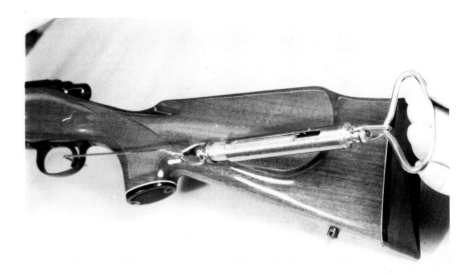

A trigger's weight of pull is expressed in pounds and ounces of pressure required to release the sear. Here, the weight of pull is being tested with a trigger scale designed for the purpose.

more, and in some cases as heavy as 10 pounds. The reason most manufacturers ship their guns with such a heavy pull is that they can rest assured that their guns won't be accidently fired by clumsy and untrained fingers. This policy also offers protection from liability suits resulting from the improper and unsafe handling of firearms. But just because a trigger weighs out heavy does not mean it is not a potentially good trigger. Almost all quality rifles, especially bolt-action models and the premier single shots, have adjustable mechanisms that can be easily reset by *qualified* persons. The reason I say qualified persons is that while anyone can stick a screwdriver into a trigger assembly and turn a few screws, you have to know what you're doing to *do it right*. The usual tipoff to bum trigger tinkering is a tendency to set the weight of pull too light and setting the sear engagement too close. Experienced gunsmiths can do the job right, as can knowledgeable amateurs. If you want to fiddle with the trigger on your rifle but aren't sure of what you're doing, be sure to read the instructions and ask for experienced advice if you can get it. The primary objective of any trigger adjusting is an absolutely safe mechanism. When the sear engagement is set for minimum contact, there is a danger of accidental release when the bolt is closed or opened. A good test for positive sear contact, along with visual inspection, is slamming the bolt closed *hard* several times. If the sear then releases, some readjusting is called for.

Never succumb to the amateurish notion that a light trigger is a good trigger. A far more important factor in trigger quality is *consistency* of pull. Any sort of junk trigger can be tinkered with until it has a light letoff, but the pulls may vary by a pound or more. A really good trigger is one that varies no more than 2 or 3 ounces from shot to shot. This sort of consistency is vital to good

marksmanship because there is no way you can fire a shot at the precise instant you want to if you're playing guessing games with your trigger.

If you check out a bunch of new rifles with a trigger scale you would find that, in addition to being overly heavy, most of them have a variance of a half pound or more from pull to pull. But don't fret. With most adjustable mechanisms the variation can be refined to acceptable levels.

In addition to an adjustment for weight of pull, most good-quality triggers will also have adjustments for *creep* and *backlash*. Creep is the perceptible movement of a trigger before the sear releases (do not confuse creep with the built-in first stage movement of a two-stage trigger). And backlash is the trigger travel after the sear releases.

Ideally, a trigger should have no motion whatever but this is too much to hope for except with a few highly specialized target triggers. When a trigger "creeps" as it is pulled, it degrades your control because you find it hard to predict when a creepy trigger is going to break. The situation is especially bad when the creep feels rough or gritty, as though you're dragging the trigger over a bumpy road. Backlash hurts your shooting in a number of ways as well, especially when the sudden backlash motion disturbs your aim and steady hold before the bullet exits the barrel.

Good quality adjustable triggers such as that on Remington Model–700 rifles (which I mention because the M–700 is especially easy to adjust), can have creep and backlash adjusted out so they are barely perceptible, even to the trained finger. With almost any good mechanism you'll make the happy discovery that as creep is adjusted out there is also an improvement in shot-to-shot uniformity of pull. But again, when trying to eliminate creep and backlash, never do so at the expense of safety.

For handguns I like a somewhat lighter pull,

with 2½ pounds being about perfect for targets, plinking and hunting. A few pistols, particularly target models, have trigger adjustments that you can reset yourself, but most handgun triggers are nonadjustable. This doesn't mean that the trigger can't be improved—just that any such projects should be done only by someone who knows what he's doing. Usually this is a professional pistolsmith with specialized equipment.

There used to be a ragtailed gunsmith by the name of Robert E. Lee Jenkins who lived in my hometown of Jonesboro, Tennessee. He specialized in "trigger jobs" on revolvers. His technique was to file the sear contact until there was virtually no contact remaining. This meant that the sear would release with only a light touch on the trigger. Some of his reworked pistols even tended to fire with *no* touch of the trigger. Anyway, he once had the bright idea that if he could get a city contract to rework the revolvers used by the police force at $10 per gun (we had three town cops then) he'd have a pocketful of money. So, being a political animal of some experience, Jenkins allowed he'd grease the town bureaucracy by doing a trigger job on the mayor's beloved single-action Colt "Peacemaker" at no charge. The mayor was delighted until his Peacemaker slipped the sear, went off accidentally and shot a hole in the only good tire on the town garbage truck. Jenkins lost the contract.

Good trigger control is a 50/50 proposition. Half the game is having a good trigger and the other half is knowing how to use it. A well-trained trigger finger works like it has a mind of its own, reacting without conscious control on your part when the sights are on the target. Such control comes with practice and experience, and there is

no better—or cheaper—way to practice than "dry" firing. Dry-firing means simply snapping the trigger on an unloaded gun. But when done right dry-firing is more than just snapping the trigger. Each dry-fired "shot" should be aimed as carefully as a live round with careful note made of where the sights are on the target when the firing pin clicks. If it clicks when your hold and aim at their best, over and over, you've mastered an essential ingredient of fine marksmanship—trigger control. A really good shot will dry-fire at least 100 "shots" for every round of live ammunition.

Shotgun triggers, with a few exceptions, can be judged about the way we judge rifle and pistol triggers. A shotgun trigger that has minimal creep and backlash is certainly desirable, as is one with a uniform pull, though these qualities are less essential when swinging on a winging target than when precisely aiming a rifle or pistol.

Weight of trigger pull on a shotgun, however, is more important to good wingshooting than is generally recognized. Of course experienced trap and skeet shooters know the value of a good trigger and sometimes make a fetish of having their shotgun triggers honed and polished to razor crispness. Some game shots I know go to similar extremes. I like a shotgun pull about 3 to 3½ pounds, and no more than 4. Fanciers of double guns with double triggers claim the triggers should have a 3½ pound pull on the front trigger and 4 pounds on the rear. I see no need for any difference and like identical pulls on both barrels, especially with single-trigger doubles. Once I had a pretty little 20-gauge side-by-side with a single trigger that weighed out at 3 pounds on the right barrel and 5 pounds on the left barrel. I never could hit very well with the left barrel because the heavy pull tended to pull me off the target.

Weight of pull is especially important on shotguns weighing less than 6 pounds. If the trigger pull is too heavy, there is a detectable tendency to pull the gun off target when pulling the trigger(s). If you happen to own one of these lightweight sweethearts that is tough to hit with, you just might check the trigger pull. For a shotgun weighing 6 pounds or less I like a trigger pull of somewhere between 2 ½ and 3 pounds.

Adjusting the trigger pull on shotguns is a serious business and should be undertaken only by a specialist. Most shotgun triggers don't take well to being tinkered with, and a bad trigger job is difficult and expensive to undo. So it's usually cheaper to have an expert work on your shotgun and have it done right the first time.

The trigger on a gun is a lot like a woman's fancy. When you keep it properly tuned and adjusted it will reward you in a thousand ways. But when it is neglected and used the wrong way there is always hell to pay.

Modern day adjustable trigger mechanisms, such as this one on a Remington Model 700 rifle, can be adjusted for weight of pull, backlash and creep. Adjustments have to be made very carefully however, as I am doing here, to avoid rendering the trigger mechanism unsafe or inoperable.

Optical Terms for the Shooter

Hugh Birnbaum

More than ever before, optical equipment of all sorts is being adopted enthusiastically by recreational shooters. Rare is the sight of a target shooter or hunter toughing it out without a spotting scope or a good binocular. Rarer still is the rifle bereft of aiming optics. Even pistol shooters are forsaking traditional low-profile iron sights for high-tech glassware, and the sight of a shotgun topped with glass no longer shocks, either. The bottom line is that shooters

This article first appeared in American Rifleman

have come to realize that just about anything the naked eye can do, it can usually do it better with appropriate optical assistance.

Along with all the sporting glassware, though, has come a plethora of often impenetrable terms and optical arcana that can leave the shooter glassy-eyed. To help cut through the haze and sharpen the optical scene, the following definitions are offered, with the caveat that they are intended to address practical concerns rather than to prepare the reader for the final examination in Optical Theory 101.

Knowledge of the basic terms and concepts of telescopic magnification—from collimation and diopters to parallax and twilight factor—can help you choose the most appropriate equipment and use it effectively.

Achromatic. A lens classed as achromatic is formulated to be free of chromatic aberration, which causes color fringing. An achromatic lens, or achromat, achieves identical focus with light rays of two different colors.

Astigmatism. Aberration in a lens or optical system that makes lines oriented in certain directions less sharply focused than lines running in other directions. Astigmatism also occurs in the human eye. A typical astigmatic effect would be to see the vertical lines on a sheet of graph paper sharply while seeing the horizontal lines less clearly, or vice versa.

Bell. In scope sights with ends flared to accommodate large-diameter ocular or objective lenses, the oversized lens housings are referred to as bells, as in ocular bell or objective bell.

Binocular Collimation. Regulating the two halves of a binocular for parallelism. If the halves are misaligned, the images they form will not merge into a single, sharply defined viewing image. Severe misalignment causes a perceptible multiple-image effect. Slight misalignment may not be specifically obvious, but will result in eyestrain during prolonged viewing.

Catadioptric Lens. A lens system containing front-surface mirrors in addition to refractive lenses. Catadioptric designs "fold" the light path internally to reduce the overall length of the lens system to a significantly shorter dimension than a conventional design would require for a given focal length. Catadioptric lenses, also called mirror lenses, are sometimes used as compact telephoto camera lenses and are occasionally employed in spotting scopes. They are relatively common in astronomical telescopes.

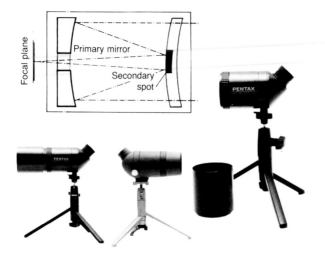

Center Focus. Refers to a type of binocular with a central focusing control that adjusts both halves of the binocular simultaneously. In center-focus binoculars, one ocular lens is individually adjustable for focus while the other is fixed. Initially, the user focuses the fixed-ocular half of the instrument with the central control, then focuses the other half with its independently adjustable ocular. Further focusing requires using only the

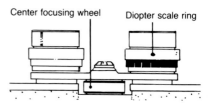

Center focusing wheel   Diopter scale ring

central control. A center-focus binocular is quick and easy to use, but is relatively complex mechanically.

Chromatic Aberration. Occurs when a lens brings different wavelengths (colors) of light to separate and distinct points of focus rather than to a common focus. Depending upon the severity, the ef-

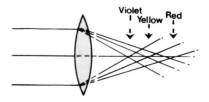

Violet Yellow Red

fect may range from slight unsharpness to gross unsharpness with visible color fringing.

Collimator. An optical device containing a lens system that bends light rays passing through it to make the rays parallel. The lens system is often coupled with a target such as a reticle or, in certain applications, a pinpoint light source. A collimator is used to "trick" another optical device, such as a camera lens, telescope, or scope sight, into forming an image of the collimator's reference target as though it were a distant target rather than a very close one. In the optical industry, collimators are widely used for visually assessing the image-forming characteristics of lenses or lens systems. In the context of sporting firearms, small collimating units, also called bore sighters, can be used to regulate a scope sight's reticle to approximately match a shoulder arm's bore axis in the relative comfort of shop or home, without making a trip to a firing range. The scope "zero" achieved by careful use of a collimator should be considered simply a rough setting that *must* be refined by actual test firing.

Coma. Off-axis lens aberration that distorts oblique light rays transmitted by the lens. Coma produces taillike smears on tiny round image details such as points of light. Under high magnification, coma may make tiny points of light resemble comets.

Crosshairs. A cruciform reticle in an optical sight, also commonly referred to as crosswires.

Curvature of Field. Off-axis lens aberration that makes light rays come to a focus at different points along a curved, rather than flat, focal plane. When viewing a flat subject, such as a paper target or a brick wall, that is perpendicular to the lens axis, curvature of field will make it impossible to obtain sharp focus at the center and edges of the viewing

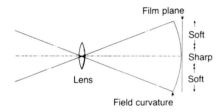

field simultaneously. When the center is sharp, the edges will be soft; altering focus to sharpen the edges of the image will blur the center.

Diaphragm. A mechanical device for reducing the amount of light entering or transmitted by an optical system. In simplest, nonadjustable form, often called a stop or Waterhouse stop, the diaphragm is nothing more than an opaque plate configured to fit in a slot or holder in the lens system, or to attach over a lens. The plate has a hole of the desired size, usually circular, that allows a limited amount of light through the optics. An adjustable diaphragm, such as found in most camera lenses and called an iris diaphragm, consists of several interconnected, overlapping movable metal or composition blades that can be opened and closed concentrically to vary the size of the central aperture.

Using a stop or diaphragm to reduce the effective aperture of a viewing system produces two immediately evident effects. First, the brightness is reduced. Second, the depth of field is increased. Depth of field refers to the zone of sharpness from near to far in the observed image. Accessory stops or diaphragms available for some target-model rifle scopes are used to enhance sharpness in depth, which is quite limited with high-magnification optics. Iris diaphragms or interchangeable stops are often used in conjunction with high-precision aperture sights on match rifles to achieve optimum clarity of front sight and target. Handgun shooters

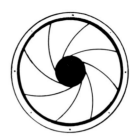

unable to see iron sights clearly without corrective spectacles that render the target unacceptably blurry may manage to sharpen sights and target adequately by placing an accessory small-aperture diaphragm or stop plate over the aiming eye's eyeglass lens.

Diopter. A measurement unit that expresses the refractive power of a lens. Focusing eyepieces of scope sights and binoculars are sometimes equipped with a scale calibrated in diopters to facilitate returning to a previously determined setting. The corrective power of simple eyeglass lenses is given in diopters. Accessory diopter cor-

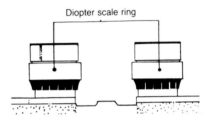

rection lenses are sometimes installed in viewing systems or sights to allow comfortable use while the owner is wearing nonprescription shooting glasses.

Distortion. A distorted image falsifies subject contours and/or proportions. Distortion is most easily perceived when viewing subjects of known shape and dimensional relationships. Two common forms of distortion are barrel distortion and pincushion distortion. Barrel distortion makes straight lines appear to bow outward toward the edges of the field. Pincushion distortion makes straight lines appear to bow inward toward the center of the field. Small amounts of distortion may be tolerable in viewing optics provided the

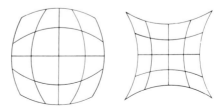

distortion remains fairly unobtrusive, as it generally does not impair overall utility. Nonetheless, the finest viewing optics are virtually free of any image distortion.

Erector Lens. Certain combinations of objective and ocular lenses yield an inverted image. An erector lens incorporated into the system serves to reorient the image right side up. In binoculars and telescopes prisms are often used to "erect" the image.

Exit Pupil. The exit pupil of an optical viewing system appears as a bright disc of light that may be seen by looking into the ocular lens from about 10 inches with the instrument aimed at a light source (not the sun!) or a bright background. Within certain limits, the larger the exit pupil the brighter the view through the optical system. You can calculate the aperture of the exit pupil in millimeters by dividing the effective diameter of the objective lens in millimeters by the magnification of the instrument. An exit pupil aperture as small as 2mm is large enough for easy viewing in good daylight conditions. An exit pupil diameter of approximately 7mm is large enough for darker environments or evening use. As the pupil of a normal human eye cannot open larger than about 7mm, there is little or no practical brightness advantage to designing ordinary viewing instruments with excessively large exit pupils.

Eyepiece. The lens or lens group through which the user of an optical instrument views the image. The term eyepiece is often used interchangeably with "ocular" or "ocular lens," but may also refer to the physical rim or mount flange that contains the outermost lens of the ocular. The context in which the word occurs normally reveals the specific meaning.

Eye Relief. The distance between the user's eye and the ocular lens at which the entire field of view of a scope sight or other optical device is visible simultaneously. Instruments described as having long or extended eye relief allow more than the usual distance between eye and ocular. Long-eye-relief rifle scopes are desirable on rifles that recoil strongly to reduce the likelihood of the ocular striking the shooter's eye or face, or on top-ejecting rifles that will not permit conventional scope mounting. Handgun scopes with extended eye relief provide a full field of view when held at arm's length. Long-eye-relief spotting scopes and binoculars allow users to see the entire field of view while wearing eyeglasses.

Field of View. The expanse of subject included within the field of an optical system. The measurement is normally taken across the diameter of a circular field and, in the U.S., expressed for scope sights in feet or yards at a subject distance of 100 yards unless otherwise stated. The field of view of binoculars is generally given for 100 or 1,000 yards. In countries using the metric system, field of view is commonly expressed in meters at a subject distance of 100 or 1,000 meters. Field of view may also be specified in angular terms, as an angle of view. Knowing the angle of view allows calculating the field of view for any subject distance of interest.

Flare. The scattering of nonimage-forming light within an optical system, caused by poorly controlled internal reflections from lens surfaces or mechanical components. Flare may be perceived as stray reflections, as a veiling glare or hazy quality that obscures detail in the image, as a loss in image contrast, or as any combination of these phenomena. It is most likely to occur when the field of view includes highly reflective, brightly lighted features or a strong light source. Some target scopes and spotting scopes are equipped with lens shades that may be quite effective in suppressing flare by preventing sunlight from shining directly on the front element of the objective lens in sidelighting or when shooting against the light. The higher the quality of the optical system, the less likely it will be to exhibit flare effects, although no optical system is immune to flare under some very extreme lighting conditions.

Focal Plane. The plane where the image formed by the lens or lens system is in sharp focus. In a camera, the focal plane is the film surface.

Focus. This term may refer to the focal point of a lens, a lens' focal length, the condition of maximum clarity of an image, or the action of adjusting a lens system to yield the clearest and best defined image it is capable of forming of a subject at a particular distance. An unfocused or out-of-focus image appears blurry, ill-defined, and deficient in contrast. An in-focus image looks sharp, precisely defined and as contrasty as the lens system and viewing conditions permit.

Focusing Scale. Scope sights with adjustable focusing objectives usually have a focusing scale on or adjacent to the movable focus control. The scale, calibrated in feet, yards, or meters, permits setting the focus rapidly for targets at known distances. When target distance is unknown, the scope is focused visually and the scale ignored. Accuracy of focusing scale calibrations should be verified when a scope is new and occasionally thereafter, as discrepancies are not unusual. This may be done by focusing the scope carefully on targets at known distances. If the focusing scale is at odds with reality, have it adjusted by the appropriate service facility or remark it with small pieces of tape or dots of nail polish for personally useful range settings. An optical instrument that focuses erratically or inconsistently should be repaired or replaced.

Haze. Light scattered by particulate matter in the atmosphere, such as dust or moisture droplets. Haze lends a foggy or cloudy appearance to distant objects or scenes, subduing colors and contrast. Haze effects are more apparent when using high-magnification optical instruments than when viewing with lower-power optics or the naked eye, and are more pronounced at long range than short range under a given set of atmospheric conditions.

Individual Focus. Refers to a type of binocular in which the ocular of each half must be focused independently each time the instrument is refocused. Adjusting the focus of an individual-focus

binocular is slower than a center-focus model, but the former is mechanically simpler and, construction quality being equal, potentially less vulnerable to hard knocks.

Lens Aberration. An optical flaw that adversely affects image quality.

Lens Coating. Antireflection layer or layers deposited on surfaces of prisms and lenses by vaporizing metallic compounds in vacuum chambers containing the optical elements to be coated. Lens coating reduces loss of light and image degradation caused by scattering of light reflected by lens surfaces. Traditional lens coating comprises a single antireflection layer applied to each significant glass surface. More modern multiple-layer lens coatings consist of three or more antireflection layers per surface. Both single and multi-layer coatings are effective when applied appropriately.

Luminosity. Radiating or reflecting light. Also a measure of the brightness of a light source or of a reflective surface expressed quantitatively according to rigorously defined criteria.

Jim Carmichel is here testing scopes mounted on a rack. Visual comparison of scopes helps Carmichel judge relative qualities of definition, field of view, and light-gathering power.

Magnification. Relationship between the apparent size of an object as viewed through an optical instrument and the apparent size of the object as seen with the naked eye. For example, a scope that makes an object look four times larger than it appears when viewed directly has a magnification of four times, usually expressed as 4×. A magnification designated by a number smaller than one indicates that the viewing device makes the subject appear proportionately smaller than when seen with the unaided eye. An instrument of 0.9× magnification reduces the apparent size of the subject to only 90 percent of what it would seem in direct viewing.

Note that the term magnification is used even when the optical device "minifies." As a practical matter, nearly all sporting optics yield positive magnification that enlarge the viewing image. The magnification bears a direct relationship to the apparent distance of the viewed object: the greater the magnification, the closer the object appears. Dividing the actual distance of the object by the magnification indicates the apparent distance of the object as viewed through the optical system. An object 100 yards distant would appear as though it were 50 yards distant when viewed through a 2× scope and just 10 yards distant through a 10× scope.

Mirage. Optical phenomenon that occurs when air near the ground is significantly denser than the air above it, creating visible reflected images of distant objects or targets. Less extreme mirage phenomena are of concern to outdoor target shooters, appearing as a shimmer that makes precise aiming difficult or impossible. Or they may cause an apparent displacement of the target that leads to erroneous shot placement as the shooter fires at the mirage image rather than the actual target. High-power scope sights make mirage more noticeable, but they also allow the experienced marksman to judge the mirage effect with greater certainty and to compensate for it to the best of his or her ability. The term mirage is also broadly applied to the heat shimmer from a hot gun barrel, which may disrupt the sighting image. Extra-long lens shades offer relief from such heat shimmer.

Objective. The objective lens or lens group forms the image of a distant target or subject at or near the focal point of the optical system. The objective is located at the front of the instrument, farthest from the eye.

Ocular. The ocular lens or lens group enlarges the image the objective lens forms and allows the viewer's eye to see it clearly despite its proximity to the eye. The ocular is the part of the optical system nearest the viewer's eye and is the rearmost lens group of a scope sight. The ocular lenses of nearly all rifle and handgun scopes may be focused to suit the user's vision, thus providing the sharpest possible view of the reticle and of the image formed by the objective lens.

Parallax. Apparent shift in position of a viewed object attributable to the difference between two separate and distinct points of view. In a scope sight, parallax can cause an aiming error, or parallax error, when the target image is not formed in the same plane as the aiming reticle. The condition may be detected by moving the aiming eye progressively away from the center of the ocular toward the edge of the lens without moving the scope. If the target and reticle shift position slightly relative to each other, parallax error exists and will cause a corresponding shift in the center of impact. The more the eye moves away from the scope's optical axis, the greater the parallax error. Parallax error does not occur when the aiming eye is well centered with respect to the ocular lens, though the conditions for a potential error are present.

With a fixed-focus scope sight that has been factory-set for optimum focus at a specific distance, the potential for parallax error exists whenever targets are nearer or farther than the range for which the optics were regulated. In most cases the amount of error will not be significant in the context of normal field shooting. Parallax error can be avoided satisfactorily by keeping the aiming eye reasonably well centered. High-power varmint and target scope sights have adjustable objectives that permit focusing the scope over a wide range of target distances. Focusing such scopes carefully assures maximum image sharpness and also eliminates potential parallax error at the distance for which the scope is focused.

Porro Prism. Used in pairs in a binocular barrel between the objective and ocular lenses, right-angle porro prisms erect the inverted image formed by the objective lens group. They also "fold" the light path, permitting the binocular barrel to be made shorter than if a nonprismatic optical design were used. The offset required between the porro prisms in each pair gives the binocular barrels a

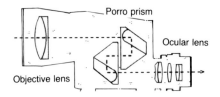

corresponding offset between the objective and ocular sections.

Relative Brightness. Relative brightness numbers are an attempt to quantify the "brightness" of scope sights and binoculars to facilitate comparison. The relative brightness number is the square of the diameter of the instrument's exit pupil, expressed in millimeters. You can determine the size of the exit pupil, if it isn't stated in product literature, by dividing the useful aperture of the objective lens, in millimeters, by the magnification, or power, of the instrument. For example, a $4\times$ rifle scope with a 40mm objective would have a 10mm exit pupil ($40 \div 4 = 10$) and a relative brightness of 100 (10^2). The relative brightness reflects the optical truth that, all other factors being equal, large-diameter objectives admit more light than small-diameter objectives. More light can pass through a large window than through a small one.

Resolving Power (Resolution). The ability of a lens or lens system to form an image in which fine subject details are clearly differentiated. The higher the resolving power, or resolution, the more precisely subject detail is rendered.

Reticle. In a rifle or handgun scope, the reticle is an aiming reference consisting of crosswires, dot, pointed post or other distinct shape that appears superimposed on the field of view. The reticle is positioned within the optical system to coincide with the plane of focus of the objective lens or lens group. Some scope sights are offered with a choice of reticle styles to accommodate subjective preferences and/or match function to application. As a rule, to which there are exceptions, hunting-style scope sights have relatively bold reticles that aid rapid aiming, while target and varmint models feature finer reticles that subtend less of the target and may be less prominent, but are conducive to precise shot placement when aiming carefully and deliberately. Some spotting scopes and binoculars incorporate a scaled reticle intended to aid in estimating target distance or size.

Roof Prism. Also called Dach prisms (Dach is the German word for roof), these relatively complex prisms erect the image in binoculars and "fold"

the light path to allow shortening the barrels. Roof prisms are more difficult, and therefore more expensive, to manufacture than porro prisms, but they allow designing the binocular with compact, straight barrels, reducing size and often reducing weight. For a given level of quality, a binocular incorporating roof prisms is likely to cost more than one of similar power and light transmission that uses porro prisms. When minimizing instrument size and weight is not a major criterion for selection, overall optical and mechanical quality are more important than prism configuration.

Spherical Aberration. Causes varying degrees of image distortion. Light rays entering the outer portions of the lens are brought to a focus closer to the lens than light rays passing through the

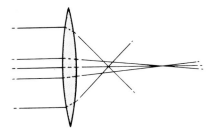

center of the lens. The resulting distortion is more likely to be noticed in photographs than when viewing through such a lens.

Twilight Factor. Most often associated with binoculars, the twilight factor is a numerical expression of the telescopic effect in dim light. It may also be calculated for scope sights. The twilight factor is derived by multiplying the magnification, or power, by the useful objective diameter, in millimeters, and then extracting the square root. In the case of a $4\times$ scope sight with a 40mm objective, the calculation would be $\sqrt{4 \times 40} = \sqrt{160} = 12.64911$. The twilight factor assumes realistically that in dim light, all other factors being equal, viewing instruments with higher magnifications and larger objectives will outperform optics of lower power and lesser light-gathering capability.

Variable Power. Variable-power scope sights, spotting scopes, and binoculars have a control that allows the user to adjust the magnification over a predetermined range, as with a photographic "zoom" lens.

Wide-Field. Wide-field viewing or sighting optics provide a broader field of view at any given distance than would a conventional non-wide-field instrument of the same magnification.

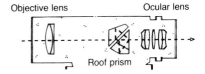

Objective lens   Ocular lens

Roof prism

A Guide to Muzzleloading

Jim Carmichel

The old saying that angels watch over fools and small boys proved true the first time I tried to load and fire a muzzleloading rifle. It was a Sunday afternoon and my parents had gone for their customary drive, leaving me at home with stern instructions to catch up on my lagging school work. For me school work was not a happy chore under any circumstances, most especially on a sunny Sunday afternoon. So before too many minutes passed I had the alarming thought that the homework might be a violation of the Sabbath. Thus fearful for my immortal soul, I closed my books and went outside where I hoped the warm spring sun would wash away any trace of the recent sin.

My salvation thus momentarily secured, I cast about for a pious activity to occupy me for the remainder of the day. Within seconds my thoughts targeted the ancient "hog rifle" that dwelt in our smokehouse. Despite grave warnings to keep my hands off the mysterious thing, it had long been a focus of my wildest imaginings. Surely it had not only provided squirrels, deer and turkey for the bellies of my forebears, it had also saved them from bears, panthers, and marauding Indians. For such a treasure to be banished to the dark recesses of our smokehouse was an insult to our heritage.

The truth was that the old rifle had been very much on my mind for several weeks. Not that I had any intention of actually shooting the thing, mind you, but as a matter of interest I *had* made a few discreet inquiries as to how one might go about loading and firing such ancient rifles. According to Alonzo Smithpeters, who lived down the creek a ways and who was over 80, the old rifles were easy to shoot. You just poured some gunpowder down the barrel and, using a ramrod, pushed a "ball" down on the powder. I didn't understand what he meant by a ball and he said it was only a round bullet. He also said that the ball would shoot straighter and farther if it was wrapped in a patch. His description of a "patch"

was a bit confusing so I didn't press him for details. Finally, a "cap" was pressed on a nipple at the rear of the barrel and the gun was ready to fire.

"What's a cap, Mr. Smithpeters?" I asked. "Wait, I'll show you," he said, and, after digging through a drawer filled with wondrous objects, produced a small white can half filled with what appeared to be tiny copper thimbles.

"When the hammer hits these," he explained, "it strikes a streak of fire that goes down the nipple and lights the powder."

With that final bit of information, everything became clear. At last I understood the workings of the old rifle in our smokehouse. How simple it was. Why I bet I could load and shoot it myself. The thought was to haunt me for days. But before I could shoot it, not that I would ever want to, I'd need some caps and some powder and some bullets. The powder was easy; I could always get some out of a shotgun shell. And finding a bullet would be no problem either. But getting caps was another problem. I'd never even heard of them before, much less had any idea of where to buy some. I'd never seen any at Sander's Feed Store or at Dave Grayson's Cash Store. But, Dave mainly sold girdles and shoes and thread anyway. (My mother refused to go into Dave's store after she heard that he offered to give Priscilla Moffheizer a pair of red lace garters if she would not tell her husband and if she would come back when Dave's wife was out of town. I figured that if all Dave had on his mind was red garters then he probably wouldn't have any hog rifle caps.)

"Mr. Smithpeters," I was almost afraid to ask, "could you spare a few of them caps? I'll pay for 'em."

"What do you want with them?"

"Oh, they're just for my collection. I collect old stuff like that."

One by one, five of the precious caps were

This article first appeared in Outdoor Life

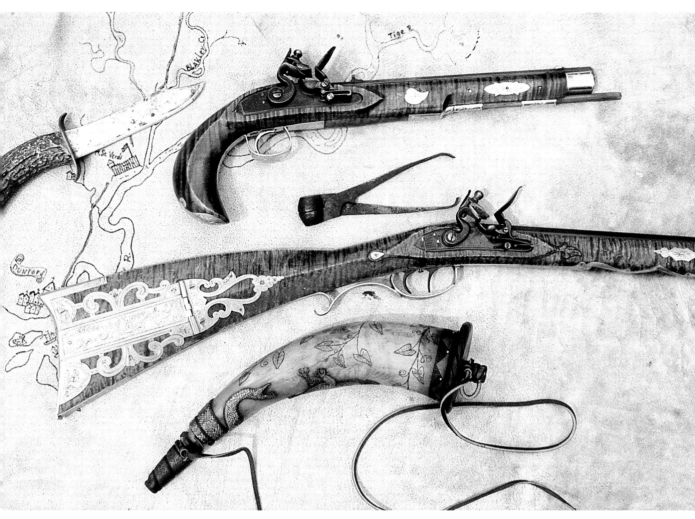

The Kentucky, or Pennsylvania, longrifle was the most accurate arm of its day, and it was one of America's first truly original art forms. Few, if any, American designs dating to Colonial days exhibit as much exquisite grace and workmanship as the Kentucky longrifle. This modern-day reproduction and the pistol were entirely hand built by Louis Smith, a master gun builder from Tennessee. Smith did all carving, inlaying, engraving, and finishing entirely by hand. The guns shoot as good as they look.

placed into my outstretched palm, each sending an electric ripple through me that made my scalp tingle and my toes itch. That had been a week before and I'd hid the caps under a bird's nest, also part of the collection in my dresser drawer.

The way I had it figured, my parents would be gone for at least another hour. This would give me plenty of time to get the smokehouse key down from its hiding place over our back porch door and give the old rifle a good looking over.

As it turned out there was also enough time to cut open an old shotshell and dump its full load of powder into the muzzle of the old rifle. There was also time enough to pull the bullet out of an old and tarnished .38 pistol cartridge and ram the bullet into the barrel, after pouring the pistol powder into the barrel, too.

Now all I had to do, should I ever decide to shoot the old rifle, was to place a cap on the nipple. Within two seconds my mind was made up. Since I obviously knew how to correctly load and handle the old rifle, what harm could be done if I fired it a time or two? I located the caps and within moments I was aiming at a white spot on a huge apple tree in our back yard.

Click! The hammer fell but nothing happened. "Must be something wrong with these caps," I thought, "try another one."

Click, again. I tried a third and fourth cap with the same result.

"Damn," I said aloud, then crossed my fingers to take it back because it was Sunday.

I carefully placed the final cap on the rusty nipple. This time I didn't bother to aim at the apple tree because the rifle surely wasn't going to go off. Anyway I drew the hammer to full cock and pulled the trigger.

"*K E E R O B L A M M!*" it went. The sound still echoes in my memory.

There, I'd done it. The rifle looked as good as ever and a thin wisp of smoke curled from the muzzle. I held my nose closer to inhale the delicious aroma. What rapture. I returned the rifle to the smokehouse, hid the key again, and disposed of the gutted remains of the shotshell. My parents would never suspect. The only problem was a continuing commotion issuing from our henhouse on the other side of the calf pen, more or less in line with the big apple tree in our back yard . . .

Oh my God!

I arrived at the henhouse door just in time to witness the final death throes of Queenie, my mother's favorite nesting hen. My bullet had missed the apple tree and a half-dozen yearlings in the calf pen, but it hadn't missed old Queenie.

During the course of this episode I violated at least a half dozen of the cardinal rules of safe black-powder shooting. That I managed to survive with my hands, eyes, and other parts intact, and without blowing the old rifle to smithereens, is proof positive that angels do guard over little boys.

Except for poor old Queenie, the affair had a happy ending, but some other black-powder shooters have not been so lucky. It is the stories of guns blowing up in shooters' hands, injuring shooters and bystanders, that keep many hunters, perhaps yourself, from enjoying the pleasures and advantages of muzzleloading. Also, depending on where you get your instructions, the loading, firing and maintenance of a muzzleloading firearm can sound as complicated as quantum physics.

The truth is that modern muzzleloading guns, especially the ones you can buy ready made at most gunshops, or build from kits, are extremely safe. They have such enormous reserve strength that it is virtually impossible to blow one up, even when grossly overloaded. So if you've shied away from black-powder shooting because you're afraid of accidents, there is little need for fear. You can also forget your concerns about muzzleloaders being difficult to load and care for. I find it more difficult to mix a good martini than to load a muzzleloader. And, come to think of it, you can load a black-powder rifle about as fast as a bartender can mix a martini.

Okay, so you're convinced that muzzleloading rifles are safe and easy to load, but you still aren't interested. After all, you have a nice breechloader for your deer hunting so why bother with anything else? Hunting with a muzzleloader just might extend your deer hunting season and could

Environmentalists might be inclined to make you put a scrubber on this chimney.

also improve your chances for success! This is because some states have special deer seasons for black-powder firearms only. This means that you get to increase your chances by spending more time in the woods and, besides, some muzzleloading hunts are during the best part of the season and in the best areas. In a recent season in Tennessee, black-powder hunters bagged nearly 12,000 deer, many of them on special black-powder-only hunts.

Lots of hunters have taken up muzzleloading rifles only as a means of taking advantage of these special hunts, but along the way they've discovered the joys of burning blackpowder and so have become confirmed muzzleloaders. The reason is simple: Muzzleloaders are fun; there is nothing that quite equals the thrill of bagging a deer, or even a squirrel, when you've done it all from scratch. One of the reasons that black powder is so exciting is that you are totally in control of your rifle's performance. When you bag a trophy buck or center a bull's-eye, it's because you've put it all together yourself.

The legend of the "Kentucky" longrifle is one of our most treasured heritages. Sadly though, as the legend has grown, myths, halftruths, and utterly silly misconceptions have been spread. Much of this misinformation has come from ill-informed outdoor writers who haven't bothered to learn enough about their subject. For example, we've all read descriptions of the ignition and firing sequence of a muzzleloader as being something of a *click-hiss-swoosh-whoomboom* (with variations) affair. From this you could get the idea that you could skin a beaver between the time the trigger is pulled and the bullet exits the muzzle. Who would want to hold onto a firearm while all those strange things were going on inside? In truth, as you will discover, there is virtually no perceptible difference between firing a muzzleloader and a modern breechloader. Even flintlock guns fire with amazing speed.

Now don't misunderstand, muzzleloaders can indeed go *click-hiss-swoosh-whoomboom*. And sometimes they only go "click," but that's their way of telling you that they haven't been loaded correctly, or that something else is bothering them.

Another myth is that muzzleloaders don't deliver enough power for serious big-game hunting. I don't know where this got started, but that sure ain't right. In fact, some muzzleloaders don't develop enough energy for big-game hunting, but that's only because they were never intended to. A little .30 or .32 caliber caplock squirrel rifle would hardly qualify as a deer rifle but neither would a breechloader in, say, .32/20 caliber. Many,

probably all, states that allow hunting with a rifle specify a minimum allowable black-powder caliber for big game. My home state of Tennessee requires that muzzleloading rifles used for big-game be of .40 caliber or larger.

The most popular calibers are .45 and .50. Here is a comparison of energy levels of different cartridges and calibers: A .50 caliber round ball weighs some 180 grains. When loaded to a muzzle velocity of 1800 fps it has a muzzle energy of close to 1300 foot-pounds. By comparison, a .30/30 with a 170-grain bullet has a muzzle energy of 1827 foot-pounds. Thus it appears that a typically loaded muzzleloader is not quite in the same league with even a .30/30, but like most experienced black-powder hunters, I don't believe that such comparisons tell it like it really is. The reason is that the formula used to calculate bullet energy is heavily biased in favor of bullet velocity. In practical terms, however, the large-diameter, soft-lead balls used in muzzleloaders are remarkably effective on game. You'll see this for yourself on your first muzzleloading hunt.

Anyway, if you want more energy from a muzzleloader, all you have to do is go to a larger caliber. Or you can substitute conical projectiles, such as Maxi-Balls, for the traditional round ball. A .50 caliber Maxi-Ball weighs 370 grains and, when loaded to a muzzle velocity of 1,500 fps, equals the muzzle energy of a .30/30. In actual practice though this load would be well suited to such game as elk, moose, and even the big bears. In terms of *real* comparisons, we've had to resort to Magnum class cartridges to equal the brute knockdown power of heavy-caliber muzzleloaders.

The classic myth about muzzleloaders is that

Don't ever underestimate the potential accuracy of a properly loaded muzzleloading rifle. This target was fired at 100 yards with a .45 caliber Thompson/Center Hawken style rifle. Also shown are precut patches, a Lyman bullet mold, powder measures and Hoppe's Number 9-Plus, a black-powder solvent and patch lubricant. Keeping the bore clean is a key to accuracy with black-powder rifles.

they aren't accurate enough for serious hunting. Ha! Anyone who says a muzzleloading rifle can't be accurate would certainly have gotten a lot of argument from a British officer named Ferguson and his troops at a place called King's Mountain during the American Revolution.

To be fair, I can understand how an uninformed beginner might conclude that muzzleloaders are woefully inaccurate. After all, it is possible to ram all sorts of poorly measured powder charges and ram ill-fitted bullets into the barrel of a muzzleloader. Yet there is no mystery about what is required to make a black-powder rifle accurate. All you have to do is use the correct powder charge and a properly fitted ball or projectile. If the rifle is a good one and your aim is true, the bullet will hit where it is supposed to. These simple criteria for good accuracy are exactly the same as with breechloading, cartridge-firing rifles and pistols. If, for example, someone loaded .30/06 ammunition with .270 bullets, he would surely conclude that the .30/06 is wildly inaccurate. Similarly, misfit bullets are bound to cause similar loss of accuracy in muzzleloaders. Happily, as we shall see later in this story, today's beginner doesn't have to worry about such problems and can expect good accuracy from the very first shot.

In my college days back in the 1950s, when I got really interested in shooting and hunting with muzzleloaders, there wasn't much to choose from in the way of guns or equipment. Some shooters used original antiques and those who could afford them had fancy reproductions made. Poor boys like I made our own rifles and pistols using combinations of new and scrap parts. Back then, a traveling jewelry salesman by the name of Turner Kirkland carried a pile of scrap gun parts in the trunk of his car. When he visited my hometown, I'd dig through his scrap pile until I found enough parts to assemble into a working caplock or flintlock mechanism. Then I'd find a barrel and build myself a "Kentucky" rifle or pistol. As it turned out, I made enough of these reproductions to pay most of my college expenses. And as it also turned out, Turner Kirkland founded Dixie Gun Works and became the world's largest dealer in muzzleloading guns, parts and accessories. Who could have predicted that the Tennessee Mountain lad and the sharp-trading jewelry peddler would someday go on African safari together and use their muzzleloaders to bag everything from warthog to elephant?

Because of Turner Kirkland, and others like him, a black-powder fan no longer has to scratch around in junk boxes as I did. Today's market offers varieties of finished guns, kits, and accessories that were absolutely unimaginable a generation ago. Recently I attempted to survey the muzzleloading rifles, pistols, and shotguns currently available but gave up when the number passed one hundred.

Many of the guns and kits are truly excellent, but what has really made black-powder shooting an expedient and worthwhile proposition for today's hunters are the accessories, components, and related equipment now available. You can walk into a gunshop and buy a muzzleloading rifle plus *everything else* you need and then go straight to the range for a hugely enjoyable and successful shooting session. Time was when getting everything together was something of a chore. One started out by melting scrap lead and casting bullets in a mold. Then one had to find the right thickness of patching material and tend to endless other details. Nowadays you can buy ready-made swaged balls by such bullet manufacturers as Hornady and Speer that are not only more convenient but also more accurate than the balls we used to cast. Honest! These swaged balls are available in narrowly graduated sizes (such as .445, .451, .454, and .457 inch) so that you can very closely match the ball to the barrel for best possible accuracy.

Good patching materials and patch lubricants are also available, along with an endless assortment of cleaning materials, powder flasks and measures, cappers, ball pullers (for unloading without firing), patch knives, and "possibles bags" in which to carry everything.

Just about any gunshop that carries muzzleloading guns and accessories will also sell you powder and percussion caps. When you survey the brands and types of powders available you may, at first, become a bit confused, but there's really no need to. Here's why: First of all, muzzleloading firearms are loaded *ONLY* with black powder or a black-powder substitute such as Pyrodex or Golden Powder. Black powder and black-powder substitutes are always clearly marked on the container. Smokeless-type powders are never used in muzzleloaders because they generate gas pressures far in excess of what black-powder rifles are made to withstand. To give you an idea of the difference, a charge of smokeless powder will generate some *5 to 20 times more internal pressure* than an equal volume of black powder. That's why smokeless and black powders must be strictly separated.

Substitute black powders are identified with such symbols as "RS" or "P," indicating that they are for rifle and shotgun or pistol use. True black powder is identified according to granulation size, with 1-F being the coarsest size. Progressively finer granulations are 2–F, 3–F and 4–F. This sounds confusing, I know, but most black-powder firearms come with instructions and a list of recommended types and charges of powder. As a good rule of thumb, just remember that the bigger

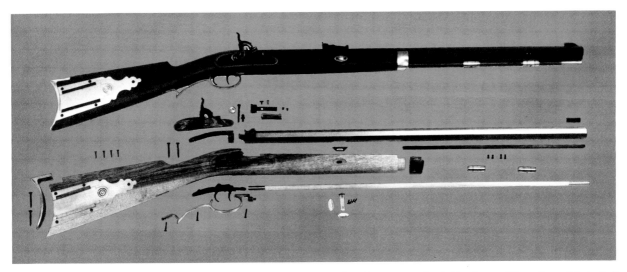

Shooting black powder is a do-it-yourself sport and assembling kits have an undeniable charm. Though prefabricated kits permit speedy assembly, and rule out most chances of errors, they still offer plenty of opportunity for the personal touches as to final shaping, finishing, and decoration. Black-powder shooters tend to have a strong streak of individualism, which is reflected in their rifles.

the bore the bigger the powder granulation. For example, 1-F powder is best for large-gauge shotguns and muskets. For rifles of .50 caliber and larger, use 2-F granulation. Smaller-caliber rifles and pistols do best with 3-F, and the fine-grained 4-F is for the priming flintlocks. Hunting rifles in the .45 and .50 class generally do best with 2-F powder.

Though it is certainly convenient to buy a finished rifle, the do-it-yourself kits have an undeniable appeal. With a kit you can carve extra flourishes or add inlays that make your rifle—like yourself—truly one of a kind. Most kits are so nearly complete that they can be finished in a weekend. These kits additionally require only basic tools unless you do a lot of extra carving, inlaying, or hand rubbing.

There are so many good rifles and kits on the market that I won't attempt to make any recommendations. I will, however, point out a few features to look for in a good hunting rifle. Good workmanship and quality are as unmistakable in a muzzleloader as they are in any other type of gun. Not surprisingly, the better-quality muzzleloading rifles also tend to be more expensive. But don't let price be your only guide.

As you would expect, the accuracy of a muzzleloader is largely dependent on the quality of its barrel. Tight or rough spots in the bore can cause severe accuracy problems, but unlike breechloaders, which allow easy inspection of the barrel, you'll have a difficult time getting a good look into the bore of most muzzleloaders. That's because the breech end is tightly closed with a close-fitting plug that can be removed only with

special tools. If your dealer will allow, however, you can learn a lot about a barrel's potential accuracy by fitting a tight patch on a ramrod and "feeling" the bore for tight spots. If the patch comes out with a scuffed look that could indicate rough tool marks on the rifling.

Another indicator of barrel quality is the "crowning" or tapering at the entrance of the muzzle. Look for a smooth and even taper. If the crowning is off-center or uneven, or if there are rough edges, you'll probably have problems. In my experience, the barrels to be most wary of are some of the imports on the low end of the price scale.

You should also pay particular attention to the firing mechanism, which in black-powder lingo is called the lock. The mechanism is manually cocked before firing by pulling the hammer back to full-cock position. Check the smoothness of the mechanism by holding the trigger back (so the sear won't catch) and rocking the hammer back and forward several times. If the internal parts are poorly fitted or binding, you'll feel a certain roughness or hesitation as you work the hammer. If your dealer has several muzzleloaders to choose from, try working all the locks. Comparing the "feel" of different locks will give you a quick lesson in what's good and what isn't. Pay particular attention to the feel of the safety, or "half cock" notch. It should feel firm and positive. While you are testing the lock be careful not to let the hammer fall full force on the unprotected nipple. Dry-firing, of course, will quickly batter the rim of the nipple and make it unusable. This nipple is usually easily replaceable, however.

Take special notice of the alignment of the hammer with the nipple. The nose of the hammer, you'll see, is somewhat cupped. When the hammer is fully down, the nipple should be well centered in the cup and the contact should be even around the rim of the nipple. The reason these details are important is for positive ignition. I'm constantly surprised at the number of commercial muzzleloaders with poor alignment and contact between the hammer and nipple.

If you are considering a flintlock rifle, check the feel of the mechanism the same as you would on a caplock. If the cock (hammer) has a flint in place, go ahead and dry-fire it against the frizzen. Several bright sparks should be visible. Also check to make sure that the hole into the barrel is well aligned with the priming pan.

Most muzzleloading rifles come fitted with double-set triggers. This type of trigger mechanism is traditional on caplock rifles and remains popular with black-powder shooters. The rear trigger is pulled to the rear until it "sets" with an audible click. The mechanism is then armed and will fire when you touch the front "hair" trigger. This type trigger is more or less independent from the lock and can be functioned without cocking the hammer. So go ahead and try dry-firing the triggers a few times; no harm will be done. If the hair trigger is too heavy or too light, you can easily adjust it by means of a small external screw between the triggers.

The sights on many black-powder rifles leave a lot to be desired. Some are non-adjustable and seem to have been stuck on as an afterthought. Hitting a target, or a deer, requires good sighting equipment, so if the rifle you like doesn't have good sights, ask your dealer if good-quality replacement sights are available. I prefer hunting-style peep sights and there are some inexpensive but excellent sights of this type available. They can be mounted on most rifles with little effort or cost.

Muzzleloading guns are so pretty to look at and so much fun to handle that it's often difficult to decide which you like best. However, for hunting purposes, the selection can be narrowed considerably. Though Brown Bess-style muskets have an impressive bore size they are smoothbores and as such don't offer much in the way of accuracy. In fact, most muskets of this type don't even have sights, making it impossible to hit a deer-size target beyond a few yards.

Rifled muskets are much better for deer hunting because they are equipped with sights (some are quite excellent) and are capable of sufficient accuracy to ensure good hits at most deer-hunting distances. Some rifled muskets, notably the Zouave carbine style, are especially light and easy to carry, making them popular for hunting in

My old hunting buddy, Buck Fleenor, one of the country's best known makers of Kentucky style rifles, shows off a string of plump bushy tails he took with a .32 caliber caplock squirrel rifle, which he built himself.

dense brush. The rifled muskets are large caliber, usually .58 bore, and fire heavy "Minié" projectiles that are loaded without patching. If you are a military buff, the rifled muskets, which are replicas of mid-19th-century infantry arms, will have a special appeal. Many of the rifled muskets on the market are especially well made and beautifully finished.

The rifles most popular with big-game hunters are the long-barreled Kentucky style and the shorter, but usually larger caliber, Hawken style. No firearm, before or since, has equaled the grace and beauty of the "Kentucky," or Pennsylvania, style rifle. This was one of America's earliest art forms; lovely to look at, delightful to hold and the deadliest firearm of its era. Today's commercial reproductions of the famed Kentucky rifle range from the good to the very bad, and when I say bad I'm talking about performance as well as styling and worksmanship. If price is no obstacle, the very best, certainly the most beautiful, muzzleloaders available are the hand-built Kentucky-style reproductions. These are made one at a time by a handful of talented craftsmen with the prices often running into the thousands of dollars.

A good Kentucky rifle can be remarkably accurate, accurate enough to clip a squirrel out of a tall hickory or to hit a deer at surprising distances. A deer hunter who knows his rifle and load well enough to make the right allowances for bullet drop can put a shot on target at 200 yards and beyond. My favorite squirrel rifle is a trim .32 caliber southern-style Kentucky built by Tennessee Valley Arms. At squirrel-hunting distances it puts the little .32 balls all in the same hole.

Larger-caliber Kentuckies in .45 or .50 caliber can do double service for both large and small game. Light loads in larger caliber rifles can be delightfully accurate, and they're fun to shoot. The main problem with Kentucky-style rifles for big game is that their long barrels, which are usually 40 inches or longer, make them awkward to carry in brush. Some states specify a minimum barrel length for black-powder hunting, in which case a long-barreled Kentucky-style rifle might be the only way to go.

The Hawken-style rifles, named after the legendary St. Louis gunmakers who made heavy-caliber rifles for the hunters, trappers and explorers who became known as Mountain Men, are considerably shorter than Kentucky-style rifles. This makes them easier to carry and faster to shoot. There are some excellent Hawken-style rifles on the market, with several makes to choose from. You'll find that they come in several calibers, but for big-game hunting the "workable" calibers are .45, .50 and .54. Most Hawken-style-rifles currently available feature a "hook" or patented-style breech that makes the barrel easily removable from the stock. This not only makes it easier to clean and service the rifle but also facilitates barrel swapping.

As you study the market you'll find that some firms offer replacement barrels that quickly interchange with the original. Thus you might have a small caliber for squirrel hunting, another barrel for big game, and yet another barrel with special sights for target shooting. When you take a close look at the black-powder market, you'll be amazed at what it offers.

If you happen by a rifle range where black-powder shooting is in progress, you just might be turned off by what seems to be the endless and complicated loading processes. This is only the nature of black-powder target shooters who sometimes go to considerable lengths to squeeze the last fraction of accuracy from their rifles. For hunting, however, the loading process is quick and easy and requires few accessories. For example, my hunting pouch contains only a half dozen items, including a small flask of powder and a pre-set measure. (The powder charge is poured into the muzzle *only* from the measure, *never from the flask or horn.*) I carry the pre-patched balls in a homemade wooden loading block as well as a "short starter" to evenly start the balls into the muzzle. My supply of percussion caps is held in a brass "capper," which is much faster and more convenient than fumbling caps out of a can. A few cleaning patches for wiping between shots completes the kit. When I'm afield I use the wooden ramrod that fits under the barrel, but when I'm shooting or doing heavy-duty cleaning at the shooting range, I use a tough fiberglass rod. These are certainly worth the investment.

My first recommendation to anyone who is in-terested in getting into muzzleloading is to order a Dixie Gun Works Catalog. It only costs $3.00 and its 600+ pages cover just about everything that is available in the way of black-powder guns, parts, tools and accessories. You haven't seen anything until you've seen the Dixie Catalog. Another book that no black-powder shooter should do without is the Lyman Black Powder Handbook. It contains dozens of loading tables for rifles, pistols, and shotguns, plus lots of useful information on how to load, use, and care for muzzleloaders of all types. Both of these books give you a lot more practical loading and shooting dope than I have room for here.

One other piece of advice: Black-powder shooting is always more fun than beginners expect it to be. So unless you want to add a lot of fun to your shooting and hunting my advice is to stay away from black powder. One whiff of that pungent white smoke can hook you for life. As an old-timer once said, "Black-powder smoke don't smell good, but nobody ever said it smells bad."

Here's a list of some makers of guns and accessories that would like to help you get started in black-powder shooting:

Blue and Gray Products, Inc., RD #6, Box 362, Wellsboro, PA 16901

Butler Creek Corporation, 290 Arden Dr., Belgrade, MT 59714

Connecticut Valley Arms Co. (CVA), 5988 Peachtree East, Norcross, GA 30071

Dixie Gun Works, Inc., P.O. Box 130, Union City, TN 38261

Euroarms of America, Inc., P.O. Box 3277, 1501 Lenoir Dr., Winchester, VA 22601

Hatfield Rifle Works, 2020 Calhoun St., St. Joseph, MO 64501

Hopkins & Allen, 3 Ethel Ave., P.O. Box 217, Hawthorne, NJ 07507

Kassnar Imports, 5480 Linglestown Rd., Harrisburg, PA 17110

Lyman Products Corp., Rte. 147, Middlefield, CT 06455

Mowrey Gun Works, 1313 Lawson Rd., Saginaw, TX 76179

Navy Arms, 689 Bergen Blvd., Ridgefield, NJ 07657

Oregon Trail Riflesmiths, Inc., P.O. Box 45212, Boise, ID 83711

Ox-Yoke Originals, 130 Griffin Rd., West Suffield, CT 06093

Ozark Mountain Arms Inc., Rt. 1, Box 44AS/Hwy. 32, Ashdown, AR 71822

Richland Arms, 321 W. Adrian St., Blissfield, MI 49228

Tennessee Valley Arms, P.O. Box 2022, Union City, TN 38261

Thompson-Center Arms, P.O. Box 2426, Rochester, NH 03867

Uncle Mikes (Michaels of Oregon), P.O. Box 13010, Portland, OR 97213

Williams Gun Sight Co., 7300 Lapeer Rd., Davison, MI 48423

Lones Wigger: World-Level Shooting Champp

J. Scott Rupp

There wasn't much fanfare—no ticker-tape parades or brass bands. But a major chapter of American sports history recently closed. Lt. Col. Lones W. Wigger, Jr., retired from world-level competition.

Wigger hung up his guns in the international arena at the 44th World Shooting Championships, shooting 300-meter rifle for the United States at Skovde, Sweden, last September.

He took four silver team medals there. Add those to the list, and since picking up his first award in 1963 at the Pan American Games in São Paulo, Brazil, Wigger has piled up 145 international medals. In his 37-year shooting career, he has held 29 world records, and he holds or co-holds 32 national records. He has won 80 national championships.

At age 49, Wigger is the most successful amateur athlete in this country. No athlete in any sport has been so successful for so many years.

The decision to retire, he said, was not an easy one.

"My performance in the '86 World Championships was not as good as I had hoped it would be," Wigger said. "I think that probably helped me make the decision that it was time to do something else." That something else is serving as director of the U.S. Shooting Team.

Wigger won his first Olympic gold medal at Tokyo in 1964, setting the world record in the process. He also took a silver and became world record co-holder in the English match. Since then he has carried the banner for U.S. Olympic shooting efforts, missing only 1976 and 1984, and has shot on 16 other major U.S. teams.

"Every time you go on the line to represent the United States, you want to do well. You don't

This article first appeared in American Rifleman

Wigger's standing position has earned him two world records, since broken. But seven of his national records still remain in force.

Wigger is the only shooter-athlete ever accorded the honor of being this country's standard-bearer at an international competition. He was selected above nominees from all other participating sports to carry the flag at the 1975 Pan American Games.

want to embarrass yourself, but also you don't want to embarrass your country. There's a tremendous amount of pressure on you to do well," Wigger said.

"And I never had such a load of pressure lifted off my mind as when I fired that last shot in the world championships knowing it would be my last shot for the United States. When that was over it was a tremendous lift because now I don't have to go through that kind of pressure anymore.

"That last shot was a 10, incidentally," he added with a grin.

Wigger's will be big shoes to fill, as an experienced competitor and a *de facto* team leader as well.

"He's the fiercest competitor of our lifetime, our generation," said David I. Boyd, assistant director of NRA's Shooting Programs Dept., who first shot with Wigger on the '63 Pan Am team. Boyd and Wigger became friends while shooting on various teams over the years. "He's the most intense individual," Boyd said. "I've met a lot of champions in my time, and he's a true champion.

"He gave more of himself to the U.S. team, more than anyone else." Much of Wigger's success, Boyd said, is owed to determination, never giving up, and always working right to the last shot. "He wouldn't accept his own best."

Boyd related a story about Wigger's early training at Ft. Benning, Ga. Wigger would be shooting standing, and his close friend, Gene Kolstad, would come in and stand right beside him. With his face just inches from Wigger's, Kolstad would

stare while Wigger was working on a shot. If the shot didn't break, Wigger would look at Kolstad, grin, then go back to working on the shot. When the rifle finally went off, the pair would start screaming and hollering at each other. Boyd considers this—friends putting pressure on each other—one of the reasons for Wigger's success.

Ernie Vande Zande, NRA shooting sports manager at the U.S. Olympic Training Center, said one can see by the way people work and prepare for something what their goals are; and he said Wigger's was clearly to be the best.

While Vande Zande was stationed with the U.S. Army Marksmanship Unit at Ft. Benning, he, Wigger, and two other shooters once traveled to a prone match in Manassas, Va. Wigger and two others shot perfect 3200s, but all lost the match because of X-count. The trip back to Georgia took two days of hard driving. The morning after their return, Vande Zande went to the range early and found Wigger and the other two at the test shed with their rifles dismantled.

"They all had 3200s, fantastic scores, but they had their guns apart trying to get more Xs," he said. It was a learning experience for Vande Zande, and he said it showed him what Wigger was all about. "He was never satisfied. He was always looking for another point, another X.

"Think about the sport of shooting, or any sport. There's no one who's done what Wigger has done. He is a man with the ability to create victory."

Wigger began shooting competitively in Montana when he was about 11 or 12 years old. His father, Lones, Sr., a longtime shooter, was his first coach. He said his son was tough to coach, as are many juniors who are instructed by their parents. Although he didn't always do as he was told, he did want to learn. Young Wigger liked basketball and baseball, but since he was neither big nor fast, he devoted himself to shooting.

His father said Wigger "was determined to do something on his own," and shooting was something he could do well, and it was a game he liked. With a chuckle, Lones, Sr., said that was the biggest problem. "When we'd go to the range, we'd be the first there and the last to leave, he liked it so much. That bulldog attitude got him to the top."

During the summers, while the elder Wigger was busy working on his ranch, young Wigger would find his own matches, often driving long distances to compete. "He'd go to Canada on his own and come back with a carload of trophies. Some of those were traveling trophies, and we would have to get them back the next year."

There were no junior clubs for him to shoot with in rural Montana, so he looked to the seniors and the scores they were shooting. "That's how I learned to shoot under pressure, to put the pressure on myself and go out and try to shoot the score," Wigger said.

Wigger went to Montana State University, then called Montana State College, where he shot for its ROTC team for five years—he stayed an extra year to shoot. It was there that he met his wife, Mary Kay. They dated for about a year, then were married while both were still in school. Wigger spent a lot of time on the road shooting, and it made for a tough first year. "Being alone a lot sure isn't a plus," she said, but over the years she's grown accustomed to his constant traveling, and on the positive side, she's had the opportunity to travel around the world with him.

During Wigger's sophomore year, he attended a shooting clinic held in El Paso, Tex., in con-

Wigger's dominance of smallbore rifle competition at the National Matches began in 1963 when he won both the prone and position titles.

junction with a big indoor match the team fired every year. The U.S. Army Marksmanship Unit instructors, Bill Krilling, Gary Anderson and Dan Puckel—all champion shooters—made an impression on the collegian. Wigger decided he wanted to shoot for the Army team.

"I probably had the idea all along, but this cemented what I wanted to do, to be on the Army team and shoot international. So I set that as my goal."

In early 1961, Wigger joined the Army as a lieutenant and was assigned to Ft. Benning's USA–MU. He said he made up his mind going in that shooting would be his No. 1 priority. He wanted to be a champion, a task to which he dedicated himself. But after the Pan American Games in 1963, he decided to leave the Army and then go back to Montana.

INTERNATIONAL MEDALS WON BY LONES WIGGER							
	Gold		Silver		Bronze		
	Team	Individual	Team	Individual	Team	Individual	Total
Olympic Games	*	2	*	1	*	—	3
World Championships	20	2	16	6	3	4	51
Pan American Games	9	4	—	5	—	—	18
Championships Of The Americas	18	10	1	9	—	1	39
CISM**	14	4	6	4	2	2	34
Totals	61	24	23	25	5	7	145

*None awarded. **Conseil Internationale du Sport Militaire (military olympics)*

"My commitment was up, and I felt like I would probably be transferred somewhere else, and I really didn't, at the time, want to make the Army a career, and I didn't want to do the other type of jobs, so I decided to get out."

While home, "all I did was go around and shoot all the matches I could find," he said. One of those competitions was the National Matches at Camp Perry, Ohio. That summer Wigger won both the smallbore prone and position titles—the only shooter who can make that claim.

When he had been out of the service for a while, the Army asked if he wanted to come back. Yes, he said, if his assignment was the marksmanship unit. So, in November, 1963, he returned.

The following February Wigger broke the 1140 smallbore free rifle mark for his first time at Ft. Benning's Parks Range. In that year, he said, every time he shot, his scores got better. The improvement culminated in his gold and silver medal performances at the Tokyo Olympics. His 1164 smallbore free rifle score shattered the world record by seven points, and his 597 in English match tied him with a Hungarian for the world record and earned him the silver medal.

After reaching the Olympic plateau, however, Wigger went into a slump; he was unsure what direction to take. Every road, it seemed, turned downward.

"I had really achieved everything and more than I ever dreamed I could, so where do you go from there," he said. "It was really hard for me to reevaluate, 'What do I do next?' It took me several years before I overcame this . . . success, I guess you might say."

The years he considered to be a downswing were not without note. At the 39th World Shooting Championships in Wiesbaden, West Germany, he was on three gold medal record-setting teams: English match, smallbore free rifle, and 300-meter free rifle. It was the last time the U.S. trounced the Soviet Union in the world shooting championships.

Aside from lack of direction, other factors contributed to Wigger's less productive years. He was, after all, an Army officer, and in those days that meant duty in Vietnam.

He did his first tour in 1967, serving as an agriculture adviser (he had an agriculture bachelor's degree from MSU) at the sector, or county, level. In addition, he worked on the S-3 operations staff—one of only 50 Americans in the Vietnamese province at the time.

He was rotated back to the States in February, 1968, and grabbed a spot on the Olympic team, English match, and headed for Mexico City. He didn't do as well as he might've expected, placing 25th with a 592.

He stayed in the marksmanship unit until after the 1970 world championships, where he took a silver for 300-meter prone and a bronze in smallbore free rifle in addition to being on three gold medal-winning teams and six silver medal teams.

After attending sniper school he found himself on a plane back to Vietnam in early 1971 as chief of a sniper team. As he wrote in an article some years later, his work was cut out for him.

"I found the average replacement (troop) could not hit a silhouette target at 25 meters, knew little of basic marksmanship fundamentals, and did not understand why he needed to zero his rifle. I tried, unsuccessfully, to change the division policy of issuing rifles to replacements after in-country training and battalion assignments, so that they could go to the field with a zeroed rifle."

The team was supposed to go to the Americal Div.—the Army was sending sniper teams to all American divisions—but was instead sidetracked to a Vietnamese training center just north of Saigon. Wigger and his team stayed two months, establishing a sniper range and building a snipertrained Vietnamese cadre of instructors.

In March they moved to Chu Lai, replacing the Americal Div. team there. When Americal stood down, Wigger took his team to Da Nang to support the snipers in the field and train a few more. After training two instructors, Wigger's team went home in December, 1971.

He did, however, manage to fly back to the States during the summer of '71 to win the Camp Perry smallbore position championship.

Wigger's longevity at the marksmanship unit, 25 years give or take, could be considered an accomplishment in itself. But, as Wigger said, "The Army felt like they were getting the best benefit out of me by keeping me in the marksmanship program rather than shipping me all over the world and doing the various jobs that a major could do."

Wigger said the years after his return from Vietnam up until '84, were his best. His performances picked up in '72, when he won a gold medal in 300-meter free rifle at the Munich Olympics, and continued to climb every year. "Up through '84 I look back and think I was shooting as well as, or better than, ever," he said.

The beginning of the 1970s saw a few changes in the rifle game. One was the loss of 300-meter free rifle as an Olympic event.

Shooting 300-meter rifle is a favorite of Wigger's. For him it was *the* game because of the challenge—the noise, the elements, the recoil. "To me, it's the epitome of what an international match should be," he said.

The year 1972 saw the last of 300 meters in the Olympics. "The handwriting was on the wall," he said. International Shooting Union (UIT) sentiment was against the big bore guns, preferring events that required less space and therefore less money. The International Olympic Committee agreed with that line of thinking and 300 meters was finished in the Olympics, but is still fired in the World Shooting Championships and Conseil Internationale du Sport Militaire (CISM) competition—the military Olympics.

The early '70s, while Wigger was getting back on track, saw a decline in American stature in the shooting world. "When we were dominating back in the '60s, there were only three or four shooting programs in the world; there're probably 15 or 20 now."

During that time frame, the cream of the crop in the U.S. shooting came from the military—primarily the USAMU. There the shooter could train full time, concentrating on training and competition. But then the draft ended; people decided they didn't need to join the service to shoot. They could shoot in their spare time. Family obligations and jobs removed shooting as top priority.

"You can't be a world champion on weekends," Wigger said.

The dry spell put the U.S. "behind the power curve" as more countries created shooting programs. The armed services in this country had to train whomever they could get; some of the best shooters remained civilians and did not receive optimum training opportunities.

This state of affairs was changed somewhat, however, with the institution of the U.S. National Team program in 1978. Much of the program's support is provided by the International Shooter Development Fund, established by the NRA to raise money through member contributions. The program provides funds for training and travel expenses for the more promising shooters. Wigger, a member of the NRA Board of Directors since 1980, resigned that position so he could take the reins of the U.S. Team as its director. He has moved from his Ft. Benning home to Colorado Springs, Colorado—site of the U.S. Olympic Committee's Training Center and the USST's resident athlete program.

His new job is to work with the national coaches and see that the U.S. gets back on top and wins gold medals. "I look at my job a lot like an athletic director of a university. All the coaches work for me, and my job is to oversee and help them as best I can and see that the school wins," Wigger said.

"I'm going to put all my effort into seeing these goals, new goals of mine, accomplished like the goals in the past when I was shooting."

Aside from a wealth of knowledge acquired competing throughout the world, Wigger brings to his new job a quarter-century's experience in training shooters.

His daughter, Deena, is a champion in her own right. She won two gold medals at the 1983 Pan Am Games and won the women's three-position and prone championships at the 1985 U.S. International Shooting Championships. The year 1985 also brought her a silver medal at the World Airgun Championships in the junior woman catagory; she was named Female Athlete of the Year for Shooting Sports by the USOC for that year. Last year she grabbed an air rifle bronze at the world championships while setting a junior women's world record.

The youngest of his two sons, Danny, clinched the Camp Perry junior three-position title in 1981. Ronald, a lieutenant at the USAMU, came within five Xs of capturing the smallbore prone title at the 1986 National Matches.

Mary Kay Wigger thinks shooting is one of the best things that their children could've become involved in. Not that they had a choice, she said, they were already in the system—that's how they spent their summers. It kept them occupied, out of trouble, and she said it helped them mature.

Wigger's Ft. Benning Junior Rifle Club has been

Wigger won his first Olympic gold in 1964. Only 11 shooters in history have won two Olympic golds; four are Americans.

LONES WIGGER'S NATIONAL CHAMPIONSHIPS	
300-Meter Free Rifle	13
Int'l Army Rifle	10
Smallbore Rifle 4-Position	10
Smallbore Rifle 3-Position	8
Int'l Smallbore 3-Position	8
Indoor Gallery Rifle	6
Indoor Int'l Smallbore Rifle	5
English Match	5
Smallbore Rifle Prone	4
Indoor NRA 3-Position	3
Int'l Air Rifle	3
Indoor Air Rifle	2
High-power Rifle Silhouette	2
300-Meter Rifle Prone	1
Total	80

a force to be reckoned with, especially the past several years. The team has won just about every national championship this country has to offer.

It's tough training juniors, he said, because not much headway can be made except for the basics of position, sight alignment, breath control, etc. To coach them mentally is another matter. He said it's not something that the coach does.

"One day, a light bulb goes off in their heads and they realize to shoot a 10 they've got to make it look like a 10. When that day dawns, things start falling into place because they realize that they're going to determine whether that's going to be a 10 or not.

"It's not whether the gun's pointed in the right direction, or that they've pulled the trigger at the right time, or that they're lucky. They're really in charge of their own destiny, and once they figure this out, then they realize in order to shoot a 10 you have to work."

Work and dedication are the cornerstones of Wigger's success.

"I don't usually worry too much about competition. My competition is myself. Whenever you're shooting, you're shooting against yourself. You're not shooting against everybody else on the line."

The shooter should contend against his own goals, his own level. What determines whether the shooter wins or loses depends on how well goals are accomplished. Goals must be constantly raised, he said, and the shooter must work toward the new goals.

"If you beat everyone else while you're doing it, that's fine." Wigger prefers score goals and when he knows what the scores are, he said it pumps him up and he uses that to his advantage. That method isn't for everyone, though.

"A lot of people would be better off not looking at scoreboards and just worrying about doing their own thing and their own performance. That's what you should be doing."

For all his achievements in the international arena, the National Matches at Camp Perry have proved to be successful turf for Wigger. He's won the smallbore three-position rifle title 18 times since 1963, never relinquishing the title twice in a row. He's also won the smallbore prone championship four times. Two other shooters have won both the prone and position titles since 1957, but Wigger is the only one to win both in the same year, once in '63 and again in '73.

When Wigger was a junior, the National Matches symbolized shooting at its highest level. It was the most prestigious match he had been to, and he decided that one day he would win.

"Camp Perry became a goal of mine every year, especially the position championships. I don't really know why, but when I drive up to the gate

Shooting is a Wigger family tradition. Lones, Sr. (right) was his son's first coach and is still coaching juniors and shooting. Ronald (second from right) nearly won a Camp Perry prone title, and Deena won an air-gun bronze medal at the 1986 World Championships.

and drive onto those grounds, I get psyched up."

His victories there contribute to that natural psyche. "I reprogram myself that I'm the guy to beat," he said.

Conditions at Camp Perry are famous, or perhaps infamous, for their ability to confound even the best shooters. Wigger said many good shooters immediately quit mentally, or make up their minds that they can't do well because of the gusting winds, hot sun, or the rain.

"To me, when people do that, it just drives me a little harder; I work harder and to the other direction because I am a result of hard work and effort," not natural talent and ability, he said.

No matter how bad it gets, somebody has to win. The shooter who wins, he said, is the one who works the hardest. "Nobody outworks me," he said.

Wigger will continue to shoot Camp Perry and any other matches he can get to. He's always had a goal to win the national high-power rifle championship and said he plans to pursue that. He said he would also like to win the smallbore rifle silhouette championships; he already has two high-power rifle silhouette championships to his credit.

But priority goes to his responsibilities as director of the United States Shooting Team. "I wanted this job. I feel like I can do this job . . . I decided it was probably time to do something a little different and contribute something else to the game other than just shooting."

PART SIX

GUNS OF YESTERYEAR

Guns of the Boxer Rebellion

Pete Dickey

At the turn of the century, the ordnance departments of the world were in turmoil. Black-powder and even single-shot rifles were still found in many national inventories, but smokeless repeaters had been and were being developed and issued in wide variety.

Ordnance boards were viewing semiautomatic pistols, and some were in the hands of officers and private adventurers; but revolvers, many of them obsolescent, were still *the* item of issue.

The summer of 1900 saw, in a small compound in Peking, a multinational assembly of clergy, diplomats, and troops that had no precedent, for all were armed.

The arms used by and against them are the subject here, but it is necessary to consider why members of this armed band were in Peking in the first place.

The foreigners came to China, in Kipling's words, "to hustle the East." The Manchu government, tenuously administered by the Empress Dowager, found its customs service, railroads,

This article first appeared in American Rifleman

banks, telegraph, seaports, and even the opium trade all under control of the "foreign devils."

In addition, the Christian churches had acquired many converts ("secondary devils"), much property, and not surprisingly, much antagonism from the established native religions.

Secret societies terrorized the foreign missions and the government itself. Always fearing them, the government first tolerated, then fostered, and finally directed their activities.

The largest of the societies was I Ho Ch'uan, this said to translate to Fists (or Bands) of Righteous (or Public or United) Harmony.

I Ho Ch'uan was a loosely organized but ultra-patriotic group that practiced ritual athletics and mysticism. Its members were said to scorn all things foreign (favoring pikes and axes over firearms) and to believe themselves to be bulletproof. Here they were mistaken.

Many other secret societies and surely some unorganized individuals, with no compunctions against firearms, aligned themselves with I Ho Ch'uan and, collectively, they came to be known as the Boxers.

In Peking they joined regular government forces in huge numbers to besiege the Catholic Cathedral (The Peitang) and the legation quarter or compound. These locations were about a mile and a half apart but both located within the Tartar City or northern half of Peking.

John Clymer's 1945 painting in the U.S.M.C. Museum takes artistic license with Marine socket bayonets and the percussion revolver. The Gatling gun was used at Tientsin, but not at Peking.

Many rifles saw duty during the rebellion; the four at left are only a sampling. From top to bottom are: a .60-caliber Tientsin-made gingall of the 1890s weighing 40 pounds; the 5-shot 6mm Lee Straight-Pull used during the siege; Mauser Model 1871 11mm single-shot that China had bought in quantity; 5-shot, .30/40 Model 1898 Krag-Jorgensen that arrived with the relief column. U.S. Marine contingent within the walls (see the inset photograph below left) used not Krags but Lee Straight-Pulls with great effect.

The "International," here manned by a British legation guard and civilian volunteer, is now an exhibit in the U.S.M.C. Museum in Washington, D.C.

Within the compound and the cathedral were thousands of Chinese Christian converts and nonconverts, as well as nonresident foreigners who had flocked into the compound as Boxer terrorism increased in the surrounding provinces.

One on-site reporter, American missionary and 29-year China veteran A.H. Smith, wrote in *China in Convulsion* (1901) of British customs officers straggling in with revolvers; missionaries with rifles *and* revolvers; and French and Belgian railroad personnel with butcher knives wired to their rifles in lieu of bayonets. They came to be known as the carving knife brigade. He said that the British legation handed out Martini rifles to volunteer Chinese converts and included a fuzzy photograph of European volunteers with holstered handguns and what looked like bolt- and lever-action sporters and Martini single shots.

The guns of the defending volunteers, then, were as diverse a collection of arms as might be expected, and their national sources were probably as numerous as the foreign ministers themselves.

In the compound were the legations of America, Austria, Belgium, France, Germany, Great Britain, Italy, Japan, the Netherlands, Russia, and Spain, plus the Korean embassy.

The diplomats and their families, as of early June, were protected by a multinational guard of about 400 troops, including 53 U.S. Marines and 3 blue-jackets. All the other countries were rep-resented by soldiers, sailors, or marines, save the Netherlands, Belgium, Spain, and Korea. Each military contingent had its own arms, and the Chinese outside the gates had theirs. The fighting broke out in earnest on June 20.

Like the volunteer defenders, the Chinese had a wide assortment of rifles. A.H. Smith tells of early use of "gingalls, two-man guns, 8–10' long" being fired into the compound, later of "Mausers," and finally "Mannlichers." As the fighting increased, and as the Boxers were displaced more and more by the Chinese armies, we are told that "the latest magazine repeating rifles" were used and some captured. No models or calibers are noted, but the "Mannlichers" far outperformed the "Mausers"—repeating or otherwise—in penetration. The latter made small chips in brick, but "Mannlicher fire rapidly cut away the walls."

Knowing that the Chinese had bought 26,000 11mm Model 1871 single shots from Mauser and others from Steyr starting in 1876, we suspect that they were the primary Chinese armament. They were supplemented first by some Model 1871/84 11mm Mauser repeaters and later 8mm Model 1888 German Commission Rifles (often *called* "Mannlichers" because of their appearance and magazine construction) and 7mm Model 95 Mausers.

It is probable that some rifles were Chinese made. Another Smith (W.H.B., in *The book of Rifles*) reports M88s were made in Hanyang, and Springfield Sporters of Penn Run, Pennsylvania, is at this writing importing antique M88 Hanyang-made rifles that may include some of the actual rifles used at Peking. It is possible, of course, that "real" Steyr-made Mannlichers and still other Mausers were in use. But in the research for this article no comment on pre-1900 "official" Chinese imports of them was found (unlike the Models 1871, 71/84, 88, and 95, and even some Sniders and Sharps Borchardts).

It must be remembered, however, that the warlords who really ran the provinces, and in some cases equipped the Boxers, had nothing against "unofficial" firearms transactions. Thus, every rifle type made from the ubiquitous single-shot Martinis and Remingtons to the then most modern Winchester lever actions *may* have seen use by the Empress's troops or the red-sashed Boxers.

As to the other Chinese armament that joined the Mannlichers in cutting down the defenders' walls, A.H. Smith mentions regular use of up to a dozen Krupp guns, occasional machine guns, flares and rockets, and even great quantities of bricks and bottles catapulted over the walls. Of them Smith said, "The Hague Conference should have condemned them along with the dum-dum bullet."

Fortunately, almost all the Krupp shells failed to explode on contact, and Chinese fire of all types, save the bricks and bottles, was erratic.

That may have been what saved the armed defenders; for according to the 1911 edition of *Encyclopaedia Britannica* they never numbered more than 500.

In addition to the miscellany of rifles and revolvers in the hands of the volunteers, the defenders had those of the guard force and a few "crew-served" guns. Smith mentions the single U.S.M.C. "Colt Automatic" as being the most effective. It was a Colt Model 1895 6mm machine gun that was moved on its carriage from place to place and was once run up a ramp to the Tartar wall to repulse a concerted attack. Then there was the "braying" British five-barreled Nordenfelt. It was 13 years old and "always jammed after four shots." There were also an "Italian one-inch quick-firer," which soon ran out of shells, an Austrian Maxim machine gun, and one which may have done more for morale than all the rest, the "International" or "Betsey."

This was a smooth-bored, iron muzzleloading barrel, apparently a relic of an Anglo-French expedition of 1860, that was strapped to a railroad tie and a pair of Italian caisson wheels. It was loaded with Russian projectiles (the Russians had brought along shells but left their gun in port) and, apparently, a mixture of powder from the Russian shells and from Chinese fireworks. It was fired, and fired often, by an intrepid U.S. Navy gunner's mate, Joseph Mitchell.

Mitchell's performance did not go unrecognized. He received America's highest military award, the Medal of Honor, and he was not alone.

For actions during the siege and including the fierce fighting at the ports in Tientsin and on the relief expeditions that followed, a total of 59 Medals of Honor were presented. Four went to U.S. soldiers (including one to Bugler Calvin Titus who was the first man to scale the Tartar wall when the relief expedition finally arrived). Navy personnel (including Mitchell) took 22, and the Marines (including the legendary two-time MOH awardee Dan Daly) took 33.

According to A.H. Smith, the International gun "recoiled" so much that it dislodged sandbags and

Boxer poster was discovered in a Manchu palace during the looting that followed the rebellion.

Japanese soldiers of the relief expedition stand guard over stacks of captured military rifles (including Model 1888s) that are dwarfed by gingalls.

broke out windows inside the walls, but it kept going throughout the siege and did not "blow up" as some accounts say it did. The original barrel on a faithfully reconstructed carriage is now on display at the USMC Museum in Washington, D.C.

The modest "armory" that assembled the International gun did other good works. The Germans had few ball but, surprisingly, many blank cartridges for their rifles. These were "bulleted" with castings made from pewter ornaments; shells for the Italian gun were recharged with Russian powder and projectiles made by local tinsmiths, and were primed with pistol cartridge cases. An attempt was made to turn the wire-bound brass boiler of a fire engine into a mortar, but was aborted in favor of the "safer" International. But the bread-and-butter work of the armory was the maintenance of the kaleidoscopic collection of military rifles that saw such hard usage.

The American contingent had not the expected .30/40 Krags (those came later with the relief expedition), but Winchester-made Lee Straight Pull rifles in 6mm caliber. The three Marine officers probably had U.S. Navy .38 Colt revolvers.

There wasn't enough ammunition to practice wall cutting, as the Chinese did with their comparatively big-bored 8mms, but the Winchesters and the similarly chambered Model 1895 Colt "Potato Digger" did great execution. Three to four thousand Chinese soldiers and Boxers were said to have died at the walls, and nobody doubted the efficiency of Marine riflemen.

In his 1901 biography of President McKinley, Marshall Everett quoted a captured Chinese soldier: " 'When we see so many falling around us that we are forced to run, then we know we are fighting Americans.' " He went on to say "This superiority in marksmanship was conceded by the allies, too. They had seen it demonstrated often, and the brave man is quick to give credit where credit is due. The Japanese gave especially convincing evidence of the opinion in which the American was held in China. They are enthusiastic fellows, and are ever anxious to learn all that friend or foe can teach them, and they gave particular attention to the methods and work of the Americans.

" 'We do not shoot as well as you,' said a Japanese officer, 'but we have seen the importance of learning it. Look out for us; in a few years more we shall shoot even as well as the Americans.'

"If imitation is the sincerest flattery, Uncle Sam's enlisted men have reason to feel proud, for no one is as quick as the Japanese to see what is worth imitating. His judgment and perceptive power in this line are what brought him so rapidly to the front.

"All in all, the people of the United States had ample excuse for pride in the men who were representing them on the battlefield in China. The record made was splendid."

Just what the other nationalities used within the walls can not be answered precisely—despite enquiries of the various embassies in Washington. Only the Austrians answered with definite information.

Printed references, few though they are, differ widely or dwell on generalities because virtually every nation was involved in small arms changes necessitated by the advent of smokeless powder, and it was not unusual to find different rifles in use by the same force.

As examples: acknowledged Enfield expert Ian Skennerton advised that the British troops may have had both Lee-Metfords and Lee-Enfields, but some of their colonial forces, including the Sikhs

BOXER REBELLION SMALL ARMS

	Rifles	Revolvers
American	Winchester-Hotchkiss/Springfield .45/70; U.S.N. M1895 (Lee Straight-Pull 6mm); M1892-1898 Krag-Jorgensen .30/40	Colt Army/Navy Models 1889–1896 .38 Long Colt
Austrian	Model 1890 Mannlicher 8mm	M1870/74 Gasser 11mm
British (incl. Colonials)	Magazine Lee-Metford/Magazine Lee-Enfield .303; Martini-Henry .577/.450	Webley Marks I–IV .455
Chinese (Incl. Boxers)	M1871, '71/84 Mauser 11mm; M1888 Commission/Hanyang 8mm; Gingalls; Martini-Henry	Mention found but no specifics
French	Lebel Modele 1886 M93/Berthier Modele 1890 or '92 8mm	Modele 1873 '74 11mm; Modele 1892 8mm
German	M1871/84 Mauser 11mm; M1888 Commission 8mm	M1879 or 1883 Reichsrevolver 10.55mm
Italian	Modello 1891 Mannlicher-Carcano 6.5mm	Modello 1889 Bodeo 10.35mm
Japanese	Murata 8mm; Type 30 Arisaka 6.5mm	S&W No. 3 .44 Russian Type 26 9mm
Russian	Moisin-Nagant M1891 7.62mm	S&W No. 3 .44 Russian Nagant M1895 7.62mm

and Bengal Lancers that came with the relief columns, had single-shot Martini-Henrys; Fred L. Honeycutt, Jr., despite his years of research on Japanese rifles, thinks it possible there were Type 30 rifles at Peking but more likely Muratas, but he is not sure; the U.S.M.C. Museum uncovered proof that even a few Winchester-Hotchkiss and Trapdoor Springfield .45/70s were still in the hands of Marines or sailors. Fortunately, many contemporary photographs preserved at the U.S.M.C. Museum in Washington, D.C., showed some details of some rifles that are reflected in the table.

The Boxer Rebellion was not "expected," and there was no apparent reason to make sure the troops there had the most modern rifles that would, logically, be better issued to more probable areas of conflict.

It will be remembered that the Americans, barely "finished" with the Spanish-American War, were thoroughly occupied in the Philippines; the British were right in the middle of the Boer War; the Sino-Japanese War had ended just five years before; the Russo-Japanese war was just four years in the future, and Germany's belligerency was on many military and civilian minds.

The Kaiser, in fact, set the tone for World War I in a July 1900 statement directed against the Chinese but remembered, in part, by the world:

"Just as the Huns a thousand years ago under the leadership of Attila gained the reputation by virtue of which they still live in historical tradition, so may the name of Germany become known in such a manner in China that no Chinese will ever again dare to look askance at a German."

The Kaiser's troops in Peking didn't have the new Model 1898 Mausers—but those of the *Ostasiatisches Expeditionskorps*, the German punitive force sent into China *after* the Rebellion, did. This, according to German rifle expert John Walter, was the Model 98's first combat use. U.S.M.C. photographs also reveal that at least one C96 Mauser pistol, with stock, accompanied the punitive force.

Thus the "listing of small arms of the Boxer Rebellion" applies only to the rifles within the walls or brought with the columns that relieved Peking. Where more than one rifle is listed, any or all *may* have been used, and there may have been others. In the case of handguns, the table is even more uncertain for, in those days, not only U.S. officers but those of most other nations bought and carried whatever they wanted.

When the relief column finally moved out of the port of Tientsin on August 4th, after an earlier expedition had failed, it was substantial.

Of the force of about 19,000 men that reached Peking 10 days later, and 55 days after the siege began, half were Japanese, 20 percent Russian, 15 percent British, 10 percent American, and the balance French, German, Austrian, and Italian.

The legation compound and the Peitang were soon relieved and their defenders, military and civilian, men and women, clergy and laity, joined their rescuers in an orgy of vandalism and looting that shocked even the hardened military observers of the day.

Each of the "civilized" nations thereupon blamed the others; however, all tried to take credit for the "victory" and forget its aftermath. The Chinese, they say, never forget.

Keeping His Powder Dry

Helmut Nickel

The necessity to "keep his powder dry" posed a considerable problem for the bearer of a muzzleloading firearm. The powder container had to be easily portable, of durable material and, above all, of watertight construction. Powder flasks made of metal, wood, *cuirbouilli*, or horn—either staghorn or bovine—were designed in manyfold shapes during the 16th century, the period when firearms became the dominant weapon for war and sport. Often two powder flasks, one of large size for the powder charge that went into the barrel, and a much smaller one for the fine-grained priming powder, were carried together. Whatever their materials and shapes, however, these early European powder containers uniformly had a nozzlelike spout, which was closed by a hinged cap that was activated by a spring lever. This fixture made it possible to measure out the precise amount of powder needed and to shut off its flow instantly to avoid dangerous spillage. The latter consideration was of crucial importance in the days of the matchlock musket, which had to be loaded while the musketeer kept its match burning.

This article first appeared in American Rifleman

Hunting bag with accoutrements is dated about 1850 and is believed to have come from North Carolina.

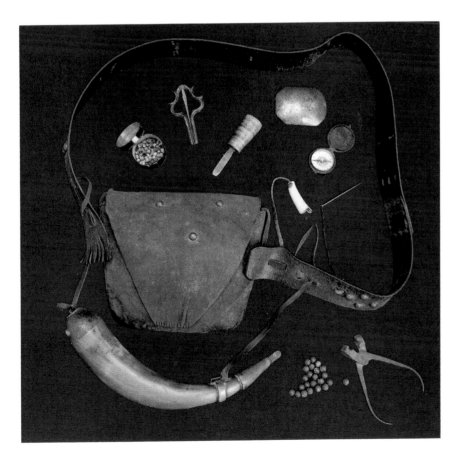

Powder flasks for fashionable huntsmen were often contrived from extravagant materials, such as hollowed-out sections of stags' antlers or the shells of large exotic sea snails. These materials gave them bizarre outlines that suited their owners' fancies and provided them with conversation pieces. Military powder flasks, on the other hand, came in two basic types. One, usually associated with matchlock-carrying musketeers, was boxlike, of trapezoidal, almost triangular outline; the other type, for arquebusiers and carabiniers equipped with wheellocks, was of a one-sidedly curved shape that was clearly derived from the natural curved form of a cow horn with truncated tip.

Horn was a material that combined durability with moisture resistance and light weight, and therefore was almost ideally suited for use as a portable container. Strangely enough though, in Western and Continental Europe, bovine horns in their natural rounded shapes were only, in exceptional cases, used as powder horns; they were usually pressed flat by heat treatment until they received an almost rectangular cross section. Invariably, they were cut off squarely at their tips, and metal spouts with hinged and spring-levered caps were mounted on their narrower ends. The metal mounts that closed tip and bottom ends were usually of matching decoration.

It was in countries with less highly developed technology than Western Europe, where the obtaining of springs for the hinged spout-caps would present a serious and perhaps insurmountable problem, that cow horns in their natural shapes were used as powder containers, with the tip of the horn itself drilled for a spout. This was the case, for instance, in Morocco, but also in Scandinavia where it became popular toward the end of the 17th century to use such "natural" powder horns. These were often richly decorated in folk art style with carvings in shallower relief, skillfully making use of the color differences between the light-hued outer layers of the horn and its darker inner core for a cameolike effect.

The motifs carved were sometimes Biblical scenes, such as Adam and Eve under the Tree of Knowledge, Daniel and the Dragon of Babylon, or the Three Wise Men following the Star of Bethlehem. At other times they were figures from popular literature such as the romantic heroes Ogier the Dane and Roland. These Scandinavian powder horns are signed and dated by their artists. The most prolific among the about 20 known carvers was Mass Massøn, whose signature, combined with a date like "1698," may mislead an elated collector to assume that he has found the earliest New England—Massachusetts—horn.

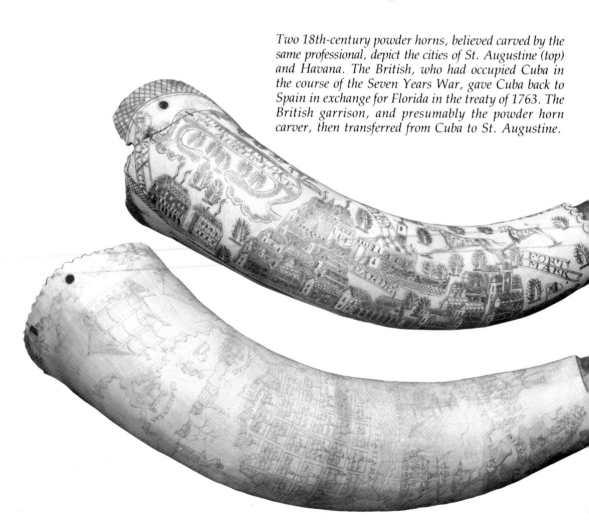

Two 18th-century powder horns, believed carved by the same professional, depict the cities of St. Augustine (top) and Havana. The British, who had occupied Cuba in the course of the Seven Years War, gave Cuba back to Spain in exchange for Florida in the treaty of 1763. The British garrison, and presumably the powder horn carver, then transferred from Cuba to St. Augustine.

Similar technological difficulties were probably the reason for the adoption of the drilled spout tip on American powder horns. There was a far greater demand for powder containers in America than in Europe, where firearms were not an everyday survival tool. Among Europeans, guns were either restricted to the military or, even more exclusively, reserved for the hunting aristocracy.

It has been long understood and is generally acknowledged that the rifle was brought to America through German and Swiss gunsmiths who settled in Pennsylvania at the end of the 17th century. However, contributions of the even earlier Scandinavian settlers in Delaware and Pennsylvania (New Sweden), who are credited with having introduced the log cabin, to other parts of early American material culture has not been fully established yet. The introduction of the powder horn as the logical and soon indispensable companion piece to the "Pennsylvania" rifle could well be one of their significant contributions.

The horns, as raw material for powder horns (but also for combs, lanthorn panes, and hornbooks), were imported from "longhorn" cattle of Spanish stock from the West Indies, Mexico, and even South America by contractors furnishing leather for the British army. The horns were an inexpensive (one penny apiece) by-product of this flourishing trade. By boiling the horn in water mixed with potash the pitch was removed. After the horn was cleaned and trimmed to size, its tip was bored for a spout and fitted with a wooden stopper, while the open bottom end was closed by a plug of wood, which was secured by pegs or nails.

In order to avoid the application of fixtures for the carrying strap such as loops (which might become inserted too deeply and might then perforate the walls of the horns and jeopardize its watertightness), the fore-end of the horn was scraped down about an eighth of an inch, with only a narrow ring around the spout left standing for a secure attachment of the strap ties. The horn's bottom end was cut in such a way that a curved lip protruded beyond the plug and this was pierced with one or more holes to tie on the shoulder strap. The scraping of the spout down to the dark core of the horn created a pleasing contrast to the light-colored outer layers, which were then smoothed with pumice and polished.

Though the sale value of a powder horn was not very great—the importing contractors sold a horn in the rough for fourpence each, and for sixpence trimmed and bored—its value as part of a man's survival kit was inestimable. In order to make sure of its ownership and to claim it when lost, it was only prudent to mark it in some way, either by simply carving the owner's name or initials on the plug or the side, or by applying some distinctive decoration.

While European powder flasks were decorated by a variety of techniques ranging from applied mountings in silver or bronze-gilt to intricate inlays in bone, wire, or mother of pearl, as well as carvings in relief. American powder horn carvers concentrated on engraved ornamentation. Engraving on European powder flasks is usually only detail enhancement on inlaid elements; overall engravings are relatively rare. Curiously, what is probably the earliest surviving fully engraved powder flask made out of a section of a bovine horn is dated April 7, 1560 (Metropolitan Museum of Art accession #21.183.2), is probably of Italian origin, and is entirely covered with scenes illustrating the contemporary best-selling romance of chivalry, *Orlando Furioso* by Ariosto. The work has as its hero the same Roland who is featured in the decoration on the carved Scandinavian horns of the late 17th century.

The settlers and townsmen of America, when called up for military service, had to supply all or part of their equipment. Many of them would have brought their own hunting knives and tomahawks as substitutes for bayonets and sabers, always in short supply, and also their powder horns. It is a truism that the soldier's life is nine

This exhibit of Southern powder horns was seen at four museums in Florida, Tennessee, and Alabama between 1985 and 1986.

The use of horn flasks for gunpowder was introduced into the New World by European soldiers and colonists. This pair of carved horns dates from the Revolutionary War period. The lower "Isaac Hay" horn was topically inscribed, "LIBERTY OR DEATH."

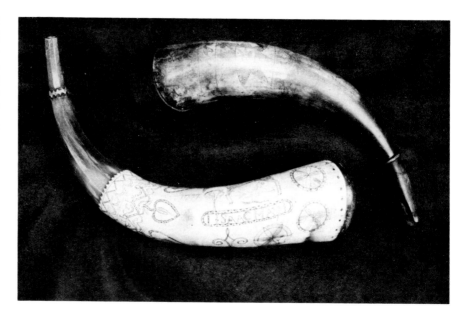

parts boredom and one part sheer terror. During the boredom periods, it was a pleasurable escape to record with pride and doubtlessly also with vast relief the terrors, i.e. the battles and campaigns luckily survived, on the most convenient space handy—on one's treasured powder horn. A sure indication that decorating a powder horn was a way of breaking the monotony of enforced inactivity is given by inscriptions, such as "made in Roxbury Camp," "made at the Garason," "Charlestun Camp No. 3 Decr. ye 17th AD 1775," or "made while lame." Sometimes the pride, the terror, and the suffering are recorded in lapidary sentences: "Marched on alarm to Ticonderoga July 8 1758 2nd Boston Regiment"; ". . . att Lake Gorg July the 8 Ano 1758. The fite be gun July the 6 and wee lorst 1947 men"; "Horne we will strife together Z.S. 1776 Noe boots or bread Dec ye 11 1777 Vallye Forge," and, added in another hand, "Ye dam rebel did make ye goode horn GR June ye 29 L.G. 1778."

This engraving was done by scratching the designs into the smooth surface of the horn with a sharp nail, a bit of glass, or simply with the point of a jackknife. The recording of campaigns quite naturally led to scratching out the lay of the land, with place names and landmarks. This developed into a specialized type of decorated powder horns bearing detailed engraved maps. Many of these elegantly engraved powder horns seem to have been executed by professional engravers. Quite possibly, they were made in England for British officers preparing for service in the North American colonies and wanting to make sure to find their way through the trackless wilderness of the Hudson and the Mohawk Valleys and beyond.

Often these map horns are further embellished by views of the cities of Albany, Boston, or Philadelphia, and particularly New York, with its windmill at the battery, its landmark in the days before the Statue of Liberty. Another standard decoration of these professionally engraved horns was the British royal coat of arms; many of the colonial horns made by local folkartists also bore renderings of the king's arms though, more often than not, only vaguely remembered.

As is to be expected, patriotic sentiments at the time of the Revolution were expressed by the watchwords "No slavery" and, of course, by the omnipresent "Liberty." One outspoken Pennsylvanian put his low esteem for King George into the pithy statement "Hure Keonig Ioerg," an epithet casting strong doubts on the moral values of the royal family.

The vast majority of powder horns for everyday use, though, would have been plain, without any decoration except the owner's name or initials and an occasional date. In his fundamental work, *American Engraved Powder Horns* (New York, 1954), Stephen V. Grancsay included a checklist of 1,152 engraved powder horns. Among these are 572 that display either maps of the Hudson Valley, the Great Lakes district, or Canada, or have inscribed place-names that refer to these northern areas. Only 24 of the 1,152 can be identified by their inscriptions or maps as having originated from territories south of Pennsylvania though, of course, many horns signed with only a personal name or initials might be of Southern origin. Occasionally a double-headed eagle, with or without an attempt to represent the Spanish royal coat of arms, appears in a horn's decoration, hinting at a connection with the Spanish-dominated territories of Florida.

Grancsay quotes one of his correspondents from North Carolina, who assures him that in the second half of the 19th century there were still many powder horns, used by hunters mindful of tradition who favored the muzzle-loading shotgun. But, he pointed out, these horns were plain because "the North Carolina (upcountry) Scots were not artistic." It is interesting that engraved powder horns made from bovine horns were popular in Scotland during the 17th and 18th centuries (the MMA owns one fine example, accession #45.160.5, decorated with a carefully executed representation of a Spanish piece-of-eight, dated 1669, surrounded by "tartan" checker patterns and "Celtic" strapwork), but these Scottish powder horns were the flattened European type.

In spite of what was said about the North Carolina Scots, one of the finest engraved powder horns in the collection of the Metropolitan Museum, accession #39.87 dated 1770, shows the walled city of "Charles Town South Carolina." It still has its original carrying strap attached, skillfully woven of black and white wampum beads. Another Southern horn, accession #37.131.6, of about 1760, displays a finely engraved detailed map of "The Middle Settlement of Cherokees" between the Little Tennessee and the Tuckasegee Rivers. When carrying firearms, Cherokees and Seminoles would also have been carrying powder horns, of course. These would have been ornamented with their own tribal totems and designs.

Deservedly famous among the Southern engraved powder horns is a small but significant group with representations of the city of Havana and other sites on Cuba, and of St. Augustine, Florida. Havana was one of the strongpoints of the Spanish trade routes in the New World. Therefore, when Spain entered an alliance with France during the erratic course of the Seven Years' War (1756–1763), a British expeditionary corps attacked and captured the city of Havana in the summer of 1762. The British held on to Cuba for almost a full year until the peace treaty of Paris, when Spain regained Cuba in exchange for giving up possession of Florida.

The British occupation army of Cuba then withdrew to new quarters in recently vacated St. Augustine. The Spanish residents, whose ancestors in 1565 had founded this oldest town in what is now the United States, had to make room and were moved to Cuba and New Spain (Mexico). Twenty years later, however, in the Treaty of Versailles (1783), Florida was given back to Spain and it was the turn of the English to pull up stakes and move on from St. Augustine to Georgia, the Carolinas, and the Bahamas.

There are more than a dozen surviving powder horns which commemorate these events; they show views of Havana, Morro Castle, and other places on Cuba, and several record in their inscriptions the pageant of illuminating the city at the embarcation of the British troops in July 1763. On two of these horns, it is specified that they were engraved in St. Augustine. One particularly elegant horn, "Engraved for Master Cuming," shows "An exact propsect of St. Augustine from the light house the metropolis of the province of East Florida," with its buildings amidst a lush vegetation of what are probably meant to be orange trees. This historically most important horn (MMA, accession #37.131.26) bears the royal arms, as do most of these horns made for British officers. Its inscription is set into a frame supported by a double-headed eagle and surmounted by a mermaid combing her hair among the churning waves.

The British expeditionary corps, which had captured the strong fortress of Castillo del Morro in a final assault after a 40-day's siege on July 30, 1762, and to which Havana surrendered on Aug. 14, was a combined force of British regulars and American provincials under the command of Admiral Sir George Pocock for the navy and Lord Albemarle for the land troops. The provincials were 2,300 men from Virginia and New England and were commanded by General Phineas Lyman from Connecticut. This Cuba campaign, incidentally, was the last overseas action in which Americans fought under the British colors. At the surrender of Havana, three million pounds sterling in minted money and bullion were seized by the victors. British commanders in chief were authorized by royal order to distribute five-fifteenths of captured booty as prize money among their officers and men, the size of the individual shares being determined by rank. Although the term "prize money" could be narrowly interpreted to apply only to goods taken in naval actions, in view of the magnitude of this booty is was decided to stretch a point in favor of a more encompassing attitude and to declare it eligible as prize money. It is said, however, that according to the grading system by rank, the lion's share was awarded to the British officers as aristocrats; a small quantity was handed to the Virginians, who counted as gentlemen, but when it came to the share of the commoners from Massachusetts, nothing was left over at all.

Although their knapsacks were not any fuller when they embarked from Havana than they had been when they set out to conquer Cuba, and their occupation of St. Augustine was only a brief interlude in the great powerplay of politics, these brave men have left to us in their faithful companions, their powder horns, a mute but nevertheless eloquent testimony of their days of glory.

Targets of Yesteryear

Ralph Lindsay

Photos by J. Dean Austin

Trapshooting got its start in the late 1700s, when English nobles practiced their hunting skills by shooting pigeons released from wire traps.

Around 1850, British sportsmen began to shoot at glass balls, thrown from catapult-like devices that retained the designation "trap." This new form of shooting was introduced into the Boston area in 1867.

As would happen in other areas of the shooting sports, the British would invent; the Americans would develop and eventually perfect.

The performance of the British traps left much to be desired. The short, straight flight of the glass balls wasn't much of a challenge to shooters in this country. In 1877, champion shooter Capt. A.H. Bogardus patented the Bogardus Trap, the first really successful target machine, and the Bogardus Glass Ball, a target ball with ridges for easy breaking.

Ira Paine, the famous pigeon shooter, patented his own target ball that same year. It had no ridges, but was filled with feathers; a hit on a Paine ball was almost like bringing down a live bird. Others used woodchips.

Other inventors were active too. Trapshooters had a wide selection of targets and traps from which to choose. Plain colored glass balls were cheap (no patent royalties) and could be used in any glass ball trap.

Pitch balls had two sellings points: they were easily seen in the air and the broken pieces were supposedly absorbed into the ground like so much fertilizer. Metal "birds" eliminated glass shards and could, after painting, be reused.

In 1880, the clay (pitch composition) pigeon was invented by George Ligowski, resulting in a target that "flew" more like a live bird than a glass ball did. Ligowski began marketing his trap and pigeons in 1881, and targets of the same shape are still used today.

Glass balls survived until World War I, used as targets in Wild West shows and circuses.

In the golden age of glass ball shooting, salesmen carried cutaway samples of shotshells (right) to promote their lines.

This article first appeared in American Rifleman

On Nov. 2, 1877, in Indianapolis, Captain A. H. Bogardus managed to break 500 glass balls in a time of 35 minutes and 4 seconds.

PART SEVEN

AMMO AND RELOADING

New Loads from Federal, Remington & Winchester

Jim Carmichel

The year is made of two parts: One part is called Hunting Season and the other part doesn't have a name. Last year, during the early part of the duck season, I had one of those days that lifetime memories are made of. Teal and woodies rocketed high and fast from behind a colonnade of tall poplars and sycamores on the river's bank. When they cleared the treetops they were almost directly overhead, so we had to shoot fast or not at all. During past seasons my favorite gun and load combination for this kind of shooting has been a 12-gauge upland gun with Improved Cylinder Choking and 1¼ ounces of Number 6s. The resulting pattern is wide enough to deal with a teal's aerobatics and dense enough to get several pellets on target even out at a goodly distance. As workable as this combination has been, it didn't always kill ducks dead in the air, resulting in "flutterers" and crippled birds that gave the retrievers a chase.

This season though, every hit bird was instantly dead, turning over and tumbling through the air before thumping hard on the ground. Easy work

for the dogs. Even Ben (my everlasting hunting pal, who hardly ever speaks, and hasn't been impressed with anything since Millicent, his brother Ralph's purebred Hampshire sow, jumped a 5-foot fence and ate Marvin Jenkins' attack dog) plucked a shell out of my ammo belt and allowed as how he'd like to see what sort of load killed ducks like double-forked lightning.

The cartridge he fished out of my belt was unlike any that has ever been offered in the past. It was Remington's new Multi-Range Duplex shell with a loading of two different sizes of shot: 4s and 6s. The teal and woodies had been killed so cleanly because of the bone-shattering energy of the larger shot, augmented by the multiple penetrations of the 6s.

Sometimes a new development in shooting technology is so obviously good that we don't even have to test it to be convinced of its advantages. Other developments have to be tested and proven or disproven in the field. This was the case

This article first appeared in Outdoor Life

with Remington's new duplex shot load. I had my doubts and assumed a cautious "show me" attitude.

The reasons for my doubts were well founded and based on both logic and experience. Though this is the first time a duplex shot charge has been factory loaded, the idea is hardly new to handloaders. By the time a shotshell reloader has accumulated a gallon of spent primers, the idea of combining two sizes of shot will probably have entered his head. Back when I was a teenager I shot crows several times a week year-round. My standard shot size was Number 8, which was great when the crows came cartwheeling through the trees, but the light shot seldom had any effect on the lone scouts that came over high and cautious. That's when I was smitten with the vision of tossing in a half teaspoon of Number 5's so as to extend my reach while at the same time retaining a peppery pattern for short-range skirmishes. As far as I could ever determine, however, the combination load was of no advantage. Another time I mixed 8s and 9s in a futile search for the ultimate clay-target buster.

From the logical standpoint, a duplex load would seem to be self-defeating. This is because a basic premise of matching the shot size to the game is to select the smallest shot that will get the job done. By using the smallest workable size of shot, we are then assured of a maximum shot count per charge volume. In other words, this is a way of getting more of a good thing. By mixing the charge with larger shot a disproportionate number of the smaller shot are eliminated. For example, an ounce of Number 4 shot contains some 135 pellets. The same weight of Number 8s has a pellet count of about 410. Thus if an ounce charge is half and half of each size shot, the pellet count is 273. In other words, the number of pellets in the charge has been reduced by a third. If we assume that a Size 8 shot is adequate for the job at hand, we then must ask what good purpose can be served by reducing the number of pellets in the charge. (I use this somewhat extreme example of shot mixing for purposes of illustration. In reality, Remington's Duplex shells use shot of more similar sizes, the charge weights are heavier and the proportions are not half and half.)

What with my previous experiences with mixed shot loads and the above-listed practical considerations, I had to wonder if Remington's Duplex load was anything more than a gimmick, just another sales strategem in the intensely competitive shotshell wars. But the guys at Remington are not inclined to be frivolous with their products, and my first test clearly told me they were on to something. But why do Remington's Duplex work so well when earlier attempts failed?

One big reason is that most experimenting

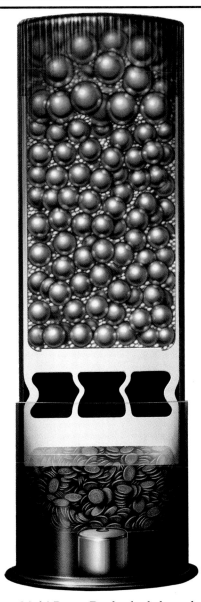

Remington Multi-Range Duplex loads have shot in two sizes. This variation has No. 2 over No. 6. The company states that smaller shot provides good pattern density, while larger pellets of course give added punch. Here you'll see that the larger pellets, which tend to retain velocity better, are loaded on top.

handloaders such as my teenage self *blended* the two shot sizes in duplex loads. The goal was to achieve a uniform distribution of the two shot sizes with the pattern. Remington's researchers discovered that for a duplex load to be workable the shot sizes have to be segregated. The results, in effect, are two-shot charges working almost independent of each other. Another important element of Remington's dual shot load is having the larger shot on top of the column. The reasons for this are rather technical, but easily explained.

Larger size shot retain their velocity better than

smaller sizes. If, for example, shot sizes 2 and 6 are mixed and fired from the same cartridge, the Number 6s would be trailing somewhat behind the Number 2s by the time they had traveled forty yards. If the larger shot were mixed with the smaller size, or positioned at the bottom of the shot column, they would create a considerable disturbance as they shouldered their way to the front of the shot swarm. Just think of it as a bunch of fat ladies stampeding to the front of a crowded bus.

By having the larger shot positioned on top of the column, they not only do not disturb the flight of the smaller shot but also better maintain their own pattern uniformity. This is why the larger shot truly adds *effective* longer range to the Multi-Range Duplex load.

To make these new loads as good as possible, Remington copper-coats the lead bullets for improved surface hardness, and the shot are nested in a granulated buffering compound. The shells themselves have a dark, nonreflective finish with the metal base having a black oxide coating.

Available in 12 gauge in both standard 2¾-inch and 3-inch Magnum lengths, the Multi-Range Duplex loads have either lead or steel shot loadings. I expect this development will be much copied by other ammo manufacturers because it appears to be well worth copying. Here's a list of the Duplex combinations.

Lead Shot

Shell Length (inches)	Shot Weight (oz.)	Duplex Combo
3	1⅞	2 × 6
3	1⅞	BB × 4
2¾	1½	2 × 6
2¾	1½	BB × 4

Steel Shot

3	1¼	BB × 2
3	1¼	BB × 4
3	1¼	2 × 6
2¾	1⅛	BB × 2
2¾	1⅛	BB × 4
2¾	1⅛	2 × 6

The Duplex loads are not Remington's only new shotshells. Keeping their research and testing departments in high gear over the past couple of years, Remington has also developed a completely new target shell. If you shoot trap or skeet you are aware that the Remington name disappeared from competition loads a few years ago with their only offering being the Peters blue hull. If you are not a target shooter, you may say "so what?" to new target shotshells bearing the Remington name. The fact is that the time, money, and talent invested in the development of a new target load

is the wellspring from which many—if not nearly all—shotshell improvements flow. To a very large extent, shotshell makers gamble their reputations on the quality and success of their target loads. That's why they make such a fuss when championships are won with their shells. As it so happens, the combination of factors that make good target loads also makes good hunting loads. Thus when a manufacturer introduces a dramatically new and better target load, it's a safe bet that better hunting loads are soon to follow. Remington's new "Premier" 12-gauge trap and skeet loads are a from-the-ground-up effort with a new wad, case, and primer. They say it is their finest target load ever. Watch for the introduction of new Remington hunting loads over the next few years and you'll see what I mean by the "spillover" effect.

Also new this season are Remington's two new hotshot 12-gauge rifled slug loads. In the 3-inch Magnum loading the 1-ounce slug has a muzzle velocity of 1,760 fps, which is some 200 fps faster than previous slug loads. The 2¾-inch load with the 1-ounce slug has a speed of 1,680 fps. These higher velocities mean a flatter trajectory and more knockdown power. At 50 yards, for example, the Magnum load delivers 30 percent more energy than previous rifled slug loads. Here's a table giving the "hard stuff" on the performance of these new big-game shotgun loads.

BALLISTICS

Remington 3-Inch Magnum Rifle Slug

Range (Yards)	Velocity (ft/sec)	Energy (ft-lbs)	Drop (In.)
0	1760	3009	0
25	1538	2297	.4
50	1345	1756	1.7
75	1189	1372	4.2
100	1075	1123	8.3

Remington 2¾ Inch HV Rifled Slug

0	1680	2741	0
25	1647	2091	.4
50	1286	1606	1.9
75	1144	1272	4.6
100	1045	1061	9.0

If you hunt with a .338 Winchester Magnum rifle, or think you might like to, you'll be interested in Remington's addition of this superb cartridge to their catalog. The new loads include a 225-grain pointed soft-point bullet with a muzzle velocity of 2780 and a 250-grain PSP bullet leaving the muzzle at 2660. This heavier bullet load is of particular interest because it rounds out, along with Federal's new Premium .338 load, the availability of good bullet weights. It is with a 250-grain bullet that the .338 Mag. does best what it does so well—anchoring big game.

Remington has quite a few other new loads, including 20-gauge steel shot combinations, a hot new load for the .257 Roberts, loads for the .357 Magnum and .45 Colt, and an improved bullet for the .45/70. Also, at last, are factory-finished cases for the 7mm B.R. Remington cartridge. Previously, cases for this wildcat had to be handmade from .308 cases. Silhouette shooters and long-range handgunners who use this popular round will be much relieved.

FEDERAL

Federal Cartridge Company is another ammo maker that has been burning the midnight powder and developing a passel of new loads. Remember when ammo makers offered only one or two steel shot loads? Federal has seven new steel shot loads, which brings to 30 the total of steel shot combinations they offer. Last year, you'll recall, Federal introduced size "F" steel shot which, with a diameter of .220-inch is somewhat larger than size BB (.180-inch). This year they also offer size "T," which, having a diameter of .200-inch, is midway between sizes BB and "F." The purpose of these larger size shot is to increase long-range punch, especially for goose hunting. Federal's new steel loads include both "F" and "T" loadings for the 10-gauge Magnum and a "T" shot load for the 3-inch 12-gauge Magnum. Also for the standard 2¾-inch 12-gauge are new loads with Number 3 and BB steel shot. Responding to requests from owners of 16-gauge guns, Federal now offers 16-gauge steel shot loads. These are available in a choice of Number 2 and Number 4 shot sizes.

Some combinations of bullet and cartridge are so obviously superior that one wonders why it ever took so long for the two to be put together. A case in point is Federal's new .338 Win. Mag. Premium loading of the 250-grain Nosler Partition Bullet. Federal has been using Nosler Partition bullets in a few select Premium loads for several years now with considerable—and certainly predictable—success in the hunting field. I can personally vouch for the superiority of the 250-grain Nosler in the .338 Mag. because this is exactly the combination I've been handloading for several years. The game I've taken range from elk to moose to Alaskan brown bear to African lion and even a couple of Cape buffalo. It is one of the most utterly reliable big-game cartridge/bullet combinations I've ever used and I predict great results from Federal's version.

Other new Federal Premium rifle loads with Nosler Partition bullets are the 7mm Rem. Mag. with 140-grain slug loaded to 3150 fps and the .257 Roberts with 120-grain bullet loaded to 2780 fps. This new .257 Roberts loading is what's known as a +p load, which means that it develops a higher pressure and velocity than traditional .257 factory loaded ammo. Sometime during the dim past of the .257 Roberts, some rifles in this caliber were marketed that were not as strong as are modern rifles. Thus, as a safety measure, ammo makers deliberately kept working pressures to minimum levels. (The .257 was not the only caliber in this category.) As a result, factory loaded .257 ammo was never what it could have been, which explains why almost all .257 fans were handloaders. Anyway, what with the introduction of extra strong rifles in .257 chambering by Remington, Ruger and Winchester, it made sense to load the

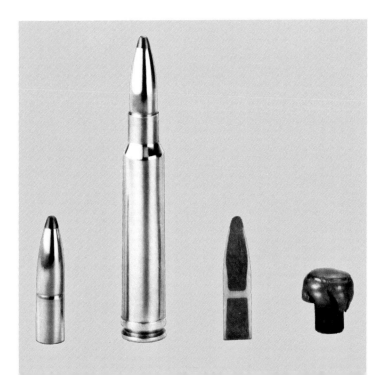

New from Federal Cartridge is a .338 Winchester Magnum with a heavy 250-grain Nosler Partition bullet.

.257 to its full potential. Now, all major U.S. ammo makers offer +p .257 Roberts ammo. If you own a .257 Roberts of good vintage the +p loads are the ones to use for best performance. Federal's new Premium load should be a winner for all deer size game.

Long-range hunters who dote on the .25/06 will go for Federal's new 117 bullet with boattail shape. This streamlined bullet shoots flatter and suffers less wind drift at the longer ranges than flat base bullets. And if you are still convinced that round nose bullets are better for hunting in brush, Federal now offers a round-nose, 180-grain bullet for the .30/06.

Another new rifle load from Federal is a 50-grain hollow point bullet for the .22 Win. Mag. Rimfire. Until now the .22 WMR has been loaded with lighter bullets that go faster at the muzzle but have less punch at longer range. This new bullet from Federal gives the .22 WMR 16 percent more energy at 100 yards than standard loads with 40-grain bullets.

If hunting with buckshot is your thing (required in some big-game areas), Federal's two new buckshot loads are worth looking at. Both are for the 3-inch 12-gauge Magnum with one loaded with Size 000 Buck and the other Size 1 Buck. The big buckshot are made of a lead alloy having a high antimony content for extra hardness. They are then highly polished and copper plated. This hardening, polishing and plating help them retain their roundness better which, in turn, improves flight characteristics for the best possible pattern density. The 000 Buck load contains 10 pellets, with the Number 1 Buck load having 24 pellets.

NORMA JOINS FEDERAL

More than a few American shooters and handloaders will be joyed to learn that Federal has acquired the exclusive U.S. distribution rights of Norma loaded ammunition and brass reloading components. Norma is an old and highly respected Swedish firm that manufactures a number of calibers not available elsewhere. This means that U.S. shooters who have relied on Norma for hard-to-get ammo and reloading items will now have a reliable source. So just tell your dealer to contact Federal for your Norma needs.

WINCHESTER

Winchester's announcement of 14 new steel-shot loads makes them the industry leader with a count of no less than 35 different steel shot loads and combinations. Particularly interesting among Winchester's new steel shot loads are those with Number 3 shot. This should be a smart alternative

for hunters who normally use Number 4 or 5 lead shot. Also interesting is Winchester's copper-plated steel shot in sizes "T" and "BBB." Loaded especially for goose hunters, these high-performance steel-shot loads are available in both 12- and 10-gauge Magnum shells. Winchester's new Super Steel shotshell packaging is marked with the recommended uses for the various loads. So choose a box marked pass, decoy, or goose and you won't go wrong. If you don't think you'll need a whole box of 25 shells to take your limit, Winchester also offers 10-round packaging with 12-gauge Magnum shells.

And speaking of compact packaging, Winchester has also expanded the number of pistol calibers that can be bought in the popular 20-round boxes. These smaller boxes are not only more affordable, but more convenient to carry. The 20-round packaging now includes more loads in .41, .44, and .45 calibers.

Boattail, or taper-heel, bullets have been slow to catch on with hunters even though they have long been popular with long-range target shooters. The boattail shape improves a bullet's streamlined efficiency so it can slip through the air more easily. Thus it retains its velocity better and thereby has a flatter trajectory, better resistance to crosswinds and greater downrange punch. Winchester's announcement of a new .30/06 load with a 180-grain silvertip boattail bullet makes a great cartridge even better. If you're wondering what load to use for big, tough-hided game such as elk or moose, this new load will be hard to beat. Also new from Winchester is a 7mm Mauser (7 × 57) load with a 145-grain bullet. Time was when there simply weren't any really good 7mm Mauser factory loads. Now the situation is much changed and this new load should be one of the best. For light- to medium-size game the old 7 × 57 is unbeatable, especially now that some excellent rifles are available.

Here's a target load that should have lots of appeal to upland hunters. It's Winchester's new AA Super-Lite 12-gauge shotshell. The reason it is called Super-Lite is its reduced recoil even though it is loaded with a full 1⅛-ounce shot charge (rather than the 1-ounce charges of some light loads). Target shooters who may fire hundreds of rounds per tournament appreciate the reduced recoil because it has been proven that in addition to contributing to flinching and other shooters' problems, recoil can also cause severe fatigue.

It occurs to me that these Super-Lite loads will be great in a dove field, where many hunters sometimes go through several boxes of shells a day. It's a proven fact that we shoot better with ammo that kicks less, so I'm going to give these new Winchester loads a try. They come in 7½, 8, 8½ and 9 shot sizes.

Factory Ammo: Better Than Handloads?

Layne Simpson

Writers are inspired to dig into a particular subject for a variety of reasons. Three shooters I observed at a local rifle range gave me the idea for this project. They were checking out their new rifles in preparation for the forthcoming whitetail season, and if memory serves me correctly, their rifles were chambered to .308 Winchester, .30/06, and .270 Winchester.

Now I see lots of people shooting at the private ranges I occasionally use and seldom pay attention to what they are doing as long as all safety rules are being observed, but I couldn't resist listening in on the heated argument this threesome was involved in. The .308 and .30/06 shooters were handloaders, and both were giving the .270 shooter a hard time for using factory loads.

Advocates on both sides of the debate made valid points. The handloaders pointed out that a number of big-game cartridges were introduced in what are now considered to be rifles of antiquated design, made of materials inferior in strength to those currently used in building rifles.

This article first appeared in Shooting Times

Tracking down the factory load that works best in your firearm takes time, but it's worth the effort.

One of the handloaders went on to say that the performance of a number of cartridges that are factory loaded to chamber pressures compatible with those older rifles can be improved by handloading to higher chamber pressures in modern bolt-action rifles, citing the .257 Roberts as an example. The other handloader pointed out that only by trying different combinations of bullets, bullet-seating depths, powders, primers, and various handloading techniques could a shooter realize the best accuracy inherent in a particular rifle. He went on to add that the big-game hunter who handloads can better match bullets of varying expansion properties to game of different sizes.

The factory load shooter had obviously done his homework. First, he countered by stating that since shooters who use factory loads outnumber handloaders by about 10 to one, factory ammunition couldn't be as bad as some handloaders say it is. Then he dropped a real blockbuster by pointing out that most investigations of blownup firearms that prove the ammunition was at fault almost always prove the ammunition involved was handloaded, not factory loaded.

The handloaders and the factory load shooter made a number of other strong points, but what really silenced the argument was my suggestion that the three compare group sizes. The .270 shooter had brought 130-grain factory loads from three manufacturers. The groups fired with the load his rifle like best were only slightly larger than the best groups fired by the .308 handloader and considerably smaller than those fired by the .30/06 handloader.

I gained a friend and lost two that day.

While driving home from the range, I decided it was time to take an objective look at factory loads. I've been loading my own for well over a quarter-century and, like most handloaders, have long had a look-down-the-nose attitude toward any ammunition not assembled at my loading bench. I have even been guilty of parroting this wornout phrase: "First I tried factory loads in the new rifle; then I got serious with handloads."

As time went on, I began to observe an across-the-board improvement in the accuracy of factory loads. Could it be that our ammomakers had finally gotten the message? Several factory loads I tried in a number of rifles indicated they had. There was, for example, a Browning B-78 single shot in .25/06 for which I spent some long hours at the loading bench and was rewarded with no better accuracy than that of the Federal 117-grain spitzer boattail load. It was the same story with a Ruger Model 77 Ultra Light in .270 and the Winchester 130-grain Power-Point load and with a Savage Model 110K in the same caliber with the Remington 130-grain Core-Lokt load.

I decided to wring out .270 Winchester factory loads for a number of reasons. The fact that it is an extremely popular cartridge among big-game hunters was one. Also, the variety of loads available from several manufacturers made the .270 an excellent candidate for my project. But possibly most important of all, the .270 is not generally thought of as an accuracy cartridge. I'm not saying the .270 isn't an accurate cartridge; I am saying it is not usually associated with accuracy of a competitive level, as is the case with cartridges like the 7mm/08 Remington, .308 Winchester, .30/06, and .222 Remington.

Initially, I planned to gather up a half-dozen new factory rifles from various makers, feed them a variety of .270 factory loads, and report on the results. Not a bad plan, but since factory rifles (even the same model from the same maker) often vary so much in accuracy, using them would have introduced variables inherent in the rifles rather than the ammunition. Besides, I wanted to compare the performance of factory loads to that of the best handload I could come up with, and the development of a best handload for six rifles would have consumed more time than I could possibly devote to the project.

At times like this, it's nice to have a friend who is also a cooperative gunsmith.

Kenny Jarrett, owner of Jarrett Rifles Inc. (Rte. 1, Box 411, Jackson, SC 29831), is a benchrest shooter with a number of accuracy records to his credit, and he also builds rifles for his fellow competitors, some of which have set new world accuracy records. But more important to this story, Kenny builds rifles for big-game hunting and varmint shooting, using the same materials and techniques employed to build benchrest rifles.

I've fired a number of Jarrett-built rifles of hunting weight, and all chambered to such cartridges as the .223 Remington, .220 Swift, and .243 Ackley Improved averaged less than ½ MOA (minute of arc) for five shots. With custom benchrest-quality bullets, some have averaged ¼ MOA. I have also worked with Jarrett rifles in .270 Winchester, .280 Remington, .280 Ackley Improved, .300 Winchester Magnum, and .338/06, all with relatively light barrels made by Hart. They averaged from .400 to .600 inch for three shots.

The rifle Jarrett built for my factory load project is typical of his big-game rifles. The locking lugs of the Remington Model 700 bolt were handlapped to uniform contact with their abutments in the receiver, and the receiver threads were chased out to perfect concentricity with the axis of the receiver. The bolt face, receiver ring face, and recoil bracket (or lug) were also turned or ground to the same degree of concentricity. After the Model 700 action was completed, Jarrett installed a 24-inch Hart stainless-steel barrel with a 1:10 twist and .720-inch muzzle diameter. The

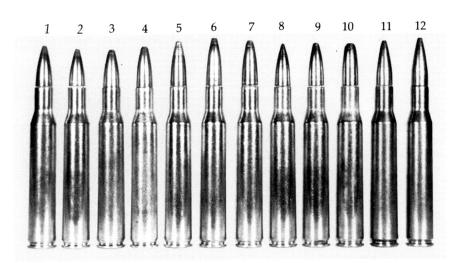

(1) Fed. Premium 130-grain SPBT. (2) Fed. 130-grain SP. (3) Norma 130-grain SSP. (4) Norma 150-grain SSP. (5) Win. 130-grain ST. (6) Win. 130-grain P–P. (7) Win. 150-grain P–P. (8) Rem. 130-grain Bronze Point. (9) Rem. 130-grain C–L. (10) Rem. 150-grain C–L. (11) Hornady 130-grain SPI. (12) Hornady 150-grain SPBTI.

.270 WINCHESTER FACTORY LOADS: ACCURACY

Load	Accuracy (Rail Gun)	Accuracy Ranking	Accuracy (Model 700)	Accuracy Ranking
Hornady 140-gr. SPBTI	0.754	1	0.992	6
Federal 130-gr. SP	0.897	2	0.813	5
Federal Premium 130-gr. SPBT	1.021	3	1.364	9
Remington 130-gr. BP	1.045	4	0.739	4
Winchester 130-gr. ST	1.048	5	1.109	7
Norma 150-gr. SSP	1.069	6	1.871	12
Norma 130-gr. SSP	1.102	7	0.562	2
Hornady 130-gr. SPI	1.129	8	0.656	3
Remington 130-gr. PC-L	1.156	9	0.549	1
Winchester 150-gr. P-P	1.183	10	1.581	11
Remington 150-gr. RNC-L	1.190	11	1.198	8
Winchester 130-gr. P-P	1.681	12	1.506	10
Control Load (Handload)	0.311	—	0.515	—

LEGEND: *SPBTI (Spirepoint boattail Interlok); SP (Softpoint); SPBT (Softpoint boattail); BP (Bronze Point); ST (Silvertip); SSP (Semispitzer softpoint); SPI (Spirepoint Interlok); PC-L (Pointed Core-Lokt); P-P (Power-Point); RNC-L (Roundnose Core-Lokt).*

NOTES: *Both guns had Hart 24-inch barrels with 1:10-inch twists. Control loads used to establish levels of inherent accuracy for both guns were 48.0 grains of IMR-4064 and a 130-grain Nosler Ballistic Tip in the rail gun and 58.0 grains of IMR-4831 and a 130-grain Nosler Ballistic Tip in the Model 700. Factory load accuracy shown is for an average of six five-shot groups in the rail gun and six three-shot groups in the Model 700. All groups were fired from a benchrest at 100 yards.*

.270 WINCHESTER FACTORY LOADS: MUZZLE VELOCITIES

Manufacturer	Bullet	Lot Number	Velocity (fps) Average	Extreme Spread
Federal Premium	130-gr. SPBT	34B-6478	2971	49
Federal	130-gr. SP	34A-4088	2984	43
Hornady	130-gr. SPI	11-224-86-8841	2981	31
Hornady	140-gr. SPBTI	02-041-87-8841	2819	57
Norma	130-gr. SSP	602619	3008	62
Norma	150-gr. SSP	611620	2684	44
Remington	130-gr. PC-L	G15-PC0377	2892	76
Remington	130-gr. BP	DO2E-C3705	2844	55
Remington	150-gr. RNC-L	FO7A-C4505	2749	66
Winchester	130-gr. ST	79XN51-52-27	2911	37
Winchester	130-gr. P-P	85YA90-25	2932	99
Winchester	150-gr. P-P	14YB21-85-25	2790	72

NOTES: *The rifle used was a custom Remington Model 700 with a 24-inch Hart barrel. Velocity shown is an average of 10 rounds clocked at 12 feet from the muzzle with an Oehler Model 33 Chronotach and Skyscreen III detection system.*

whole works, bedded into a fiberglass stock, weighed slightly over 7½ pounds.

Jarrett also builds machine-rest rifles (rail guns, as benchrest shooters who use them in Unlimited class competition often refer to them). For the second phase of my project, he fitted a new bolt and a 24-inch Hart barrel in .270 Winchester to one of those iron monsters. The Hart barrel was left at 1½ inches in diameter along its entire length, bringing the total weight of the rail gun and its Leupold 36× scope to 65 pounds.

The rail gun was Jarrett's rifle, one he had used in two matches since building it a few months prior to my using it in the .270 project. In a 200-yard match, he posted a .2623 MOA aggregate for 50 shots (five 10-shot groups), with his smallest group measuring .1581 MOA. In a 300-yard match, his aggregate for 50 shots was .3478 MOA, with the smallest 10-shot group measuring .2280 MOA! In other words, while wearing its Hart barrel in 6mm PPC, the gun had already proven its accuracy capabilities in competition.

I rounded up a dozen .270 factory loads: two each from Federal, Hornady, and Norma and three each from Winchester/Olin and Remington. Before trying the factory loads, I also developed a handload for the two guns. Of several bullets tried, both guns seemed to prefer the Nosler 130-grain Ballistic Tip seated out to lightly kiss the rifling. For powders, the rail gun indicated a preference for IMR–4064; the sporter, IMR–4831. Federal cases and 210M primers were used.

I decided to shoot all groups with the handloads and factory loads when wind conditions at Jarrett's range were at their best. This meant early morning, late afternoon, and nighttime shooting. I was able to shoot at night because the benchrest shed and target butts on Jarrett's range are artificially lit for just that purpose. In order to give each load a fair shake, I fired groups with each during the day and at night.

I had assumed my best groups would be fired at night, when there was practically no wind except for a slight, shifting breeze, but this did not prove to be true. When shooting in daylight, I was able to observe wind flags positioned at 15, 50, and 80 yards, which enabled me to fire each shot of a particular string during the same prevailing condition. When shooting at night, I had less wind to contend with but was unable to see the wind flags. As it turned out, aggregates fired at night measured about the same as those fired during the day.

When shooting groups with the two guns, I adhered to the same criteria used in wringing out factory rifles: three-shot groups with light-barrel rifles and five-shot groups with heavy-barrel rifles. After settling on a handload for the two guns, I fired a total of 20 five-shot groups in the rail gun

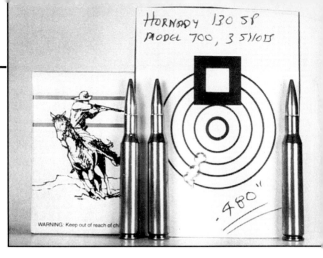

Hornady factory 130-gr., 140-gr. spire points printed . . .

and the same number of three-shot groups in the Model 700. I didn't fire the groups consecutively; I fired individual groups with the handloads throughout my shooting sessions with the factory loads in order to ensure that all were subjected to the same shooting conditions and factors like shooter fatigue and barrel wear.

Both guns liked my handloads. The 100-shot aggregate for the 130-grain Ballistic Tip seated atop 48.0 grains of IMR–4064 in the rail gun measured .311 inch. The smallest five-shot group fired measured .245 inch; the largest measured .402 inch. Needless to say, this is outstanding accuracy from a bullet made for big-game hunting and not competitive shooting. The Model 700 chalked up an aggregate of .515 inch with its load of 58.0 grains of IMR–4831 and the 130-grain Ballistic Tip. Its smallest three-shot group was .398 inch; its largest was .657 inch. This was outstanding accuracy from a hunting bullet and a rifle of hunting weight.

Six groups were fired with each factory load in strings of two groups with each load. Since the shooting consumed the better part of two days and two nights, and since conditions varied somewhat during that period of time, it would have been unfair to completely wring out one factory load under one range condition and then work with another factory load under totally different conditions many hours later. For this reason, shooting of the 12 different factory loads was spread out over the entire session.

After firing two groups with a particular factory load, I cleaned the barrels of the two guns before firing two groups with the next factory load. When working with handloads in the guns, I had observed that neither had any tendency to fling its first bullet from a clean barrel out of the group formed by its mates that followed. This, by the way, is a sure sign of an extremely well-built rifle and a top-quality barrel.

Rather than dwelling on the accuracy of individual factory loads in the two guns, I believe the remainder of my alloted space is best devoted to general observations. First of all, I'm more than

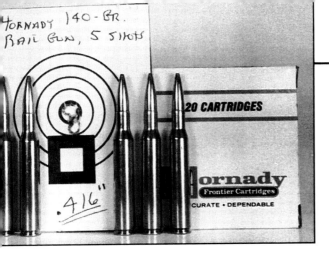

Handwritten note on image: "HORNADY 140-GR. RAIL GUN, 5 SHOTS   .416""

. . . under half-inch in Rem. M700 (left) and rail gun.

a little amazed at the small differences in accuracy among most of the factory loads in the rail gun. The loads that ranked three through 11 in accuracy varied by a mere .169 inch. When looking at the loads the rail gun liked best and worst, there is an accuracy spread of .856 inch, which is still not bad.

In contrast, the six best factory loads in the Model 700 varied in accuracy by .443 inch, with a total variation among the 12 loads of 1.011 inches. This tidbit of data tends to confirm something that shooters have long known to be true: given two rifles of equal quality, the one with the heavier barrel will often show less variation in accuracy with different loads than the one with the lighter barrel. It would also seem that a shooter has to work much harder and try a greater variety of factory loads when seeking the best accuracy from a light-barrel rifle than is the case with a heavy-barrel rifle. Of course, few of us would choose the latter when climbing a mountain; so the name of the game is to try a variety of loads.

There's something else the factory load shooter should take note of: a load that works best in one rifle may not in another rifle. This fact of life becomes quite evident when reading the accompanying accuracy comparison chart. Factory loads that ranked first, second, third, fourth, and fifth in accuracy in the rail gun respectively ranked sixth, fifth, ninth, fourth, and seventh in the Model 700. On the other hand, loads that ranked first, second, third, fourth, and fifth in the Model 700 ranked ninth, seventh, eighth, fourth, and second in the rail gun. Again, this serves to tell us that several factory loads should be employed and their accuracy compared before the owner of a new rifle decides on a load.

Now . . . here comes the monkey wrench to foul up the works. . . . Before you rush out and buy a lifetime supply of the ammunition ranking highest in accuracy in my chart, you should know that factory ammunition from the same maker often varies considerably in accuracy from lot to lot with the same load. I have no idea why, and

none of the manufacturers have enlightened me on the subject, but you can safely bet that it does.

When working with many rifles on numerous occasions, I have experienced a difference in accuracy as much as 1¾ MOA when using different lots of the same factory load from the same manufacturer. In fact, if I were to go through the same exercise with the rail gun and the custom Model 700 and with the same ammunition but with different lot numbers printed on the end flaps, it is likely that the accuracy rankings shown would be entirely different. So, if after trying various factory loads in your rifle you find one that outperforms the others by a considerable margin, jot down the lot number on that box of ammunition, run back to the dealer you bought it from, and hope he still has several boxes left.

The rail gun and Model 700 also serve to illustrate that some guns like factory loads better than others do, even when two guns are built by the same gunsmith and use barrels from the same maker that are chambered with the same reamers. When shooting handloads in both guns, I found the rail gun's aggregate accuracy for five-shot groups was 40 percent smaller than that of the Model 700 with three-shot groups. The Model 700 averaged less than MOA with six factory loads, while the rail gun managed to squeeze only two factory loads into less than an inch. My handload in the Model 700 beat the best factory load in accuracy by only .034 inch; the difference between handload and best factory load accuracy in the rail gun was .443 inch. The Winchester 130-grain Power-Point load is a classic example of what I'm talking about. Neither gun liked Winchester's load, and yet another lot I tried about a year ago in a Ruger Model 77 averaged .796 MOA for five three-shot groups.

Every experienced big-game hunter knows that velocity and bullet style are also important in a load. The advertised muzzle velocities of .270 Winchester 130- and 150-grain factory loads are 3060 and 2850 feet per second (fps) when fired in 24-inch pressure barrels. In the Model 700's 24-inch barrel, some factory loads fell short of those speeds by as much as 200 fps. Since most bolt-action rifles in .270 have 22-inch barrels, we can deduct another 60 fps or so.

This is not a case of ammunition makers attempting to intentionally deceive the consumer. Pressure barrels used to test ammunition are bored, rifled, and chambered to absolute minimum SAAMI dimensions. As a result, those barrels produce higher chamber pressures (and velocities) than the typical barrel on a rifle.

What does all this mean to a hunter in the field? My most accurate handload in the custom Model 700, using a 130-grain spitzer, wallops a 300-yard target with 1600 foot-pounds (ft-lbs) of energy. Zeroed 3 inches high at 100 yards, its point of impact is about 2 inches low at 300 yards. A decrease in muzzle velocity of 100 fps translates to trajectory and residual energy differences of one inch and roughly 100 ft-lbs. A decrease of 200 fps results in reductions of 2 inches in trajectory and about 200 ft-lbs in striking energy. Even if a 130-grain spitzer leaves the muzzle at only 2900 fps, it still delivers almost 1400 ft-lbs at 300 yards. Such differences in performance are important to some hunters.

I should also point out that velocity, though important to the hunter, is of secondary importance to the ammunition makers. Their first priority is to produce ammunition that is safe to use in a bewildering variety of rifles, some of which have been in use during most of this century. The ammunition must also function reliably in bolt actions, lever actions, pumps, single shots, and autoloaders. A tall order, indeed.

When we consider that six of the 12 factory loads I tried in the Model 700 averaged less than MOA and none exceeded two MOA in accuracy, it becomes clear that the accuracy of any load depends greatly on the quality of the rifle it's fired in. Of course, this applies to handloads as well as factory loads. By the same token, the accuracy spread between the various factory loads in the Model 700 and the rail gun indicates that even when using the best materials available, all assembled with great precision, the inherent accuracy of a rifle will emerge only when it is fed ammunition it likes.

Ideally, the factory-load shooter searching for the best accuracy at his disposal would try all available loads in his rifle, but we must be realistic. Considering the cost of factory ammunition, such a program would be far beyond the reach of many shooters. There is also the possibility that the first load tried will satisfy the shooter's requirements. Even so, the more different loads a shooter tries, the higher his odds of discovering that No. 1 load. Perhaps other companies will follow Remington's lead and offer rifle cartridges in cartons of 10, allowing the factory load shooter to try a greater variety of loads at less cost.

Any handloader who says factory loads don't offer enough variety in bullet performance probably hasn't looked at what is available. Remington .270 factory loads are good examples. The Bronze Point bullet has been around since before World War II and is constructed to expand at low-impact velocities. It's an excellent choice for shooting deer-size game at extremely long ranges. The highly successful Nosler Ballistic Tip bullet is the same idea, only with the nose cavity filled with polycarbonate instead of bronze.

For shooting heavier game or game of any size

at closer ranges where deeper penetration is desired, the Remington Core-Lokt bullet is of controlled-expansion design and enjoys an excellent reputation as a big-game bullet. The same applies to Federal and Weatherby ammunition loaded with the Nosler Partition bullet. And we must not overlook Hornady ammunition loaded with bullets of Interlok design, the same that is available to handloaders.

All of this is not meant to say that we should give up handloading and switch to factory loads, even though some fellows I know would be better off doing so. Performed properly, handloading offers the shooter many options not available in factory-loaded form. But I can say without reservation that the fellow who patiently tries a number of factory loads and then stocks up with the load that shoots best in his rifle doesn't need to hang his head in shame or hide his ammunition under the bed when a shooting pal who handloads rings his doorbell.

PMC AMMO RESULTS

Several weeks after wrapping up my .270 project, I received ammunition in various calibers, including two .270 Winchester loads, from PMC. I was unable to try the PMC ammunition in the custom Model 700, but I did wring it out in Kenny Jarrett's rail gun. In all fairness, however, I must point out that since I fired all groups with the PMC loads consecutively (under excellent range conditions), the end result is less than a true apples-to-apples comparison of what I came up with for the other brands of ammunition. But since PMC is considered to be one of the "Big Six" producers of sporting ammunition for the U.S. market, its absence from my report would have made the project incomplete.

Aggregate accuracy for the 130-grain pointed softpoint (PSP) load (Lot No. 270C-042) was 1.204 inches. The 150-grain PSP load (Lot No. 270D-048) printed 1.577 inches. Advertised velocities of the two loads are 2816 and 2547 feet per second (fps). The loads I tried exceeded these figures in the rail gun's 24-inch Hart barrel. More specifically, the 130-grain load clocked 2851 fps on my Oehler Model 33; the 150-grain load moved out at 2619 fps. Their extreme velocity spreads were 74 and 48 fps respectively.

I was puzzled by the discrepancy in velocities until I checked PMC's brochure and found the velocities listed for all ammunition were obtained in off-the-shelf rifles and handguns rather than pressure barrels. For example, PMC used a Remington Sportsman 78 with a 22-inch barrel when chronographing its .270 Winchester loads. This explains why both loads were generating higher-than-advertised velocities in the rail gun.

When the Bullet Gets There

Jim Carmichel

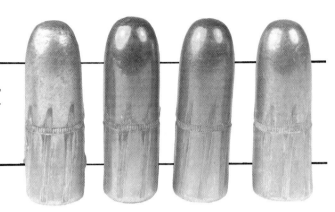

These Hornady .45 caliber steel-jacketed "full patch" bullets were recovered from elephant skulls. Often steel-jacketed bullets appear to have ordinary copper jackets because of a thin copper coating. You can check with a magnet. Despite their rugged construction, some full-jacketed bullets bend, flatten, and even break up on contact with the superstructure of heavy game.

About a half dozen events are absolutely guaranteed to hold a sporting man's attention. Some I haven't tried but a few I have: Once a charging lion arrested my attention for a few seconds and another time a murderous elephant rudely interrupted my peace of mind for what seemed like several minutes. And then there was the time when I witnessed a bull moose falling madly in love with a saddle horse. Normally, I don't find affairs of the heart of others of much concern. This time however I found myself intensely involved in the flirtation because I happened to be riding the object of the moose's ardor. Though I have no firsthand experience in this area, I have it on good authority that a jealous woman coming at you with a butcher knife can also hold your interest for a time.

Another episode that is bound to hold your attention is the handloading of ammunition that will be used to hunt dangerous game. Make a mistake at the loading bench, and it can cost you your life. I know a knowledgeable handloader in New Jersey who has a dozen or so African safaris under his belt. Even so, he frankly confesses to having a fit of the clammy sweats when faced with the chore of loading ammo for animals that are big and mean. That's why he always uses store-bought cartridges for game that is inclined to have ugly temper fits.

I take the opposite view. Even though I have tremendous respect for the reliability of factory-loaded cartridges, if something is going to go wrong, I want to know whom to blame—not that it would make any difference. That's why every one of the lions, leopards, Cape buffalo and elephant I've collected were taken with my handloads.

Ordinarily, these carefully assembled big-game loads have been pretty things, put together with surgical cleanliness and care. Each component is checked and rechecked before being committed to the loading process. No dirty fingers are allowed to touch a primer or smudge a gleaming brass case. Even the slightest cosmetic defect is reason to toss the round into the reject box, to be used for practice or zeroing. Only the brightest and slickest make their way to the African bush.

That's why a few .458 Win. Mag. cartridges I loaded last summer were so peculiar. Rather than gleaming with virginal radiance, the bullets were as tarnished as a harlot's sorority pin. Deep scars slashed into their jackets and their noses looked like they had smashed into brick walls. Which wasn't all that far from fact for, in truth, the soiled and scarred bullets had been recovered from elephant skulls.

Over the years I've made determined efforts to recover the bullets, or fragments thereof, from every head of game I bag. This exercise is a form of homework for gun writers. I've found myself sifting through elk lungs during Montana blizzards and splitting the bones of cape buffalo under a blistering African sun, hoping to find a bullet, or a piece of a bullet, that might have a story to tell.

The 500-grain FMJ (Full Metal Jacket) Hornady bullets I had loaded for the second time around had been chopped out of elephant skulls in such remarkably undamaged condition that the challenge of using them to bag yet another tusker was

This article first appeared in Outdoor Life

A recent and very effective "solid" design is this monolithic bullet manufactured by the A-Square Company. This space-age bullet has no jacket or core but, rather, is composed of a homogeneous leaded bronze alloy.

irresistible. I don't know if this stunt has been tried before. But given the peculiar notions of hunters who seek dangerous game, I expect it has.

To save you the suspense, I did take the second-time-around bullets on safari, but no, there were no elephants worth the taking. Perhaps another time. Anyway, the subject of this essay is why that small handful of bullets was recovered in such wonderfully reusable condition and why other bullets split and shatter beyond recognition upon impact with a deer or bear. Here we're discussing *bullet performance* and the way a bullet behaves—or misbehaves—when it hits a game animal. This determines to considerable extent whether the animal will fall where it stands or whether you will have to track it into the next county.

The journey of a bullet is divided into three segments. The first of these, the short trip through the rifled barrel, can be predetermined with a high degree of exactitude. The second part of the trip, from muzzle to target, can be plotted with mathematical precision. However, the third part of the bullet's flight, known as *terminal ballistics*, occurs when a bullet strikes and enters the target, and this continues to be the cause of rampant puzzlement. I've fired scores of identical bullets at identical game, but on recovery no two had performed in identical fashion. The remaining structure of every expanding bullet I've ever seen is as individualistic as a fingerprint.

For purposes of discussion, the rifle bullets used for hunting can be divided into three general types. One of these is nonexpanding, full-jacketed solids such as the ones I briefly discussed earlier. At the other end of the rainbow are bullets designed to expand and fragment so rapidly on impact that their disintegration can be likened to a small explosion. Between these extremes are the bullets most of us use for most of our hunting.

These are controlled-expansion-type bullets. These are the bullets that account for most of what we think we know about bullet performance—and almost all of what we don't know.

The purpose of full-jacketed bullets, commonly called "solids," is to penetrate as deep and as straight into bone or tissue as possible. Generations of experience have taught us that the bullets that penetrate best are those that best maintain their original shape and weight. To this end bullet makers have historically busied themselves with the design and construction of projectiles that can deliver thousands of pounds of energy without being mangled or squashed in the process.

Unlike expanding-type bullets that are usually constructed with the jacket material covering the base and closing at the nose, the jackets on solids cover and protect the nose and close at the base. Also the jackets of many solids are made of steel, which is stronger than copper jackets and thus more resistant to damage. Often these steel jackets are coated with a layer of copper so about the only way to be sure of steel is with a magnet. Though there is a small cadre of hunters in North America who prefer using "solids" on all game from whitetail deer on up, the real home of the non-expanding bullet is Africa.

Hunters of dangerous game, especially elephant and buffalo, prefer solids for a number of good reasons. The most publicized use of solids is for elephant hunting when a bullet must penetrate a foot or more of skull in order to reach the brain. A soft point, expanding-type bullet fired into an elephant's skull would, in most instances, simply expand or fragment in the honeycomblike bone structure and never reach the brain. Even body shots at these huge mammals call for hard-coated bullets to penetrate the tough hide and go deep enough to reach the vital organs.

Similarly, full-metal-jacketed bullets are the preferred medicine for Cape buffalo. Whereas soft-pointed bullets may be stopped by the critter's massive bones, a good solid into the shoulder area will bust up enough bone structure to disable or at least slow him down a bit.

Though relatively few American hunters will ever feel the urge to use a "solid" bullet, it is worthwhile to have some understanding of how they perform. That is, an understanding of solids helps us better understand how expanding bullets work because of the contrasts in the way they perform.

First of all, the terminal performance of any bullet depends on how it utilizes the energy that has been imparted to it in the form of velocity. In the case of solids, the idea is for it to penetrate as deeply as possible, regardless of what obstacles lie in the bullet's path. When bullets are broken, or become flattened or otherwise deformed, their

I handloaded this .458 Winchester Magnum cartridge with a 500-grain Hornady steel-jacketed bullet I recovered from an elephant's skull. Even full patch "solids" are rarely recovered in such remarkably undamaged condition. If the opportunity arises, I'll use this "recycled" bullet to bag another elephant or a Cape buffalo.

ability to penetrate is impeded. And that, in a nutshell, explains why the very best solids, such as the steel-jacketed 500-grain Hornady bullets I described earlier, are those that retain their original shape.

On the other end of the performance scale are the expanding or "mushrooming" bullets so familiar to American big-game hunters. Over the decades enormous amounts of time and money have been invested in the development of bullets that will reliably expand upon impact with a big-game animal.

A common misconception among big-game hunters is that we want a bullet to expand so it will punch a bigger hole. This in turn is supposed to cause greater tissue damage and increased blood loss. If, in fact, these were the only reasons for using expanding bullets, we could easily achieve the same effect simply by using large-caliber rifles.

In actual practice, the functioning of an expanding bullet is considerably more complex than is generally realized. For example, a widely held misconception is that an expanding bullet does what it is supposed to do only after it has expanded. Actually, the interval most critical to an expanding bullet's success lasts for only a small fraction of a second and occurs while the bullet is in the process of expanding. This is the period of maximum energy transfer, the moment when a tremendous jolt of energy is delivered to the animal's body tissue as hydrodynamic shock. This is commonly called "knockdown power." By the time the bullet has expanded, or mushroomed, it has lost much of its velocity and the shock effect is much diminished.

Pondering this bit of information, one might conclude that the only trick to making a truly wonderful expanding bullet would be to give it a thin copper jacket that would quickly split or rupture on contact, thereby accelerating the expansion of the lead core.

But it's not nearly so easy as that because if the jacket material is too thin, or easily stripped away, the unprotected lead core will be fragmented by the impact forces. When fragmentation occurs, the terminal efficiency of the bullet is severely reduced. That's why bullet makers seek not to just develop bullets that expand. With even greater fervor they try to invent ways of *controlling* the way their bullets expand. Ideally, a bullet should expand into a mushroom shape two or three times larger than its original diameter without any fragmenting or loss of weight (mass) whatever. In simple terms, a bullet that retains all, or a high percent, of its original weight will penetrate deeper and transfer energy better than a bullet that loses part of its mass.

We know by examining and weighing recovered bullets that many of them lose a lot of their original weight, often as much as 50 percent or more. The fact that the partially fragmented bullets are recovered from successful kills tells us that a technically imperfect bullet can still do a good job. But this also has to make us wonder what percentage of weight loss a bullet can suffer before its effectiveness is severely curtailed. In other words, at what point can we declare that a bullet is not a good one, even when it has been recovered from an animal it has killed?

Before we can deliver a firm opinion on such a weighty matter, let's consider what experience has taught us. Several years ago some ingenious bulletmakers came up with the idea of gluing a bullet's jacket to the lead core. Best known of these bulletmakers is Bill Steigers who handmakes his legendary Bitterroot bullets virtually one at a time. With jacket glued around the core with space age glues, pieces of core will remain attached to the jacket even after it splits and peels back in the classic mushroom pattern. The result of this core-attaching technique resulted in recovered bullets that retained over 90 percent of their original weight. A weight retention of over 95 percent is remarkably good and represents about the best weight retention we can expect in an expanding type bullet. Bitterroot, Bearclaw, and Swift bullets all offer such exceptional weight retention. But they are expensive and available only in a limited range of calibers and weights.

Despite the phenomenal characteristics of these few custom-made, core-bonded bullets, the hunting projectile that has become the standard by which all others are compared is the Nosler Partition bullet. The distinguishing feature of this

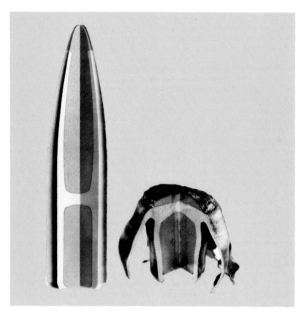

Nosler Partition bullet has a metal-jacket separation between its front and rear parts. Cutaway bullet (above right) shows how rear part remains intact behind the mushroomed front section.

highly successful and much respected bullet is a partition, or divider, near the center of the bullet that divides the core into two sections. The front section is much like other expanding bullets. On impact the front part of the copper jacket splits and peels rearward, exposing a lead core that fragments or mushrooms, or performs a combination of both, depending on impact velocity. The rearward half of the core is almost completely encased in the jacket and thus protected from fragmentation. This means that a certain percentage of the bullet is almost certain to remain intact regardless of the stresses and battering of high-velocity impact.

Back when I was a lot younger and considerably leaner, I spent a couple of years scaling Asian peaks and stalking African plains in search of every sort of huntable critter. I collected upwards of two hundred head of game during this busy time, mostly with 7mm Nosler Partition bullets of 140- and 175-grain weight. I recovered quite a few of these bullets considerably amazed that remaining weight was seldom over 70 percent. Some of the recovered slugs had scarcely more than half their original mass yet their performance had been entirely satisfactory. This led me to the inescapable conclusion that if a bullet is sensibly matched to the game it can shed at least half of its weight and still be considered highly efficient. By "sensibly matched" I'm talking about 140-grain bullets used for game weighing up to 300 and even 400 pounds. Translating these observations into a

typically American hunting situation, it is safe to conclude that a 150-grain bullet from a .308 rifle can lose half its weight and still yield deadly results on whitetail-size game.

A while back I was on a combination pronghorn and mule-deer hunt with a whizz-bang handloader who had concocted a super velocity load with 100-grain hollow-point bullets in his .25/06. He's a good shot and took a nice pronghorn at about 350 yards with a single, well-placed bullet. A couple of days later he took an easy shot at an exceptionally good mule-deer buck at only about 100 yards. Though obviously hit, the buck didn't seem to be seriously hurt and was in the act of making a clean getaway when another hunter in our party stopped him cold with a .270 slug.

That night, when we pulled the deer's hide off, we found that the lightweight thin-jacketed bullet had been blown into tiny fragments on impact. The wound, which was a bloodied mass of tissue as wide as a man's hand, did not extend into the chest cavity deeply enough to do any real damage.

Obviously, the bullet's construction had not been strong enough to withstand the high velocity impact and simply blew apart. Why then did an identical bullet perform well on the pronghorn? Because at the longer range the impact velocity had been considerably less.

Mushrooming of a bullet from a .30/06. Bullets were fired straight down into water with reduced charges to produce mushrooming equivalent to that at 50 yards (left), 150 (center), and 250.

This incident illustrates the main problem facing bulletmakers. Since they cannot predict the range at which their bullets will be fired, they have only an approximate idea of the impact velocities their bullets must withstand. Therefore, the art of making expanding bullets is, to considerable degree, something of an art of compromise.

Distance is enough to worry about on say, a bull elk with a 7mm Super Slammer. But manufacturers also have to fret about making the bullet accurate enough to punch the ace out of a playing card at 300 long paces.

Many of us are still wondering how much the spin of a bullet affects expansion. Tests I'm currently conducting at Briarbank Ballistic Laboratory, *Outdoor Life*'s firearms test facility, will shed new light on this much debated topic.

The CHeetah Mark II: One Hot Wildcat

Layne Simpson

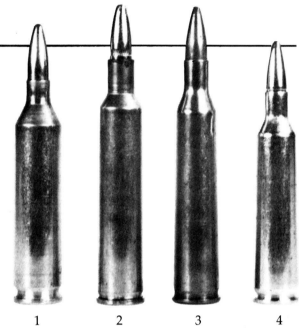

The .22 CHeetah (1) and some of its competitors, including (2) the .220 Weatherby Rocket, (3) the .220 Swift, and (4) the popular .22/250.

One of the many things I love about being a gun writer is the opportunity to keep my finger on the pulse of America's shooters. Mainly, I'm able to do so by digesting letters received from readers and taking note of where their interests lie. This gives me a rather broad overview of which cartridges are hot and which are not. Simply stated, the .22 CHeetah is as hot as a firecracker—and I'm not talking solely about its performance.

To see if what I suspected to be true about the CHeetah was anywhere close to fact, I called Jay Postman of RCBS and asked him about reloading die sales. According to Jay, .22 CHeetah die sales are still far behind those of old-timers like the .22 K-Hornet and .35 Whelen, but the CHeetah is moving up fast. Based on this information, plus the amount of interest I see among our readers, I'd say that with the exception of the introduction of the .220 Swift and .222, and the domestication of the .22/250, the .22 CHeetah has caused more excitement among varmint shooters than any other cartridge of its caliber.

Since its designer and developer, Jim Carmichel, published material about the whys and hows of the CHeetah (CH represents Carmichel and Fred Huntington), I'll move directly into handloading the cartridge. But first, the rifle.

For quite some time I planned to build a rifle in .22 CHeetah, but more pressing business kept the project sitting on the back burner. Eventually, there came a time when reader questions about the cartridge became so frequent, I started planning what action, barrel, and stock I would use in putting together a rifle for the big .22. Even before I decided which gunsmith would do the work, Jim Carmichel graciously offered the loan of one of his rifles; so the .22 CHeetah project started picking up speed.

The rifle used for developing load data was a Remington 40X single-shot action sitting in its factory stock. The barrel was a heavy, stainless steel Hart, 27 inches long, with a rifling pitch of one turn in 16½ inches. After wringing out the cartridge, I didn't mind returning the rifle, but I sure would like to have horse-traded the scope from Jim. It was one of those massive but beautiful Bausch & Lomb BALvar 24s. In case you're too young to remember that one, it's a 6–24× variable made from 1950 until 1969 or so. Looking into that big chunk of steel and glass sure took me back to more innocent times.

The rifle was chambered for the .22 CHeetah Mark II, with a 28-degree shoulder angle. I don't know how it compares in capacity with its Mark I mate with the 40-degree shoulder, but I suspect any difference between the two is in favor of the Mark II.

Basically, the .22 CHeetah is a necked down, blown out Remington BR case. Either of two methods can be used to form cases: the hard way or the easy way. First, I tried the hard way by

This article first appeared in The Handloader

running some .308 basic cases through a .308 Winchester full-length resizing die. That trued up their mouths. Then I continued necking down with 7mm/08, .243, and .22 CHeetah sizing dies, in that order. It didn't work. Due to extremely thin brass in the shoulder area, 9 out of 10 cases collapsed. I added a fourth step by using a 6.5/308 sizer die between the 7mm/08 and .243 dies. That helped but case loss still ran about 10 percent, and the formed cases were anything but pretty.

When CHeetah cases are formed that way, each sizing die leaves a small, additional shoulder. Once the case is fireformed, the ripples disappear, of course. Even so, it's unlikely that the average handloader would have .308, 7mm/08, 6.5/08, .243 and .22 CHeetah resizing dies in his inventory; so I believe it's best to go ahead and take the plunge with RCBS forming dies.

The RCBS set has two forming dies, a trim die, a reamer, and a neck reamer die. If, like me, you prefer to turn case necks, a few dollars could be saved by ordering the die set without the neck reamer die and its reamer. In addition, those who have case trimmers could get by with nothing more than forming dies Numbers One and Two, along with a full-length resizer and bullet seater dies.

Before I leave the subject of case forming, I should mention that when the cases emerge from

Although Remington discontinued the basic BR case in favor of the 7mm BR, Sako-made .308 cases with small primer pockets are now available.

their final forming die, the inside diameters of their necks won't allow entry of the case trimmer and outside neck turning pilots. Since I never ream case necks, I have a set of case neck expanders of various calibers. My expander for .224 caliber cartridges opens up the neck for an easy but snug fit with standard diameter turning and trimming pilots. After the CHeetah necks were ex-

Test rifle combined Rem. 40X single-shot action with 27-inch Hart barrel and BALvar 6–24× variable scope.

To form a .22 CHeetah case the hard way, run the BR Basic case through 7mm/08, 6.5/08, .243 Winchester, and .22 CHeetah full-length resizing dies. The wrinkles in the shoulder (center case) will disappear when the case is fireformed (right).

panded, I turned them down to an outside diameter of .248 inch (with a .2239-inch bullet seated). That allowed a neck expansion of .002 inch in the chamber. In case you're interested, the custom neck expanders and the neck turning tool I used are available from Jarrett Rifles, Inc., Rte. 1 Box 411, Cowden Plantation, Jackson, SC 29831.

After all cases were formed, trimmed, and neck turned, I loaded 39.0 grains of IMR–4064 behind some 50-grain bullets and fireformed them in the CHeetah chamber. Out popped cases with an average weight of 158.2 grains, including the spent primer. Gross water capacity of full-length, resized cases, filled to the brim, averaged 54.6 grains with an incredible .3-grain variation in capacity. That is good brass!

I decided to see how the CHeetah's boiler room capacity compared with that of the three other .22s. Remington .22/250 cases averaged 157.8 grains with a water capacity of 45.3 grains, or 9.3 grains less than that of the CHeetah. Winchester .220 Swift cases averaged 165.4 grains with a water capacity of 49.1 grains. The same lot of Swift brass blown out in my .220 Rocket Weatherby held 53.4 grains of water, giving 97.8 percent of the CHeetah's capacity.

This is a good place to mention that the objective in creating the CHeetah was not to gain a substantial increase in powder capacity over that of existing cases. Instead, Jim's thinking was to combine the latest ideas from two different worlds into one compact package. What we have in the CHeetah might best be described as a varmint cartridge built by a benchrest shooter. In fact, the Mark II version could also be described as a stretched version of the Remington .22 BR car-

tridge, replete with small primer pocket, short fat case, and short neck.

My father once told me that the only thing worse than borrowing another man's rifle is borrowing another man's rifle and not returning it to him promptly. I'll have to confess to violating both good-neighbor laws. I worked with the CHeetah off and on for close to a year, mainly to delve into the capabilities of small rifle primers in igniting large charges of powder under various conditions. I learned a thing or two, but unfortunately if I included it all here, there would be room for little else. That being the case, I'll simply hit the high spots, those which handloaders who are yearning for a CHeetah should keep in mind.

Rule number one for living happily ever after with the CHeetah is (with one exception): any propellant that will not fill at least 90 percent of the case will, at one time or another, absolutely give you fits. Maybe not this afternoon, maybe not next week, but you can bet lunch money that if this rule is broken, you will eventually regret it. For reliable and uniform ignition with most propellants, the rear of the charge must rest against the flash hole when the primer fires. Anything less and the cartridge will be plagued with hangfires and misfires. Let me give an example of what I'm talking about.

You might note that I have included load data for RL–12 with a 50-grain bullet, but not for a 55-grain bullet. The maximum load I settled on with the 50-grain bullet filled 80 percent of the case. That load works fine until ambient temperature drops below 50°F or so, at which point erratic ignition and hangfires tend to disrupt your concentration on the target. On the other hand, I experienced no ignition problems with the load at more typical groundhog-shooting temperatures.

With the 55-grain bullet, a maximum charge of RL–12 decreased load density to 76 percent and increased hangfires to 100 percent, even at temperatures as high as 96°F. Consequently, I did not include that load in the data chart.

Contrary to what many handloaders think, the burning rate of a powder does not always indicate its ignition characteristics. One might assume, for example, that since IMR–4350 is a slower burning powder than IMR–4064, it would take more spark to ignite it. In my experience, that does not hold true—at least not in the CHeetah. I tried every available small rifle primer behind 100-percent density loads of four different lots of both powders at various temperatures and experienced no hangfires with IMR–4350 so long as the temperature was above 40 degrees or so. I did, however, reach a point with IMR–4350 where an increase in charge weight yielded little to no gain in velocity. By way of contrast, two lots of IMR–4064 were plagued with hangfires even when the mercury was hovering in the 90s; yet when the right primer was used, two other lots ignited uniformly at temperatures close to freezing.

I tried every spherical powder that could be loaded to 90 percent or greater density but only H–380 proved satisfactory. In fact, H–380, along with the next propellant I'll discuss, produced the best accuracy with the fewest ignition problems of all powders tried. That includes ball and stick powders. Ignition characteristics of H–380 came as somewhat of a surprise. Before I tried it, I had doubts about small rifle primers being able to set off such large charges with any degree of ignition uniformity. Every .22 CHeetah shooter should have a supply of this powder sitting on the shelf.

When everything is taken into consideration, including accuracy, bore fouling and ease of ignition with small rifle primers, IMR–4320 is the single best propellant for the .22 CHeetah. Something else I like about this powder in the CHeetah is its progressive and predictable increase in chamber pressures as the charge is increased. Even when boosting charges beyond those listed, there was no sudden skyrocketing of chamber pressures.

IMR–4320 is the only powder that would ignite when loaded to extremely low density. I reduced some charges down to 70 percent density with the Remington 7½ primer and experienced no ignition problems at temperatures as low as 40F°. However, I found that to be true only when using two of the various primers tried.

Based on my experiences with various powders in the .22 CHeetah, the only primers I can recommend for the cartridge are the Remington 7½ and CCI 450 Magnum. When using the CCI BR–4 and Federal 205M benchrest primers behind the five powders loaded to 100 percent density, I experienced 100 percent misfires with IMR–4064 and RL–12 and up to 80 percent hangfires with IMR–4350, IMR–4320 and H–380—at an average temperature of 96°F too. I won't elaborate on the other primers I worked with simply because none I tried did the job as well as those from CCI and Remington.

One last comment on primers. The ignition

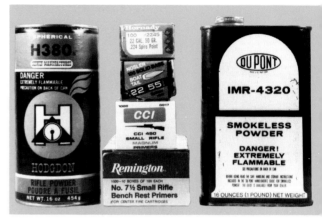

Author's choice of powders and primers for loading the .22 CHeetah include H–380, Remington 7½, CCI 450 Magnum, and IMR-4320.

problems under discussion are an inherent characteristic of the .22 CHeetah cartridge, not the fault of primers that wouldn't work. It should go without saying that we are simply asking small rifle primers to do something they were not designed to do. When combined with the right powder, Remington 7½ and CCI 450 primers solved the ignition problems, not because they are necessarily superior to other primers but because they are hotter.

Those who have already worked with the .22 CHeetah may be puzzled by the velocities I have listed. One of my criteria for any varmint cartridge has to do with case life. Any load that generates chamber pressures so high that cases cannot be loaded at least 12 times is considered excessive. Although I was able to reach 4,200 fps (feet per second) with 50-grain, and 4,100 fps with 55-grain bullets, case life decreased to five firings. That may be the fault of the rifle rather than the cartridge, of course.

A groundhog shooting pal of mine bought a Model 700 with a heavy barrel in .22/250 and had its chamber reamed out to accept the .22 CHeetah Mark II. His rifle will digest heavier powder charges than the 40X, and case life is entirely ac-

Mating a Small Rifle primer to the BR Basic case (left) enhances accuracy, but experience has revealed that under certain circumstances ignition can be a problem. A misfired bullet (right) has been pulled apart to show that a full-density load of IMR–4064 has not even been scorched by a CCI BR–4 primer.

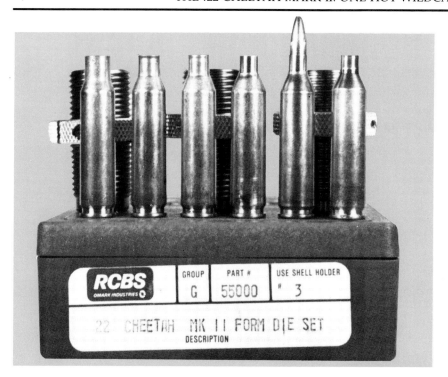

An easier way to form .22 CHeetah cases is to employ a form-die set from RCBS: The BR Basic case is first forced into two forming dies and a trim die. It is then neck-turned and fireformed.

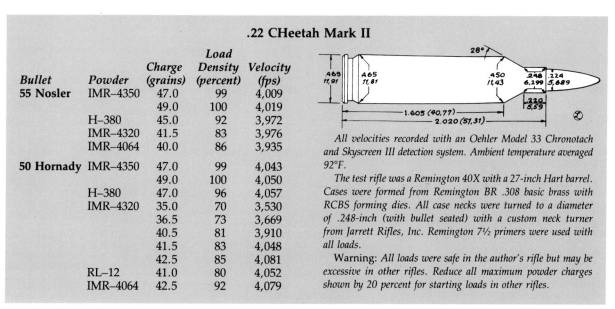

.22 CHeetah Mark II

Bullet	Powder	Charge (grains)	Load Density (percent)	Velocity (fps)
55 Nosler	IMR–4350	47.0	99	4,009
		49.0	100	4,019
	H–380	45.0	92	3,972
	IMR–4320	41.5	83	3,976
	IMR–4064	40.0	86	3,935
50 Hornady	IMR–4350	47.0	99	4,043
		49.0	100	4,050
	H–380	47.0	96	4,057
	IMR–4320	35.0	70	3,530
		36.5	73	3,669
		40.5	81	3,910
		41.5	83	4,048
		42.5	85	4,081
	RL–12	41.0	80	4,052
	IMR–4064	42.5	92	4,079

All velocities recorded with an Oehler Model 33 Chronotach and Skyscreen III detection system. Ambient temperature averaged 92°F.

The test rifle was a Remington 40X with a 27-inch Hart barrel. Cases were formed from Remington BR .308 basic brass with RCBS forming dies. All case necks were turned to a diameter of .248-inch (with bullet seated) with a custom neck turner from Jarrett Rifles, Inc. Remington 7½ primers were used with all loads.

Warning: All loads were safe in the author's rifle but may be excessive in other rifles. Reduce all maximum powder charges shown by 20 percent for starting loads in other rifles.

ceptable. Interestingly enough, even with its shorter barrel and quicker rifling twist, his rifle zips both bullet weights out the muzzle from 100 to 125 fps faster than the 40X did. As a note of interest, his rechambered 700 averages .568 inch for five-shot groups with loads consisting of Remington 7½ primers, IMR–4320 and 55-grain bullets from Hornady and Nosler. Practically every bullet he has tried averaged less than .750 inch.

The 40X was also extremely accurate with some loads. No load based on IMR–4350 or RL–12 broke the .600-inch barrier, even when using various custom benchrest quality bullets. With the two best lots of IMR–4064, accuracy with several mass-produced bullets snuggled close to ½ minute of angle. When it came to serious business though, IMR–4320 and H–380 had no peer. Nosler, Hornady, and Sierra bullets of 50, 52, 53, and 55 grains consistently shot into less than ½ minute of angle, with individual groups measuring from .350 to .484 inch. Groups fired with Remington 52-grain benchrest bullets ranged from .296 to .324 inch. Who says the big .22s won't shoot?

The .338 Winchester Magnum

Finn Aagaard

Of all the belted magnum cartridges that have appeared since WWII, the 7mm Remington Magnum is undoubtedly the most popular. The most useful of them, however, might well be the .338 Winchester Magnum, which excepting the phenomenal .458 Winchester Magnum and the semi-proprietary Weatherby cartridges is also the only postwar magnum cartridge over .30 caliber that is still a going concern.

The failure of the potentially great .358 Norma Magnum, the 8mm Remington Magnum, or even of the little nonmagnum .350 Remington Magnum may puzzle and sadden us, but there are good reasons for the modest success the .338 Magnum has enjoyed. One may guess that the Winchester creation filled the slot between the .30 caliber magnums and the ancient but still renowned .375 H&H so adequately that there simply was no room for another cartridge to grow there. For all big-game hunting purposes, the .338 Magnum matches anything its competitors could do, and it was there first.

Winchester developed the cartridge by necking down its 2½-inch-long .458 Magnum case to hold .338 inch diameter bullets. They gave it the same 25° shoulder angle that was subsequently employed by the .264 Winchester and 7mm Remington Magnum. Why they chose .33 caliber rather than .35 is unknown to me, but possibly the excellent reputation held by the wildcat .333 OKH Belted in those days had something to do with it. Also, .338 bullets have better sectional densities than those of the same weight in .358 inch diameter. To equal the 250-grain .338 bullet's sectional density of .313, a .358 bullet would have to weigh 281 grains, for example. All else being equal, the heavier the bullet, the greater the recoil.

The only other standard American .33 caliber cartridge was the rimmed .33 Winchester designed early in the century for the 1886 lever-action rifle. It used bullets of .338 inch diameter, rather than the .333 inch common to the OKH cartridges and

This article first appeared in American Rifleman

Aagaard favors the .338 only where really heavy bullets are advisable. He took his 6 × 6 elk in British Columbia's Muskwa River region. The Mauser 98 rifle has since swapped its walnut stock for one of fiberglass.

the British .333 Jeffery, and the .338 Winchester Magnum followed suit.

The .338 Magnum was first available with a 200-grain Power-Point bullet at a listed 3000 fps (feet per second). Muzzle velocity and a 250-grain Silvertip at 2700 fps. Later, a 300-grain Power-Point at a claimed 2450 fps was added. In its 1986 catalog, Winchester listed only the 200-grain Power-Point at 2960 fps and a 225-grain spitzer soft-point bullet at 2780 fps.

Remington offered neither rifles nor ammunition in .338 until 1987. Not only was the annual limited edition Model 700 Classic made for 1987 in .338 Winchester, Remington's Custom Shop also chambered for the round. Additionally, Remington offered two .338 loads, one with a 225-grain Hornady bullet that starts at 2780 fps, and a 250-grain Speer Grand Slam bullet load with an initial velocity of 2660 fps.

Until recently Federal had only one loading, with the 210-grain Nosler Partition bullet at 2830 fps. Recently, though, Federal announced the addition of a load employing the 250-grain Nosler Partition bullet at 2660 fps.

Besides Nosler, all our other major bullet makers also offer .338 bullets. Hornady has 200- and 225-grain Spire-Points, a flat-nosed 200-grain softpoint for the .33 Winchester, and a roundnosed 250-grain soft-point. Hornady once made 250-grain roundnosed, full-metal-jacket solids for use on thick-skinned African heavyweights like elephant and rhino, but it no longer does so. Sierra

These cartridges were used for the .338 ballistics comparisons that are shown below.

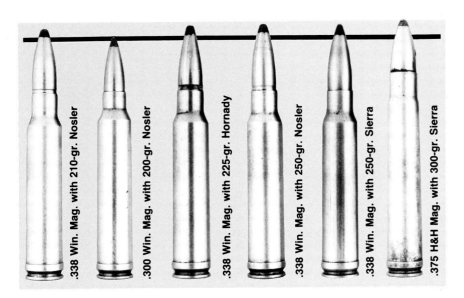

.338 Win. Mag. with 210-gr. Nosler | .300 Win. Mag. with 200-gr. Nosler | .338 Win. Mag. with 225-gr. Hornady | .338 Win. Mag. with 250-gr. Nosler | .338 Win. Mag. with 250-gr. Sierra | .375 H&H Mag. with 300-gr. Sierra

.338 WINCHESTER MAGNUM BALLISTIC COMPARISONS

Cartridge/Bullet Type		Range 0	100	200	(Yds.) 300	400
.338 Win. Mag. 210-gr. Nosler Part.	Velocity (f.p.s.)	2900	2653	2419	2199	1994
Sect. Density .263	Energy (ft.-lbs.)	(3923)	(3283)	(2729)	(2255)	(1854)
Ballis. Coef. .386	Trajectory (ins.)	−1.5	+2.9	+2.4	−4	−17.5
.300 Win. Mag. 200-gr. Nosler Part.	Velocity (f.p.s.)	2850	2687	2579	2378	2234
Sect. Density .301	Energy (ft.-lbs.)	(3609)	(3208)	(2843)	(2514)	(2217)
Ballis. Coef. .585	Trajectory (ins.)	−1.5	+2.8	+2.3	−3.7	−16
.338 Win. Mag. 225-gr. Win. Factory	Velocity (f.p.s.)	2780	2572	2374	2184	2003
	Energy (ft.-lbs.)	(3862)	(3306)	(2816)	(2384)	(2005)
	Trajectory (ins.)	−1.5	+3.2	+2.5	−4.2	−18.5
.338 Win. Mag. 250-gr. Nosler Part.	Velocity (f.p.s.)	2700	2517	2340	2170	2007
Sect. Density .313	Energy (ft.-lbs.)	(4047)	(3515)	(3040)	(2612)	(2237)
Ballis. Coef. .491	Trajectory (ins.)	−1.5	+3.3	+2.7	−4.3	−19
.338 Win. Mag. 250-gr. Sierra Boattail	Velocity (f.p.s.)	2700	2550	2405	2264	2129
Sect. Density .313	Energy (ft.-lbs.)	(4047)	(3609)	(3210)	(2846)	(2515)
Ballis. Coef. .587	Trajectory (ins.)	−1.5	+3.2	+2.6	−4	−17.5
.375 H&H Mag. 300-gr. Sierra Boattail	Velocity (f.p.s.)	2550	2401	2257	2118	1985
Sect. Density .305	Energy (ft.-lbs.)	(4332)	(3841)	(3395)	(2990)	(2624)
Ballis. Coef. .468	Trajectory (ins.)	−1.5	+3	+1.5	−6.8	−23

Trajectories based upon 250-yd. zeroes for all but the .375 H&H, calculated on a 225-yd. zero. Data approximate only and based upon various industry catalogs and Philip Mannes' "Tables of Bullet Performance." Trajectories are in inches above or below the line of sight.

makes only one .338 bullet, a superbly shaped 250-grain spitzer boattail. Speer has a conventional 200-grain spitzer and the premium-grade 250-grain Grand Slam. It also offers the 275-grain semi-spitzer with a sectional density of .348 that used to be Elmer Keith's favorite bullet in this caliber. In addition to 210- and 250-grain bullets, Barnes Bullets, Inc., (P.O. Box 215, American Fork, UT 84003) has 300-grain roundnosed soft-points and solids (sectional density .375!), and can provide .333 inch bullets as well.

Magazine editor Col. Charles Askins took a preproduction .338 Winchester Magnum to East Africa in 1957 or 1958. He wrote an interesting account of its performance with 250-grain Silver-tips on 19 animals ranging in size from little gazelles and a leopard, to tough zebra and oryx, and up to a moose-size eland. Thirteen of them required only one shot, and Askins declared that the new cartridge "performed admirably."

Kenneth Waters reported shooting a whitetail buck at 110 paces with the 200-grain Winchester factory load. Despite passing through a 1½-inch thick tree limb before reaching the deer, the bullet did not expand too violently, and it dropped the animal where it stood with less meat damage than a .270 Winchester round might have caused.

The .338 Magnum was soon hailed by many as the best all-around cartridge for this continent's larger beasts, just the thing for elk, moose, and big grizzly bears. I was curious to watch one do its stuff, but because Kenya's game regulations declared that nothing less than a .375 H&H was legal on dangerous game, most of my clients chose to bring the old Hollands' cartridge.

Finally, in 1976, Bill Zybura came on a two-week hunt with just one rifle, a .338 Winchester Magnum. His ammunition was handloaded with 250-grain Nosler Partition bullets, and I agreed to let him use it on buffalo, provided I could collaborate with a .458 as backup.

We started the safari in the high, cool forest of the Loita Hills, which are full of buffalo, colobus monkeys, bushbuck, turacos, and stinging nettles. Walking back along a ridgetop towards the Toyota right at dusk the first evening, I saw a bushbuck. As soon as I had glimpsed its horns I commanded: "Shoot that bushbuck! No, not the one against the sky on top of the rock, the one in the shadows below it." Zybura was not too sure which end was which, so he shot it more or less in the middle. I don't recommend that, but the big bullet put it down well enough this time. The horns were long enough to have qualified for Rowland Ward's *Records of Big Game.*

Several days later we ambushed a small herd of buffalo as they came out into a glade. Zybura shot a fair-average sort of bull, the best in the bunch. He hit it three times in the chest from about 50 yards, the first shot having pretty much anchored it. We discovered that the first shot had entered just behind one shoulder, where it broke the very heavy upper leg bone just below the shoulder joint. I was impressed! None of the Noslers exited. We found all just under the skin on the far side, expanded back to the partition.

The next morning we came upon a very big lone buffalo bull in thick timber. As he had a second buffalo tag, Zybura decided to take it. The bull was turned partly away from us, so he shot it some ways behind the near shoulder. It immediately swung around to face us, as if it meant to come over and flatten us for our impudence. I slammed a .458 bullet into it, which stopped it long enough to allow Zybura to finish it off. We were not able to ascertain exactly what Zybura's shot had done, and one cannot reach any firm conclusions from the taking of just two animals. But my impression was that the .338 Magnum seemed to thump the buffalo only a little less hard than a .375 would have done.

Zybura took eight other gazelle and antelope with the 250-grain Noslers, and as Askins had found with Silvertips of a like weight, they performed admirably in the field.

Some months later, the same year, Dunlop Farren also brought a .338 to Kenya for his safari. He had hunted with the rifle for 16 years, and besides probably 40 whitetail and 7 or 8 mule deer, he had used it to take a huge 52-inch 7×7 trophy elk at extremely long range across an open "park" in Alberta. Shooting from prone, he tried to hold 18 inches over its back. The bull stumbled forward one step, and stood, so he gave it another, at which it turned to face him. He put his third shot into the center of the chest, and that was it.

Farren was using 210-grain Nosler Partition bullets. The first two wrecked the elk's lungs and penetrated through the far side ribs, while the path of the third was traced into the paunch, where it was lost. The range? Well, the rifle was sighted for 300 yards, and the bullets had dropped at least 30 inches below the point of aim, so it was a considerable distance. Too far, it may be said, but Farren is one of the best game shots I know.

He used a .416 on his buffalo, but took nine head of lesser game, including Grant's gazelle, an ostrich, another record-book bushbuck, oryx, and an eland with the .338 Winchester Magnum. We recovered only one of his 210-grain Noslers, from a coup-de-grace shot on the oryx. All the rest gave complete penetration, even on the eland.

A few years ago I put together a .338 Winchester Magnum for myself, using a Mauser M98 action and a 24-inch Douglas barrel. For a long time it had one of Fajen's inexpensive Rebel walnut stocks, but eventually I decided that a serious, rough-country big-game rifle such as this one

Now fitted with a fiberglass stock, Aagaard's .338 has proved to be very effective on big game.

needed a fiberglass stock. Steve Sharpe, who operates Bear Creek Custom Rifles (106 East Texas St., Grapevine, TX 76051), claims to put a superior finish on his stocks, so I sent the rifle to him.

Many replacement fiberglass stocks have a wrinkle spray-can paint job that is easily scraped off and needs to be redone after every hunt. Sharpe says he textures his stocks with epoxy before applying a superior quality paint, and thus gets a very durable finish. His stocks are foam-filled in the forend and buttstock, but are solid fiberglass through the action area, so that the receiver is firmly supported without any tendency to bend or twist as the action screws are drawn up. It should be an extremely stable stock that will promote good accuracy and help the rifle maintain its zero.

I ordered Sharpe's classic stock, which with its trim lines, its slender pistol grip with quite an open curve, and its high, straight comb handles very nicely for me. It was painted a light gray (camouflage and other colors are available) over a textured finish that gave a good grip without being overdone. Apart from the free-floated barrel, the stock fits the metal closely with no visible gaps, and the bedding is precisely done.

With a matte-finish Leupold 4× scope and three rounds in its magazine, the rifle weighs a very portable 8 pounds. It kicks more than, say, a .30/06, but when it is held as firmly as a rifle of this nature should be held, its recoil is entirely innocuous in the field, and is quite tolerable for five-shot strings at the shooting bench.

I lent the .338 Magnum to Ron Murdock for our elk hunting this past season. It came through a wet hunt on foot in quite rugged country, where it was dragged through the alders, banged against branches, and rubbed against backpacks, without suffering a single blemish to the stock finish.

Murdock used 250-grain Nosler Partition bullets loaded up to about 2680 fps. He was in thick stuff near the bottom of a deep canyon when a glint of ivory caught his eye, and he saw a 5×4 bull 40 yards away standing on a trail and swinging its head about. Murdock shot it close behind the shoulder. The Nosler put a 3-inch hole into the rib cage, a much larger one through the lungs, tore open the top of the heart, and went out just in front of the opposite shoulder. The bull ran perhaps 20 yards the way it was pointed, turned downhill, fell, and slid down the steep slope until it came to rest against a tree with all four feet in the air, ready to be field dressed.

Another friend had previously taken two Canadian moose with this rifle, and I have used it on a 6×6 bull elk and on two whitetail deer. I killed one of the deer with a .33 Winchester-equivalent load, using Hornady's 200-grain flat-nose bullet at approximately 2200 fps. The small spike buck was hit a touch far back from about 80 yards, but the slow-moving bullet still made a mess of the rear lobes of both lungs. The buck ran 60 paces, but left a good blood trail and was dead when he was found.

Everything else killed with this rifle has been taken with Nosler 250-grain Partition bullets at about 2700 fps, which is my standard use-it-on-anything load in the .338 Winchester Magnum.

A lot of fellows, including Dunlop Farren, have enjoyed great success with 200-grain, or 210-grain bullets, and see no need for heavier projectiles. My own feeling is that if I am going to use 200-grain bullets, I would prefer to do so in a .300 Magnum, where they will have a greater sectional density and a far better ballistic coefficient to allow them to deliver more energy at long range.

The only reason for choosing a .338 caliber cartridge over a .300 Magnum is to obtain the enhanced stopping power its heavier bullets are thought to provide on the largest game. When it comes to lighter bullets, most of the advantages lie with the smaller caliber.

Nevertheless, if a .338 is one's only big rifle, then there are many situations where 200- or 210-grain bullets might be the optimum choice. I have no experience on game with 225-grain bullets, but they could well be the best compromise for an all-around load in this cartridge.

Formerly the 250-grain Nosler Partition bullet had a round nose, causing it to lose velocity rather quickly, and giving it quite a curved trajectory compared to the 210-grain Nosler. This is no longer the case; the present 250-grain Partition

.338 WINCHESTER MAGNUM HANDLOADS

Bullet (grs./type)	Powder Type	Powder Charge (grs.)	Velocity (fps)
210 Nosler Partition	IMR 4350	73.0	2894
" " "	IMR 4831	75.0	2857
225 Hornady Spire Point	IMR 4350	72.0	2855
250 Nosler Partition	IMR 4350	70.0	2701
" " "	IMR 4831	72.0	2684
275 Speer Semi-Spitzer	IMR 4350	68.0	2551
" " "	IMR 4831	71.0	2605

Reduce all beginning loads 10% and work up, watching for pressure signs. Particular caution should be used in loading for the .338 Winchester Magnum as there is considerable disparity in published data. The loads listed were under maximum in the author's rifle, which is long throated, but could be excessive in others. Cartridge overall length 3.38" imposed by Mauser magazine length. All cases Winchester and primers Winchester 120 Large Rifle.

bullet is of spitzer form and has as flat a trajectory for all practical purposes as the lighter one. The prime projectile for long-range shooting with a .338 Magnum is most likely Sierra's streamlined 250-grain spitzer boattail.

The capacity of the .338 Winchester Magnum case is such that powders like IMR 4350 and IMR 4831 give good results with most bullet weights. Hodgdon's H4831 is a touch on the slow side—I could not get enough of it into the case to produce other than modest velocities, even with the 275-grain bullet. Du Pont's IMR 4831 did well with this heavy Speer bullet, but otherwise I got the best accuracy with IMR 4350 powder. A very accurate load in my rifle is the 250-grain Nosler with 70 grains of IMR 4350. It averages close to 1¼ inches extreme spread for five-shot groups at 100 yards from the bench. (Warning: this load is close to maximum, and it may be excessive in some rifles.)

Debating the best all-around single cartridge for American big game is a favorite pastime of gun writers. It allows us to display our erudition with soaring arguments that need seldom touch down on the hard ground of reality. Although great fun, it is rather a silly game.

Nevertheless, I'll play it briefly. If I could have but one rifle for all my big-game hunting, it would not under my present circumstances be a .338 Magnum. The great preponderance of my hunting involves deer, pronghorn, hogs, and exotic game of similar size, with only an occasional foray for elk, and possibly for moose and caribou. Thus a .30/06 with suitable handloads would be sufficient.

But if I lived where I could hunt elk and moose as often as deer, or where grizzly or brown bears were definitely a factor to be reckoned with, then a .338 Winchester Magnum would be my choice. I would most probably load 200-grain bullets down to around 2300-2400 fps for whitetail in the brush. I might use 220- or 225-grain spitzers at full velocity for pronghorn and open-country mule

deer, but in practice I believe I would tend to use 250-grain Partition bullets on everything.

A superior, but expensive, alternative to the Noslers for some purposes would be the Trophy Bonded Core bullets that Jack Carter turns out (P.O. Box 262348, Houston, TX 77207). They expand to a greater diameter than any other bullets I am familiar with, but typically retain 90 percent of their original weight and give deep penetration (though not quite as deep as do Noslers).

In any event, a two-rifle battery for all North American big game is a much more realistic concept. Two rifles could indeed handle it all. The smaller one might be anything from a 6mm or a .257 Roberts on up to a 7mm Magnum or a .30/06. I would take a 7×57mm Mauser or a 7mm/08 myself, but from a purely pragmatic point of view the .270 Winchester would seem to be the best choice. A lightweight .270 with a 22-inch barrel works as well in deer cover as it does on a pronghorn prairie or a sheep mountain, and it's plenty enough gun for anything up to and including caribou (and the medium-size African antelope and zebra).

For the very largest game, cartridges like the .375 H&H and the .340 Weatherby Magnum do have advantages. Brown bear guides like them, I am told, though some of them prefer the .458 Winchester Magnum. But these are generally large and heavy pieces, and they do kick. In contrast, it is my observation that after a little practice the majority of hunters can become well enough accustomed to the recoil of a .338 Magnum to do good work with it.

Stopping power on large or dangerous game derives far more from bullet placement than from any other factor—hitting the right spot is the secret to staying out of trouble. Therefore the old axiom that for such beasts one should use the most powerful rifle *he can shoot well* is still sound advice. For most of us the .338 probably comes closer to the ideal than any other cartridge.

PART EIGHT

GUNSMITHING AND MAINTENANCE

Scope Mounting Made Easy

Bob Milek

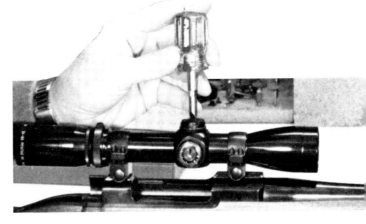

Mounting a rifle scope at home is actually an easy operation if you are set up for it. You should have a sturdy workbench and a good vise with blocks to prevent scratching your rifle.

When you get right down to it, the rifle scope sight is one pretty rugged piece of equipment. The same scope that holds together under the mild recoil of a .223 Remington will take the pounding of a .338 Winchester Magnum in stride. But it's not just recoil that it must stand up to. Hunters are notoriously rough on equipment. The scope sizzles in the hot sun, freezes in winter, and drowns in rain and wet snow. It's banged against rocks and trees, slammed on the ground, and mashed under the bulk of a spooked horse frantically writhing to regain its feet. Through all of this a good scope keeps right on working and we shooters get to taking it for granted. Sure, some scopes fail, but by and large they provide service all out of proportion to their cost.

However, when a scope does fail in the field, it can be a costly failure, bringing an expensive hunt to an abrupt end. The trouble with most scope failures is that the shooter seldom realizes that anything's wrong until he's ready to shoot or has missed a shot. Even then it's not always apparent that the scope is out of whack. Often it takes several missed shots before the shooter even

thinks of checking to see if the scope is all right.

It's been my experience that most scope failures are the result of a poor mounting job, not of mechanical failure in the scope itself. Production rifles available today come right from the factory with provisions for scope mounting—either with the receiver drilled and tapped to accept a scope mount or milled to accept rings of the manufacturer's own design. The receivers on Ruger's rifles are milled to accept Ruger rings and a set of rings is provided with the rifle. Sako receivers have special rails that accept the company's own rings. Other rifles will have rails integral with the top

This article first appeared in Guns & Ammo

Receivers on Ruger bolt-action rifles are machined at the factory to accept Ruger rings. Rings are furnished with the rifle and can be installed easily. Installation requires only a screwdriver.

of the receiver so that a variety of rings can be clamped on. Whatever the system, it's a far cry from the days when every rifle receiver had to be drilled and tapped before a scope mount could be attached. These days only military surplus rifles and those vintage sporter models require drilling and tapping to facilitate scope mounting. Should your rifle be one of these, take it to a competent gunsmith and have the drilling job done right.

This article, though, is intended to help those thousands of shooters who each year mount scopes on rifles already drilled and tapped or otherwise set up at the factory for scope mounting. So what's to know? You screw the base onto the rifle, secure the rings to the base and clamp the scope in the rings. It's no big deal. Don't you believe it! Even as convenient as scope mounting is today, there are a lot of tricks to the job that save you time, money, *and* failure. With this in mind, let's run through the job of mounting a scope and see just what is involved.

The job begins before you buy your scope and

mount. First you must decide which scope you want on the rifle. Will it be a full-size scope or one of the compact designs that are becoming so popular? Will it be of fixed or variable power? I'm not going to try and tell you what to buy or which one will do the best job. That's a completely different subject. All I'm saying is that it's important that you make this decision *before* you purchase a mount.

Why? Because the mount system you choose is dependent to some degree on the dimensions of the scope. If your rifle has a long action, it's likely that bases with standard ring spacing won't accept compact scopes or any scope with a short body tube. The rings will be spaced so far apart that only one ring will fit on the body of the scope. The other will be positioned where it falls around the larger eyepiece or objective bell. This won't work. What's needed is a mount with an extension, usually up front, that extends back over the cutout in the receiver, thus placing the rings closer together. This is accomplished in one of two ways depending on the mount manufacturer. Some make the extension provision in the base, others make a special ring that extends rearward. Both systems work. The important thing is that you be aware of the need for an extension base or ring before you buy the mount system.

Another thing you need to know about your scope before you buy the mount is the diameter of both the objective lens and the eyepiece. Most rings are available in three heights—low, medium, and high. If the scope you select has a rather large objective, it probably can't be used with low rings because the objective will touch the barrel and prevent the tube from seating in the ring. As a general rule, most fixed-power scopes up through 6× magnification as well as all compact scopes will have an objective small enough to use with low rings. A good share of the variable-power

Top left: This is what happens when you try to mount a short-bodied scope onto a long-action rifle using mounts with standard ring spacing. Bottom: The EAW scope-mounting system is one of the finest quick-detachable mounts on the market. The mount shown utilizes a front extension.

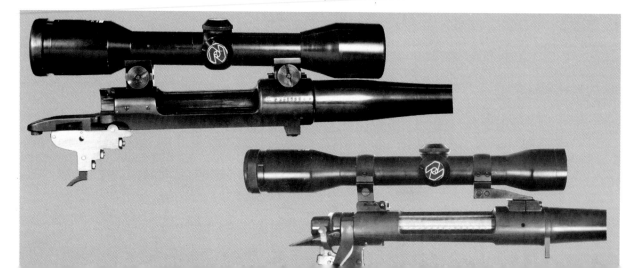

Top: When proper ring height is selected, there will be some clearance between the barrel and the scope objective. Bottom: Low rings cannot be used with a scope that has a large objective because the objective touches the barrel.

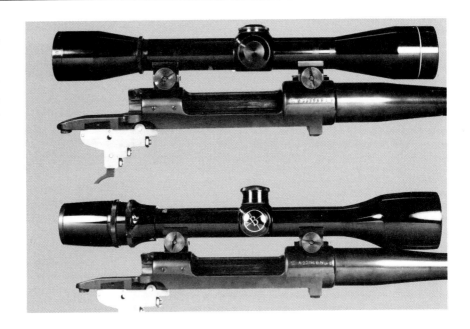

scopes intended for big-game hunting have objectives that work in medium height rings, while most varmint scopes require the use of high rings. This is a generalization, or course, and you'll find exceptions. The only way to be sure of getting the correct ring height is to know the objective diameter of your scope. Mount the scope as low as possible, but be sure there is clearance between the objective and the barrel.

It's also possible that, because of the angle of the bolt handle on a particular rifle, a medium, or high, ring system is required to allow the handle to clear the eyepiece when it's raised. This is particularly true on sporterized military rifles whose bolt was bent in the customizing job. It's seldom a problem with modern production sporters, but again there are exceptions to the rule.

Once you know what's required in the way of mounts, you must decide which particular style and make you want. Again, I'm not going to try to tell you which is best for what purpose. I personally believe that most of the mount systems sold today are excellent. However, there is one situation where you have to really give the matter some extra consideration. This is when you intend to scope a rifle so that you can remove the scope quickly and use the open sights and then replace the scope so it can be used again. This requires a mount that allows quick, easy removal and replacement of the scope and one with bases low enough that the rifle's open sights can be seen over them. This mount must be manufactured with such precision that the scope can be removed and replaced without any appreciable shift in zero.

Such mounts are few and generally quite costly, so we have innovations like the "see-through" designs that are intended to allow use of both the scope and open sights without removing the scope. With these you look under the rings to see the open sights. The scope is mounted above the see-through provision. It works but requires mounting the scope very high. The reverse of this idea is the new Scope–Site from Millett. This consists of a set of 1-inch rings, at this moment only available for use in Redfield-type bases, which have open sights built on top of the rings. Atop the front ring is a tapered 1/8-inch-wide blade with an orange insert and atop the rear ring is a square-notch rear sight fully adjustable for windage and elevation. When in place this system gives quick access to a very accurate set of open sights that will suffice for occasional close-range work. With this design the scope is mounted low, the auxiliary open sights high. I'm not saying that either see-through mounts or the Millett Scope–Site will replace a good quick-detachable mount system, but they offer a low-cost alternative.

Millett's Scope-Site is designed for quick access to open sights. Raising your head a bit when aiming allows use of high-profile sights.

Conetrol mount system's rings attach from the sides rather than top to bottom. This results in sleek rings.

Do you buy a one-piece or two-piece base? I don't think it matters. We've all heard those arguments that a one-piece base is stronger and more rigid than a two-piece base. Probably, but both are stronger than the scope itself; so I've yet to be convinced that one is superior to the other. Personally, I like two-piece bases because they leave the loading port unencumbered.

Okay, you've chosen your scope and the mounts, so it's time to install them on the rifle. You'll need a few basic tools and supplies. If slot-head screws are used in the base and rings, you need hollow ground screwdrivers whose blades fit the slots closely. Where hex-head screws are used, be sure that the wrench fits snugly. In addition, you should have a small hammer with a nylon head, some degreasing solvent, a bottle of red Loctite, and a small strip of 400-grit wet-or-dry sandpaper. For drilled and tapped receivers you'll want a 6–48 bottoming tap on hand. Finally, and you can get by without this one, a bore sighting device will save you time and ammo when it comes to sighting-in later.

If the receiver is drilled and tapped, remove the plug screws from the screw holes and position the base or bases to be certain that the holes in the mount match those in the receiver. Also check to be sure that the bases are of the proper height so that the scope will sit level with the bore line. With the 6–48 bottoming tap held in a tap wrench, clean up the threads in the screw holes. This step isn't essential, but I've found that if the threads are dirty or have any burrs in them, the screws will never tighten properly. Chase the threads in each hole and, when you're finished, spray some solvent into each hole to remove any oil or grease. Allow time for the solvent to evaporate. Using a solvent-soaked rag or paper towel, clean the top of the receiver to be covered by the bases.

Remove the base (or bases in the case of two-piece design) from the factory packaging and thoroughly clean both the bases and screws with solvent. Allow them to dry thoroughly. Position the base, insert a screw into the front hole, and carefully tighten it. Try shaking the base from side to side and up and down. If there is any movement, the screw is too long for the hole and is bottoming rather than clamping down on the base. Grind or cut the screw off until it tightens the base securely. Repeat this for each screw. For those holes that go all the way through the receiver, simply run your finger along the underside to be sure that the screw doesn't protrude below the inner surface where it could interfere with bolt movement. If a screw protrudes below the inside surface, remove and shorten it. When you've finished, each screw will be matched to a particular hole. Don't mix them up. The best way to be sure that each screw is replaced in the hole it matches is to leave the screws in their respective holes when the base is removed.

Now, remove one screw at a time and put a tiny drop of thread locking compound on the threads. Most people have a tendency to use too much locking compound. This is messy because it will seep up around the screw head, making screw removal doubly difficult later. In the case of blind holes, too much compound will run down into the hole and the screw will bottom against it and be prevented from locking securely. Use just enough thread locking compound to coat the threads.

As each screw is replaced, snug it down but don't tighten it. Then, when all of the screws have been installed, tighten each securely by holding torque on the screwdriver and tapping the top of the screwdriver handle with a nylon or plastic hammer. This tapping helps mate the threads and tighten the screws securely. You need not beat hell out of the screwdriver with the hammer. Just tap lightly as you apply pressure. Be sure to use the proper size of screwdriver or hex wrench. If you use poorly fit screwdrivers or wrenches, you will burr or ruin the heads of the screws and then you will really have trouble.

Now it's time to fasten the rings to the base. Because of the great variety of ring designs available, I won't even try to go into detail on each. Enough said that most rings come in two pieces. The important thing is to follow the manufacturer's instructions for ring assembly and installation.

There are a few tricks worth mentioning, though. First, be certain that you wipe the inside surfaces of the rings with a degreaser. Also de-

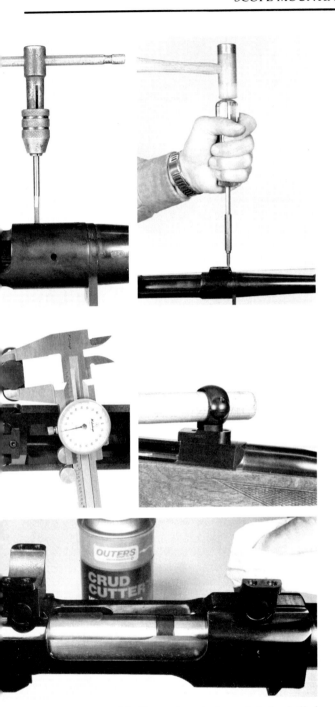

(1) *Chase threads in each hole drilled and tapped with a 6–48 tap to guarantee clean threads.* (2) *To thoroughly tighten screws, hold torque on screw and tap top of screwdriver.* (3) *Windage screws must not butt together when mount base is installed.* (4) *Use a wood dowel to rotate the front ring on Redfield-type bases. Lubricate stud first.* (5) *Degrease inside of rings as well as scope tube.* (6) *Mike the tube of your scope to be sure of diameter. If it is undersized, shims may be needed.*

grease the scope tube itself. This helps keep the scope from sliding forward under recoil. Second, mike the tube diameter of the scope. Not all tubes will be 1 inch in diameter. Some will, but you'll encounter scopes with tubes both over- and undersize. You needn't worry if the tube is 1 inch or larger. However, if it mikes out less than 1 inch, it may be necessary to place a thin shim inside the bottom half of the ring to guarantee that the rings grip the scope tube securely. On rifles that generate a lot of recoil I use a shim, even though measurements indicate that one isn't required. Burris furnishes a self-sticking shim with each of their rings; however, most manufacturers don't. Electrical tape makes a good shim, but my favorite is 400-grit wet or dry sandpaper cut to fit and placed inside the bottom half of the ring with the grit side against the ring, not against the scope. You may wonder where a shim is placed on rings that clamp together from the sides rather than top to bottom. It's been my experience that these, represented by such designs as Buehler, Conetrol, and Kimber rings, are so made that shims aren't required. They'll clamp securely, even around scopes with tubes that are a few thousandths undersize—providing you follow the manufacturer's installation instructions.

The front ring on mounts of the Redfield, Leupold, and Burris type fit into a recess in the base and must be rotated 90 degrees to line up for scope installation. Don't use the scope to turn this ring into position for the first time. Instead, assemble the ring, place a little grease on the stud before inserting it in the base, slip a wooden dowel just under 1 inch in diameter into the ring and rotate it into position. Turn it in and out several times to break it in. It takes quite a bit of pressure to rotate the ring the first time or two and using the scope could bend the tube. After break-in, it's okay to use the scope to rotate the front ring for scope removal.

Redfield-style mounts, as well as those from Buehler, have rough windage adjustments built into the rear of the mount. These come in handy, particularly if the bases happen to be a little out of line with the receiver or the barrel and receiver aren't in perfect alignment. Most scopes don't have enough windage adjustment built into them to compensate for such misalignment. By using a bore sighter you can get the windage close using the rough adjustments on the mount, then fine-tune with the scope adjustment. But, there are two possible problems to watch for with such mounts. First, be certain that the windage screws, which oppose each other in a common hole threaded all the way through the rear of the base, don't butt together. This can sometimes be detected by simply setting the rear ring in place, tightening the windage screws, then checking the

Integral ⅛-inch-wide tapered blade tops the front ring. Rear sight adjusts for windage and elevation.

ring for any movement. If there is any perceptible movement, the mount windage screws are butting together, not tightening against the ring. A more precise check for this trouble requires use of a good caliper. With the ring removed, turn the windage screws in until they tighten. Since the ring isn't in place, the screws tighten only when they butt against each other. Using the knife edges of the caliper, measure the distance between the inside of the screw heads. Now, again using the knife edges of the caliper, measure the distance between the inner surfaces of the milled recesses in the bottom of the rear ring. If the distance between these two surfaces is greater than that between the screw heads when they're butting together, you have no problem. However, if it's apparent that the windage screws will butt together before they tighten against the ring, simply shorten the screws a little.

The second thing to watch for is placing the scope tube under stress when using the mount to make coarse windage adjustments. If the front ring is still very tight where it cams into the base, it's possible to move the rear of the scope via the windage screws, but not rotate the front ring at all. When this happens, the scope tube is under pressure. To avoid this, give the front ring a few gentle taps with a nylon hammer to rotate it the same direction as the rear of the scope was moved by the windage screws. This will remove any tension that might be exerted on the scope tube.

On Redfield-style mounts, position the rings, then remove the top halves and lay the scope in place. It should fit down into the bottom half of each ring perfectly. If it doesn't, you may have to rotate the front right slightly so that the front and rear rings are in alignment. When this is done, position the top half of each ring and insert the screws that hold the two halves together. Tighten them just enough that the scope is held, but can still be turned in the rings.

Now, position the scope so that the reticle is square when you aim the rifle and so that the eye relief is right for you. These things can only be done properly with the stock on the rifle and you holding it to your shoulder. The eye relief is right when you throw the rifle to your shoulder and instantly see the entire field of view. If you have to move your head forward or back on the stock to see the entire field, the scope is improperly positioned and must be slid forward or backward in the rings.

When you're certain that the eye relief is right for you and that the reticle is square, tighten the rings down securely. Do not use thread locking compound on the ring screws, but do tap them tight with a hammer as described for base screws.

Your scope is now mounted, but you have no idea if it's set even close to zero. You can bore sight the rifle, of course, but a much more accurate method is to use a bore-sighting device like those available from Bushnell or Redfield. The most accurate of these bore sighters are pretty expensive—too expensive for the individual who occasionally mounts a scope. However, Bushnell markets a relatively inexpensive little device called the TruScope which I highly recommend to the amateur. The TruScope comes complete with three adjustable mandrels that cover every bore size from .22 up through .45 caliber.

To use any bore sighter, you select the proper size mandrel, mount the bore sighter on it, and insert the mandrel into the bore from the muzzle. Then you look through the rifle scope and adjust the screen of the bore sighter until the lines on the screen are in vertical and horizontal alignment with the reticle of the scope. Next you turn the elevation and windage adjustment screws on the scope until the reticle is aligned with the zero line representing the distance you want to sight-in for. Theoretically, your scope is now sighted-in for point of aim at this distance.

I've never found bore scopes to produce results quite this accurate. However, when properly used they will set the zero of your scope so that your shots will at least be on the paper. From there on it's just a matter of a few shots to finish sighting-in. One thing to remember when you use a bore scope: be sure the bore of the rifle is clean. If it isn't, the mandrel isn't positioned perfectly and the error of your bore sighting job will be much greater.

As you can see, there's nothing difficult about mounting a rifle scope. However, the job does require some forethought, a few tools and patience. It's not a job you can rush. Because of the variety of scope mounts available today, it's essential that you follow the instructions for assembly furnished by the manufacturer. Read these carefully and then apply a few of the tips we've been discussing. If you do, you'll find that your scope is properly mounted in a manner that guarantees rugged reliability in the field.

How to Clean and Protect Your Firearms

Rick Jamison

It once was a serious offense if you didn't clean your gun *each* time you used it. It was serious during the learning years if your father found out, and it was serious later on because it would ruin a good-shooting gun. Black powder and corrosive primers were the major culprits at one time. Today's shooters of modern ammunition don't need to worry about these culprits, but a fine firearm can still be ruined by neglect.

There are three basic areas of firearms cleaning:

Bore. A fouled barrel causes an accurate rifle to shoot *patterns*, not groups. A fouled chamber can prevent a round from chambering in a handgun.

Action. Sand, dirt, and weed seeds can cause a semiauto to malfunction. They can cause a bolt action to be difficult and slow to cycle. Lead, wax, and carbon fouling can make a revolver action feel gritty.

Exterior. In a humid climate, acidic fingerprints and sweat can cause a gun to rust in short order. Rain or snow that isn't wiped off can have the same effect.

Keeping a firearm clean and lubricated is easier today than ever before. Load components are less corrosive, and modern technology has provided a lot of excellent solvents and protective coatings that are easy to apply.

The more shooting you do, the more you'll have to clean the bore and other interior parts of a firearm. Higher bullet velocity generally means more fouling too. In addition, the smaller the caliber, the more critical a clean bore becomes and the greater effect a fouled bore has on accuracy. Bullet jacket, lead, and powder fouling are easily removed—unless they're allowed to accumulate; then removal becomes increasingly difficult.

To give you some idea of how often to clean a bore, I'll tell you what I do. When I review loads

Here is an inside view of a dirty rifle bore.

at the range, I usually fire three five-shot strings with a given load on a single target. After 15 shots, I change targets and scrub the bore. When I'm prairie dog shooting and fire a lot of shots, I may stop shooting and clean every 50 rounds or so. My big-game rifles may be cleaned only once after the hunting season, and they probably won't have had many shots fired through them. The exception is if I hunt in rain or snow; then I clean the gun as soon as I get back to camp or home. When I'm shooting a revolver or semiauto handgun for enjoyment, I clean it after each range session because I usually shoot it a lot and the lead and carbon really build up.

Let's get to the specifics of cleaning two of the most popular types of firearms: a bolt-action rifle and a revolver.

In order to clean the bore of a bolt-action rifle, you need a cleaning rod, a brush, jag, or slotted tip, patches, and solvent. If it's a varmint rifle, a gun that is often cleaned, avoid the use of jointed cleaning rods and coated rods. The joints on jointed rods often don't quite match up and form crevices to accumulate abrasive grit. Plastic or fi-

This article first appeared in Shooting Times

Some bore brushes have a looped tip (left), while others are cut off. Use the latter type with care because its sharp edges can scratch the bore.

jag tip, the patch is pushed through the bore from the breech to the muzzle, and when the rod is withdrawn, the patch is pulled off the jag tip by the crown.

I've recently been using a combination slotted tip/jag by Ox-Yoke Originals. It has a tip with a jag at either end of a slot. A special patch is inserted through the slot, and the double jag is used in a two-way motion.

For cleaning revolvers, revolver cylinders, and semiauto pistols, I generally use a loop tip, pushing and pulling the patch through the bore several times.

You can either purchase patches or make them. If you prefer to make your own, flannel is a good choice. I like a fairly tight-fitting patch, one that wipes the bore clean of residue loosened by solvent. If a single patch thickness isn't tight enough, fold it over so there are two layers; you can also use two patches or a larger jag.

In addition to these tools, I use a bore guide, sometimes called a "throat saver," when cleaning

berglass-coated rods have a habit of accumulating grit that becomes embedded in the surface. A smooth one-piece steel rod is the best choice. It can be wiped clean after each use. One with a swiveling handle helps prevent the rifling from unscrewing the tips as the rod is passed down the bore.

Cleaning rod brushes are made with metal or plastic bristles intertwined in twisted steel or brass wire cores. Some of these wire cores are looped around at the tip; others are cut off. The latter ones have a sharp-pointed surface which could be jammed into the rifling and possibly scratch it. Avoid brushes that have cut-off wires at the tip.

Make sure the brush used is the right size for the bore. A brush should require a *little* force to push it through the bore. If a brush is too small, it won't do much scrubbing of difficult-to-remove fouling; if the brush is too large, it could become stuck in the bore if you try to reverse its motion while it's inside the barrel. Also, using a brush that's too large for the bore tends to wear the brush out prematurely, and one or two cleanings make it useless for the right bore.

When you purchase brushes, purchase good ones. Inexpensive brushes and those that are too large will shed bristles in the bore and chamber. If you fire a case with a bristle in the chamber, it will leave the imprint of the bristle on the outside of the brass case. Loose metal bristles in the bore can't have any positive effect on accuracy or bore life.

When cleaning a bolt-action rifle, I generally use a jag tip for accepting the cloth patches. With the

Author recommends using an abrasive cloth, such as this one made by Lyman, to remove lead buildup from the face of a cylinder, rear of a barrel, inside of a top-strap, and similar places.

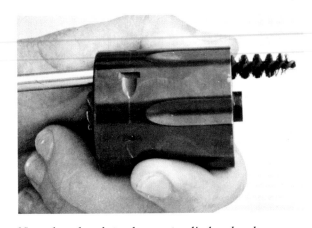

Use a bore brush to clean out cylinder chambers.

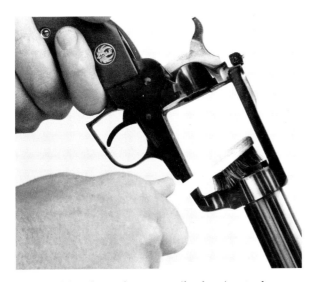

Old toothbrush can be a versatile cleaning tool.

a varmint rifle or benchrest rifle which is fired and cleaned a lot. The bore guide centers the rod as it enters the bore and prevents jamming the hard steel tip into the origin of the rifling. A bore guide also serves to keep solvents out of the trigger mechanism. Some solvents are known to build up a lacquer coating if left uncleaned from a trigger mechanism, and this could eventually gum up a trigger.

In addition to these tools, it helps to have a "vise" to hold a firearm for cleaning. For rifles, I use a Gun Cradle, which is made by Mountain Meadow Enterprises, and I like it a lot. This tool is also useful for mounting scopes, bore sighting, and similar jobs. At the range, I use sandbags to hold a rifle while I'm cleaning it.

There are plenty of good solvents available. I'm not equipped to evaluate them or determine which is best. Some seem to clean stubborn fouling better than others, but I haven't found *any* that are unsatisfactory.

Before cleaning the bore of any gun, make sure it is unloaded. When cleaning a bolt-action rifle, clamp the rifle in a device like a Gun Cradle, or a padded vise, or leave it in sandbags on the bench-

The clamp on the gun cradle will hold the rifle securely and free both your hands.

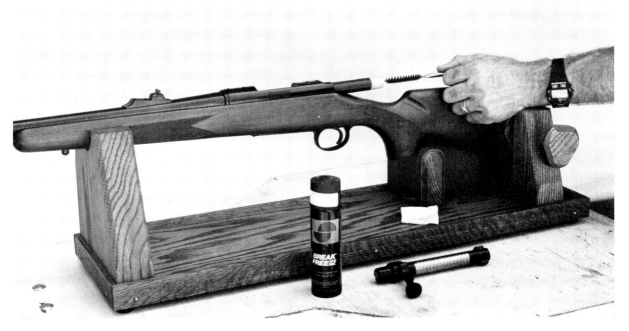

A gun cradle helps make rifle cleaning a breeze.

rest and remove the bolt. Then insert a cleaning rod guide if you have one. If you're cleaning a revolver, make sure the gun is unloaded, swing out or remove the cylinder, and clamp the frame in a padded vise.

Whether you're cleaning a rifle or handgun, attach the proper brush to the rod and dip it into the solvent. Pass the wet brush back and forth in the bore several times. I'll generally make 6 back-and-forth passes after a 15-shot string. If the gun has been fired a lot, you may wish to let the solvent-dampened bore sit for a while and then repeat the process.

Next, replace the brush tip with a jag or looped tip and fit it with a dry patch. Pass the patch through the bore and remove it. The first pass through the wet bore will probably soak the patch. Attach another dry patch and pass it through the bore, repeating the process until a patch comes out clean. In most cases, I use three patches before one is fairly clean.

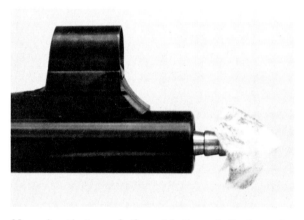

Use a jag tip to push the patch through the bore. Let the crown pull the patch off the jag.

If you're going to store the gun, pass an oily patch down the bore to coat the interior and protect it. Just clean the oil out with a dry patch before you fire it. If you're not going to store the gun, omit the oil.

If you clean your guns regularly and often, you may never need to use anything but a good solvent to clean the bores. However, if you fire a lot without cleaning, or if you fire ultrahigh-velocity rifle cartridges or a lot of lead-bullet pistol loads, bore cleaning won't be as simple as I've outlined.

In a handgun, a few jacketed-bullet rounds help remove a lot of the fouling from lead-bullet loads. Lewis Lead Remover is an abrasive mechanical means of removing lead which also works. Riflemen generally use stronger cleaners, such as the Australian-made Sweet's, and a lot of scrubbing to remove bullet jacket fouling. This will remove a great deal of copper fouling in a hurry.

There are cleaners with an abrasive mixed in the liquid. These cleaners are often used with a lead billet molded inside the barrel around an old cleaning rod brush. The lead billet is smeared with the abrasive and passed back and forth inside the barrel. Be advised that this process can easily be overdone; it will wear out your barrel faster by cleaning than by shooting.

For revolvers, use the brush and patch to clean each chamber in the cylinder. The face of the cylinder may also have a lead buildup, as may the rear of the barrel, and the inside of the topstrap. An abrasive cloth, available from Hoppe's, Lyman, RIG, or other sources, works wonders. Simply wipe off the lead smears with the cloth.

After a bolt-action rifle's bore is cleaned, I use a lug recess cleaner, which consists of a dowel rod with a hole drilled through it crosswise near one end. A gauze plug is inserted into the hold and sprayed with solvent; then it's passed into the action like a bolt, allowing the gauze to clean

Bore guide centers rod as it enters the bore to prevent the steel tip from damaging rifling. The guide also keeps solvents out of the trigger mechanism.

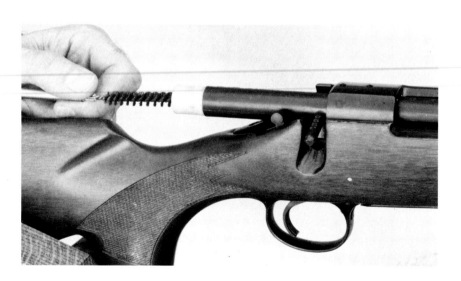

Lug recess cleaner gets hard-to-reach places.

the lug raceways, and then rotated around in the locking lug recesses to clean these hard-to-reach places. Next, a dry gauze billet wipes everything dry.

The bolt body is wiped with a solvent-dampened rag, and any interior parts of the action are wiped or brushed clean. An old toothbrush works well for many hard-to-clean areas. This works particularly well inside a revolver frame, around the recoil plate, or on the cylinder.

If you've been hunting in the rain, unload the rifle, remove the barreled action from the stock, and dry both wood and metal. Next, coat the metal with one of the new exterior coatings. While you've got the action out of the stock, clean it of any weed seeds or sand. Check the trigger to make sure it's absolutely clean and dry. With a revolver, it's a good idea to remove the grip panels, dry the underside of the wood and metal, and then coat the metal.

Keep any cleaning solvent or oil away from the stock wood as much as possible. Don't get solvent or penetrating oil on a scope lens, and be sure to keep any oil or solvent away from ammunition. Solvents can cause scope sealants to deteriorate and don't help lens coatings either. Be particularly careful with the new spray cans. It's all too easy for a scope to be unnoticed in the background while you spray solvent on a brush. Oil or solvent can render the primer and powder ineffective. Ammonia in solvents can cause brass to become brittle. Don't store ammunition where even fumes from solvents can reach it.

Once you have the bore and action cleaned,

you're ready to clean and protect the outside. Wipe the entire exterior clean and apply a protective oil to metal surfaces with a cloth. It's generally best to put nothing on the stock unless the wood has an oil finish and is drying out. In this case, a coating of linseed oil can help restore it.

Whenever you handle a stored gun, touch only the wood or stock. If you touch the metal, be sure to wipe the area with an oily rag so that it doesn't rust. This is particularly important in a humid climate.

If you put the gun away for an extended period of time, make sure all metal surfaces, inside and out, are coated with a long-lasting protective coating. It's also a good idea to inspect a stored firearm periodically so that you can ensure that corrosion is not taking place.

MANUFACTURERS LISTING

Birchwood Casey, 7900 Fuller Rd., Eden Prairie, MN 55344

Blacksmith Corp., (Arctic Friction Free, gun-cleaning equipment), Box 424, Southport, CT 06490

Break-Free San/Bar Corp., 1035 S. Linwood Ave., Santa Ana, CA 92705

Chem Pak Inc., 11 Oates Ave., Box 1685, Winchester, VA 22601

Decker Shooting Products, 1729 Laguna Ave., Schofield, WI 54476

Gun Cradle Mountain Meadow Enterprises, Rt. 1, Box 158, Priest River, ID 83856

Hoppe's Penguin Industries Inc., Airport Industrial Mall, Coatesville, PA 19320

J-B Bore Cleaner, 299 Poplar St., Hamburg, PA 19526

Jet-Aer Corp., 100 Sixth Ave., Paterson, NJ 07524

Lewis Lead Remover, LEM Gun Specialties, Box 31, College Park, GA 30337

Lyman Products Corp., Rt. 147, Middlefield, CT 06455

Outers Omark Industries, Box 856, Lewiston, ID 83501

Ox-Yoke Originals Inc., 130 Griffin Rd., West Suffield, CT 06093

Rem-Oil, Remington Arms Co., 1007 Market St., Wilmington, DE 19898

RIG Products, 87 Coney Island Dr., Sparks, NV 89431

Rust Guardit Schwab Industries Inc., Box 1269, Sequim, WA 98382

Sweet's, Sinclair International, 1200 Asbury Dr., New Haven, IN 46774

APPENDIX

NEW GUNS

To be quite honest, writing about the new guns hasn't always been a labor of love because there haven't always been many new guns worth falling in love with. In past years if you read between the lines in my annual updates, you must have noticed that I seldom had difficulty containing my enthusiasm. In fact, some of my less than effervescent comments got censored out.

The new guns I described last year were more interesting, and a lot better looking, than they had been for most of this decade. Apparently our gunmakers got their heads out of the ground and gave some serious thought to what a gun ought to be. This year there are more good guns and more of the *right kinds* of guns on the market than since the early 1960s. And that, come to think about it, is about a quarter of a century. This year I have no trouble generating enthusiasm for the new guns—the guns do it for me.

Since space won't allow me to describe all the new guns this year, I'm only hitting the highlights.

ANSCHUTZ

Does $1,290 sound like a lot of money for an air rifle? Maybe so, maybe not, depends on what you want to shoot. I doubt if Ace Perkins, down at Perkins' Feed, Seed and Sports, will stock many of the new Anschutz Model–2001 Air Rifles, but dealers in accuracy equipment will keep you supplied. Air rifle and pistol are now Olympic events, and there's a better than even chance that this state-of-the-science rifle will win some medals. If you are unfamiliar with the nuances of air rifle accuracy, the M–2001 will probably look something like an orthopedic boat paddle. But if you're up to speed on high-tech air guns, you know they live up to their reputation for being the world's most accurate class of rifles. At 33 feet (10 meters) they shoot every pellet into the same hole. All competition is offhand, and at 33 feet the 10-ring bull's-eye looks about the size of the period at the

This article first appeared in Outdoor Life

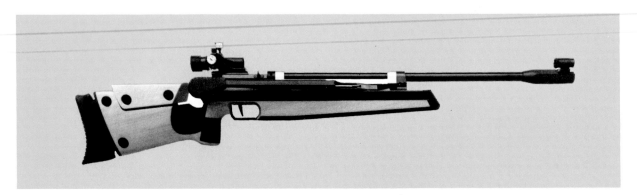

Pro shooters, in demanding Olympic-style air-rifle competitions, don't consider $1,300 a lot for an air rifle. Especially when they get the last word in high-tech air rifles, the Anschutz Model 2001 shown here.

Top to bottom: Sigarms Model 90 bolt-action rifle, available in 10 calibers, including .458 Winchester—scope is the new Redfield Ultimate Illuminator 3×-to-12× Variable; Ithaca Deerslayer II pump shotgun with a 12-gauge rifled barrel; Kimber big-game rifle in .416 Rigby; Browning Model 12 pump shotgun, a re-creation of the legendary Model 12 Winchester; Improved Ruger Model 77 rifle in .233 Remington; Thompson/Center .50 caliber Pennsylvania Hunter, available in flintlock or percussion-cap ignition; Marlin Model 1894CL in .25/20 or .32/20 Winchester; Smith & Wesson .44 Magnum Classic Hunter with bright blue finish and integral scope-mounting system.

New Anschutz Model 54 "Bavarian" has Old World styling and space-age accuracy. The Bavarian-style cheekpiece will appeal to shooters who appreciate Germanic styling, and the crisp Anschutz trigger will appeal to lovers of fine accuracy. The Model 54 comes in .22 Rimfire, .22 Magnum, .22 Hornet, and .222 Remington calibers.

end of this sentence. The mechanism is air compression with side lever operation. The trigger adjusts down to a 2.1 ounce letoff. Weight is 10½ pounds. And caliber, of course, is .177. You have to see one of these rifles to believe it.

Also new from Anschutz is .22 Hornet chambering in their bolt-action Exemplar pistol. This is a sensible combination handgun for varmint hunters because the Hornet has almost no recoil, yet it offers all the range most handgunners make use of. Built on Anschutz's super-accurate Model–54 action the Exemplar Hornet is clip-fed and comes in either right- or left-hand configuration.

Also built on the Anschutz Model–54 action is their new Bavarian-style rifle stock. As aficionados of Germanic stockmaking know, the Bavarian stock is characterized by a fuller, more stylized cheekpiece that harkens back to Schuetzen rifle days. The pistol grip has a closer curve and, of course, a schnaubel fore-end tip styling, without which no Bavarian stock would be complete. Calibers are the same as for other Model–54 sporters.

For more information on Anschutz guns and accessories, write Precision Sales International, P.O. Box 1776, Westfield, MA 01086.

BERETTA

Though the venerable firm of Beretta dates back more than 500 years, they have some up-to-date ideas about making and selling guns. Perhaps this is best demonstrated in their increasing share of the U.S. handgun market, especially their much publicized and controversial inroads into the police and military segments of the market. There's no controversy about their shotguns however. Beretta over/unders, side-by's and autoloaders have a well-earned reputation for dependability and shootability, and you are going to be seeing more and more of them on dealers' racks.

New for '88 is the Onyx series of shotguns, which the folks at Beretta claim were designed for American tastes and preferences. I'm not quite sure how they figured that an American's taste in shotguns is different from that of, say, an En-

glishman's or a Montenegrin's but the Onyx guns are stylistically different from other Berettas, and they do look nice. Perhaps that's Beretta's way of saying that Americans have better taste in smoothbores.

Aside from somewhat different stock styling, which is more classic than Beretta's usual contours, the distinguishing feature of the Onyx models is the black, rather than silver, color of the receivers, and the reason they are called Onyx. The three guns that make up this series are two over/unders and a side-by-side. Each comes in either 12- or 20-gauge and all have 3-inch chambers. Barrel lengths for the over/unders are a choice of 26 inch or 28 inch in either gauge, with the side-by coming only in 26. All three models come with Beretta's screw-in choke system, single triggers, and automatic ejectors. The fanciest of the trio is the Golden Onyx, which has a gold pheasant inlay on the receiver and figured wood. Beretta's catalog is a delight to peruse because there are so many different good-looking shotguns. Beretta U.S.A. Corp., 17601 Beretta Drive, Accokeek, MD 20607.

BROWNING

The Model–12 shotgun is back! This most honored of pump-action shotguns has been reintroduced by Browning and the answer is, yes, it looks just like it used to. In recent years Browning has offered limited runs of some of the classic Winchester guns. Without exception these have been beautiful recreations, suffering only, if you can call it that, from being too slickly finished. On the other hand, Browning's recreation of the legendary Model–12 Winchester, based on the samples I've seen, is right on target. If you loved the old Model–12 you'll love these new ones as well. Available in 20-gauge only, Browning's Model–12 is available in Grade–I, which looks like the original Skeet grade, and a Grade–V, with original Winchester-style engraving and gold inlays. Barrel length is 26 inches, and choking is modified. The production run is limited to 8,500 Grade–I models

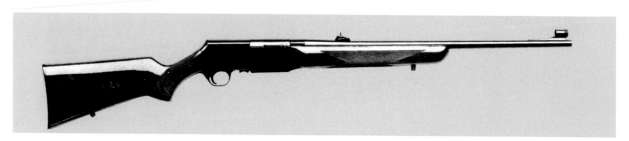

Browning's popular BAR autoloader is now available in .280 Remington chambering. A fine rifle combined with a fine cartridge, this is an outstanding hunting rifle.

and 4,000 of the Grade–V, which is a shame because anything this good should be made in unlimited numbers.

Stand back, the 10-gauge pump has arrived. When you consider the number of waterfowl hunters who prefer pump-action shotguns, plus the rapidly increasing popularity of the 10-gauge Magnum shell, putting the two together makes a lot of sense. I wonder why a major manufacturer didn't do it sooner. The gun is Browning's popular, bottom-ejecting BPS design in kingsize dress. The standard barrel length is 30 inches and comes with three Invector screw-in chokes. Extra barrels in 28- and 32-inch lengths are available as well as a 24-inch buck special for slugs. Weight is 9 pounds, 8 ounces. This is a good-looking, well-styled shotgun that avoids the "bloated" look typical of some 10-gauge magnums. It comes with vent rib and tang safety and is a natural for shooting steel shot.

Browning's centerfire autoloading rifle (BAR), which is the most consistently accurate autoloader I've ever tested, is available this year in .280 Remington chambering. Which means a good gun is even better. The .280, .270 and .30/06 look like they came out of the same litter, but the .280 has the edge in several ways. That's why the BAR is better than ever. Speaking of which, the BAR is once again available in .338 Win. Mag. chambering. If you want to hunt big North American game (elk, moose, grizzly, brown bears) with an autoloader, this is the way to go.

Also dressing up Browning's line are some additions to the A-Bolt series of centerfire and rimfire rifles. The improvements are several, beginning with an upscale Gold Medallion Grade in both centerfire and rimfire versions. This fancier grade comes with better stocking and other nice details. The A-Bolt Composite Stalker is a centerfire with a fiberglass-graphite composition stock. Also, Browning's Stainless Stalker now comes with the composite stock, which is about as weatherproof as a rifle can get. Browning Arms, Route 1, Morgan, UT 84050.

CLASSIC DOUBLES

What's this? A new gunmaker? Well, not exactly. An old company with new ideas is the best way to describe Classic Doubles. For the record, the firm once known as Olin-Winchester is no more. This was the firm that has, for the past several years, imported the Winchester Model–101 over/ unders and the M-23 side-by's. They were stylish guns, well made and sensibly priced, but Olin made the decision to get out of the gun business and concentrate on making ammunition.

Happily, these good guns weren't allowed to

die. Dean Jendsen, formerly a Winchester executive, stepped in and took over the line, and he's the right man for the job. A dedicated shooter himself, he has a vision of the future of shotgunning in America and some great ideas for keeping the models 101 and 23 on track. The shotguns will still be known by their traditional model numbers and they will still be made in the same factory that has been making them for the past quarter century. If you're a fan of the M–101 and M–23, just wait until you see—and feel—Jensen's improvements. Classic Doubles, 1001 Craig Road, Suite 353, St. Louis, MO 63146.

COLT

Colt has expanded the variations of their King Cobra revolver. This is the gun they introduced in 1987 as a replacement for their Trooper and Peacekeeper lines of revolvers. The King Cobra has the look and feel of traditional Colt gunmaking. When you thumb the hammer, there's no mistaking the Colt touch.

The concept behind the King Cobra, which comes only in .357 Magnum caliber, is to offer shooters a dependable Colt revolver at an affordable price. Thus the King Cobras cost roughly half as much as Colt's top-of-the-line Pythons. This year's additions to the King Cobra series amount to five variations; one in blued finish and four in stainless steel. The new blue model has a 4-inch barrel and contoured rubber grips. Two of the new stainless models have Colt's "Ultimate" bright polish, which looks like bright nickel plating. Barrel length choices in the bright stainless steel are 4-inch and 6-inch. There is also a 4-inch King Cobra in a soft matte-finished stainless steel and a little 2½-inch snubby. All have the contoured rubber grips and adjustable rear sights. If you like bright and shiny .45 autos, take a look at the stainless steel Gold Cup .45, which this year is being offered with the dazzling "Ultimate" finish. Colt Firearms, P.O. Box 1868, Hartford, CT 06161.

CROSMAN

Have you been paying attention to the air-gun market in recent times? I grew up in a generation when air guns were collectively called "BB" guns and were considered toys for little boys. But like the little girl next door, "BB" guns have grown up and, *wow*, you should see them now. Talk about sex appeal. I mean real grown-up shootin' stuff. One of my favorite air pistols is a CO_2-powered Crosman Model–357 revolver. It looks and feels like a Colt Python revolver and even has a six-shot pellet clip that rotates when the gun is thumb-cocked or fired double action. It has ad-

Crosman's new Model–357 CO₂-powered pellet gun has the look and feel of a high-powered revolver. The improved cylinder system now offers 10 shots.

justable sights and a surprisingly crisp trigger, and it's great for indoor or outdoor practice.

New is a Model–357 with an 8-inch barrel and a silver matte finish that looks like the stainless steel Python. Also, the clip has been changed to a 10-shot capacity, which is a great improvement. (If you own an older Model–357 the new clips will work in your gun too.)

When you are next at your gun dealer's, take a look at all the Crosman air guns. You'll be amazed at what you see in the way of "adult" products. If I'd had one of their powerful Challenger 6000 rifles when I was a boy, there wouldn't have been a squirrel left in East Tennessee. When you write to Crosman, ask about their Bikathlon. It's an exciting and healthy way to involve youngsters in shooting. Crosman Air Guns, Routes 5 & 20, East Bloomfield, NY, 14443.

DAISY

Better sit down for this bit of news, and get a grip on yourself, especially if you owned a Daisy Red Ryder carbine back when the world was young. The Red Ryder has been around for a half century! Congratulations to Red, and all the good people at Daisy who made the carbine a part of growing up in America. Like Colt's Peacemaker and the '73 Winchester, Daisy's Red Ryder is a shooting legend.

Daisy's big announcement for '88 is not an air gun, but a brand new line of .22 rimfires. There

are three basic rifles: a bolt-action single shot, a bolt-action repeater and an autoloader. Respectively, they are the models 2201, 2202, and 2203. The bolt-action repeater feeds from a 10-shot rotary magazine, while the autoloader has a seven-shot clip or longer-shooting banana clip.

Quite a number of things differ in these rifles, which were designed by Jerry Haskins (of Champlin rifle fame), beginning with the dual-barrel system. The standard rifled barrel, which is actually a sleeved arrangement, can be easily removed and replaced with a smoothbore barrel for shooting shot cartridges. The trigger assembly, which can be adjusted for a 2- to 5-pound pull, can be quickly removed for separate storage. This is a significant safety feature if youngsters are about. And speaking of youngsters, the new Daisy rimfires have an adjustable buttplate that "grows" with the child. Stop by your local gunshop and have a look at Daisy's interesting concept in .22s. Daisy is making a serious commitment to the shooting sports. Young ideas from an old company—they are 101 this year. Congratulations again. Daisy Manufacturing Co., Rogers, AR 72756.

ITHACA

Remember Ithaca guns? This grand old company almost disappeared a few years back, but now they're back doing what they do best: making their famous pump and that wonderful single barrel trap gun. Their pump gun is a John Browning design, introduced in 1937, hence the Model–37 designation. Last year was the 50th birthday, so the folks at Ithaca celebrated the occasion by renaming it the Model–87. It's still the same fine gun though, with the bottom ejection feature and super-slick action. The receiver, as always, is machined from a solid block of steel. The only exception is their Ultralight model, which is milled from solid aluminum. At 5 pounds, in 20-gauge, it's the lightest pump gun of all.

Several variations of the Model–87 range from camouflage-colored 12-gauge Magnum, to the rich-looking Supreme, with a couple of items I can't resist talking about. One is the screw-in choke tube system, which is standard on all field-

Daisy's entry into the rimfire rifle market includes this Model–2201 bolt-action rifle. It has an adjustable stock and separate barrels for bullets and for .22 Rimfire shotshells.

grade guns. This is a worthwhile feature on any gun, especially when the barrels are made thicker, as Ithaca's are to resist damage from steel shot.

Ithaca's new Deerslayer II can be called the state of the art in slug-shooting shotguns because of four very important features. First among the improvements is a *rifled* barrel. Over the past three or four years, a lot of gunmakers have experimented with shotgun slugs. And rifled barrels have proven significantly more accurate. The new high-tech sabot encased projectiles deliver rifle-like accuracy out to 100 yards, and even old-style rifled slugs do measurably better. What this means is that well-placed slug shots on deer-size game at 100 yards are now a realistic proposition. What it *does not* mean is that the range of shotgun slugs has been increased. This gets us into a point of law: Some states and localities prohibit the use of rifles for big-game hunting. These regulations usually prevail in densely populated areas because the lawmakers don't want high-velocity rifle bullets whizzing through the woods and over the countryside. Shotgun slugs and buckshot have significantly less velocity and range than centerfire rifles and are thereby presumed safer by some lawmakers. As a means of simplifying the wording of the regulations, laws only prohibit "rifled barrels" for hunting. Until now, such wording served the purpose of the law. But now comes Ithaca with a rifled *shotgun* barrel, and Mossberg, and a number of custom barrelmakers. These rifled barrels certainly abide by the intent of the law but run afoul of the unfortunate wording. It can be argued that rifled barrels are even safer than smoothbores for slug shooting simply because they permit more accurate shot placement. Anyway, before buying a rifled barrel for hunting with slugs, check the wording of local ordinances. And if there is a prohibition, you might want to get on your soapbox and campaign to have the wording altered.

Another feature of Ithaca's Deerslayer II is a "locked-in" barrel. With barrel rigidly fixed in the receiver, accuracy is improved considerably. Of course this eliminates the takedown feature, but the advantages are worth it. How important is a stiff barrel to receiver union? Just imagine how poor the accuracy of a rifle would be if its barrel wobbled around in the receiver. The third feature of Ithaca's Deerslayer II is a solidly fixed rear-sight base that doubles as a scope base. This goes a long way toward getting a scope to stay put on a shotgun. Another feature of the Deerslayer II is a higher combed Monte Carlo stock, which gets the shooter's eye closer to the center of the scope. And in case you are wondering, Ithaca still makes the older style, interchangeable, unrifled Deerslayer barrel. For more information, write Ithaca Guns, 123 Lake Street, Ithaca, NY 14850.

KIMBER

Clever fellows, those guys at Kimber. Every year they manage to come up with a showstopper. This year they have a real stunner. Kimber, you know, is the outfit that proved that shooters have much better taste than generally given credit for and, given the opportunity, will opt for classic styled, quality-built Rimfire rifles. Kimber's classy rimfire sporter is a landmark in rifle design from the 1970s and subsequent years have seen similar advances from Kimber. Last year Kimber unveiled a full-blown high-powered hunting rifle based on an action that doesn't look all that different from the much-favored "Pre-12964" Winchester Model-70 mechanism. With Kimber's classic woodwork, the combination is lovely, but where could Kimber possibly go from there?

I got an idea of what Kimber was up to when I ran into Greg Warne, bossman at Kimber, at the Chicago airport. He allowed that he was on the way to Africa to do some field-testing of a new rifle. There wasn't time for questions but I figured he was working on something in the dull, medium bore chambering like the .375 H&H. As it turns out Kimber has much bigger things in mind. At this year's SHOT Show, where shooting goods manufacturers show their stuff, Kimber took the wraps off a pump splitter in .416 Rigby persuasion. Also in the works are even more powerful rounds: the .460 Weatherby and awesome .505 Gibbs.

You might wonder how there could be much of a market for rifles in these enormously powerful cartridges, which are useful only for stopping Africa's biggest and meanest game. The peculiar fact is that these, and other, phallic cartridges are very much in vogue now. The reasons for this phenomenon are rather esoteric, and require more explaining than I have room for here.

Anyway, now is the time to sell big-caliber rifles, and the guys at Kimber are smart to be ready to supply the market. They are even smarter to know what a big-caliber rifle is supposed to look like because the fascination with heavy calibers is due to the rifles even more than the size of the cartridges. For example, if you chamber an ordinary hunting rifle for one of the super-big rounds, you still wouldn't have a "proper" heavy-caliber rifle. They have a distinctive look and style, a style that has been captured only by the best British gunmakers and a handful of specialty riflemakers in America. The required touches, in addition to a very distinctive stock style, include express sights on contoured quarter ribs, banded front sights, barrel-mounted sling swivels, drop box magazines and *veddy, veddy* British-style checkering patterns. The list goes on. Kimber has captured the essence of the heavy rifle in masterful style. Pick up one of these rifles in, say, .416 Rigby caliber, and you'll want to own it even if you never intend to be charged by a Cape buffalo.

Eventually, Kimber's big-game rifle will be made in three action lengths to handle short, medium and long cartridges. Kimber of Oregon, 9039 S.E. Jannsen Road, Clackamas, OR 97015.

MARLIN

Just wait and see, some old fuddy-duddies are going to come grousing into your local gunshop about Marlin's new 1894CL lever rifle in .25/20 and .32/20 calibers. "Who wants these old calibers?", they'll say. But fuddy-duddies are the lost souls who have forgotten that shooting is fun. For every complainer there will be a dozen guys who can't wait to get ahold of one and head for the woods. The .25/20 WCF and .32/20 WCF (for Winchester Center Fire) have been around for a hundred years or so and are the stuff of shooting legend. Once guns in these calibers were standard equipment on every trail in every camp, and in every shooting and hunting household. An outdoorsman with a .32/20 revolver in his holster and a .32/20 rifle in his scabbard was pretty well outfitted for a stay in the wilderness. They put small game in the cooking pot and came to be known as "pot guns."

If you're a handloader the .25/20 and .32/20 are special delights, especially when you cast your own lead bullets. That gets the cost down to about that of .22 Rimfire ammo, and that means you can do a lot of shooting with this new Marlin.

Also new from Marlin is a compact version of their Model–336 lever gun. Called the 336LTS, it has a stubby 16¼-inch barrel with a slenderized forearm and straight-grip carbine-style stock. Comes in .30/30 only.

Another scaled down Marlin, the Model–39TDS, is a takedown version of the popular M–39 Rimfire, with a 16½-inch barrel and comes in a padded Cordura nylon case that will float when your canoe overturns. It's a great traveling kit.

Also, Marlin is offering the Model 1894 carbine in .45 Long Colt chambering. With one of these, and a .45 Colt "hawg laig" revolver you're ready for almost anything. Like other gunmakers, Marlin has been uptight as a three-string banjo for the past few years. Happily, it looks like they want to have some fun for a change, and their new guns

show it. Marlin Firearms Co., 100 Kenna Drive, North Haven, CT 06473.

MOSSBERG

The 1988 Mossberg catalog shows nothing but shotguns and, beginning this year, every shotgun they sell they will make themselves. Gone are the imported rifles and shotguns. Replacing them are dramatic new ideas in design and performance. The hottest item is a new shotgun in a new gauge, the 3½-inch 12-gauge Magnum. Some years ago I editorialized that a sensible way to solve the steel-shot dilemma would be to introduce a new gauge—the idea being to have a shell with larger capacity than the existing 3-inch 12-gauge Magnum. One very positive thing we've learned about hunting with steel shot is that we can come close to duplicating the performance of lead shot by using larger sizes of steel. But when these extra-large sizes are loaded in standard-size cases, the shot count—and therefore the pattern density—is unavoidably reduced. So to get around this problem, I suggested a large-capacity shell, and that is exactly what Federal Cartridge Company, in concert with Mossberg, has achieved with the 3½-inch Magnum. To give you an idea of how this new shell stacks up, a 1¼ ounce load of size BB steel shot in a 3-inch shell contains 90 pellets. The 3½-inch Federal Magnum holds 1⁹⁄₁₆ ounces of BBs for a count of 112 pellets. That's a 24 percent increase. Federal is loading their 3½-inch Mags with sizes 2, BB, T&F steel shot.

Mossberg's gun for this new shell is the Model–835 Ulti-Mag. It is pump action, comes with vent rib and Accu-Mag screw-in choke tubes, which are not damaged by steel shot. Barrel length is 28 inches and weight is about 7¾ pounds. You have a choice of the traditional finish or a camo design with weather-resistant synthetic stocking. And yes, the gun will also function with 2¾-inch and 3-inch shells as well as the new 3½-inch Mag. We'll probably see a lot of these in the field come waterfowl season.

Mossberg has also introduced a rifled barrel for their Model–500 Trophy Slugster. You can get it with a plain smoothbore barrel or the new rifled tube, which significantly improves accuracy. Either barrel comes with an integral scope base. Five BR1 Sabot slug loads in the rifled barrel have

Mossberg's new Model 835 ULTI-MAG is chambered for the new 3½-inch 12-gauge shotshells and features ACCU-MAG choke tubes for use with steel shot.

Mossberg's Model 500 Trophy Slugster features a new 24-inch rifled barrel with an integral scope-mounting system. With scope mounted directly to the barrel, you'll get much improved accuracy.

been grouped inside a 3-inch circle at 120 yards. And that's worth bragging about. O.F. Mossberg & Sons, Inc., 7 Grasso Avenue, North Haven, CT 06473.

PARKER REPRODUCTIONS

These pretty doubles keep getting prettier and prettier, and this year there's a lot more to choose from. You can have screw-in choke tubes now, plus a waterfowl gun for steel shot. *Outdoor Life* editor Clare Conley and I tried these on Eastern Shore honkers last season, and I could not have been more pleased with the way they handled.

Parker Repro now has a top-flight, European-trained engraver on board and so can offer truly custom touches to suit collectors' whims. Their new B-Grade gun with banknote engraving is enough to make a shotgun lover swoon, and the forthcoming .410 is breathtaking. They also offer one of the best-looking catalogs. Dial toll-free 1(800)647-2898. Parker Reproductions, 17th & South Hall St., Webb City, MO 84870.

REMINGTON

Remington has more new guns, modifications, loads and accessories than I can begin to describe on these few pages, so the best thing for you to do is take it all in at your dealer's. The Remington catalog runs 48 pages.

You've no doubt heard that they have reintroduced the original Parker side-by-side double. Back when the old Parker Bros. Company was on the skids, Parker was bought by Remington and, in fact, the last of the "old" Parkers were actually made by Remington. Now Remington is making them again, but only on a one-at-a-time basis in their custom shop. They can be built to your specifications, just the way Parker used to do it. Owning one of these beautiful doubles requires three steps: (1) talk to your florist; (2) talk to your wife; (3) talk to Remington.

If you are a rifle buff, you know about the .35 Whelen. It is, or was, a wildcat cartridge dating back to the early 1920s and is made by simply

opening up the neck of the .30/06 case to accept a .35 caliber bullet. Designed by James Howe, of Griffin & Howe fame, it became one of the all-time most popular wildcats because it is a sensible and efficient cartridge and the .35 Whelen name honored Townsend Whelen, who wrote about guns and hunting for *Outdoor Life* when the world was innocent and gun writers were literate. So Remington once again has made a good wildcat "legitimate," just as they did with the .22/250 and .25/06. The .35 Whelen name will remain unchanged, and the two rifles currently offered in this caliber are the Model–700 Classic and the Model–7860 pump. The Whelen is offered in two loadings: a 200-grain pointed slug at 2675 fps and a 250 soft point at 2400 fps, which means it will handle anything that walks on North America.

Also new from Remington is a short-action version of their trim Model–700 Mountain Rifle. This means that .243, 7mm/08 and .308 calibers have been added to the Mountain rifle selection. And too, .338 Winchester Magnum chambering is now available in the Model–700 BDL. This is a wonderful combination.

Speaking of caliber additions, the .280 Remington has been reunited with the Model–7600 pump rifle. The combination didn't fly last time because shooters didn't know how well the .280 could perform. Now that the word is out, with the .280 becoming more popular every season, pump rifle shooters can again share the benefits of this great cartridge. And if by chance you've been looking for a short barreled autoloader, take a look at Remington's new Model–7400 carbine with 18½-inch barrel. It comes only in .30/06 this year.

Also added this year is the Model–700 ADL bolt rifle with a laminated stock. Laminated stocks were all the rage among target shooters back in the 1950s and '60s but in today's high-tech context they are neither fish nor fowl. They are not as efficient as a true synthetic stock. And while they are more stable and weather-resistant than traditional wood, they aren't as warm and pretty. To be sure, however, the color lamination can be quite eye-catching. Generally speaking, laminated stocks represent a sort of halfway house for shooters who crave the advantages of synthetic stocks but can't tear themselves away from wood.

A Remington catalog will keep you up all night. Remington Arms Co., Wilmington, DE 19898.

RUGER

Unlike most gunmakers who introduced their new products all at one time, Ruger tends to announce things as they become available. That's why their hot new 9mm autoloading pistol, the P85, was much discussed by the gun press before the catalog came out. The same with Ruger's .44 Magnum Super Redhawk. But don't be disappointed, Ruger's '88 catalog has some really new items, and I'll hint at what's going to be new *next* year.

Shotgunwise, Ruger now offers their Red Label 12-gauge over/unders with an eye-catching stainless-steel receiver and screw-in tube choking. The gun comes in 3-inch chambers and choice of 26-inch or 28-inch barrel lengths. If you prefer integral chokes the standard combinations are available in both barrel lengths. The Red Label with screw-in chokes is a smart choice for Sporting Clays.

Ruger is also offering their Model–77 bolt gun with a laminated wood stock in a brown and tan color combination called Desert Camo. And before too long you'll be seeing a whole new Model–77 in .223 Rem. chambering. This new rifle is quite a bit different from Model–77s of the past, and I think you'll like the changes. I'm going to use one of these new M–77s in this summer's prairie dog wars. I think it will be one of the all-time most desirable varmint rifles. Just wait and see what I mean. Sturm, Ruger & Co., Lacey Place, Southport, CT 06490.

SAVAGE

Ever wonder what happened to Savage Arms? For the past few years they have been missing from this column simply because I couldn't figure out what they were doing. Now everything seems to be in good order. Their '88 catalog lists some fond old favorites as well as some interesting and worthwhile additions. First of all, their Model–99 lever rifle is still being made in a clip-fed version that comes in .243 or .308 calibers. This is one of the strongest lever-action rifles ever made and would adapt very nicely to the 7mm/08. Now there's an idea to conjure with.

Also the ever-so-popular Model–24 over/under combination now comes in three versions. The M–24 has a 20-gauge shotgun barrel over which is a rifle barrel in either .22 Long Rifle or .22 Mag. caliber. The M–24V gives you a choice of the 20-gauge shotgun barrel with a rifle tube in .222, .223 or .30/30. The M–24L is a compact camper model in .22 Long Rifle and 20-gauge shotgun with 20-inch barrels. The other two models have 24-inch barrels. Another combination gun, introduced this year, is the Model–389. It is a streamlined, hammerless gun that combines a 25-inch, tube-choked, 12-gauge barrel with a rifle barrel in .222 or .308. This is a slick-looking combo, with cut checkering on real walnut stock and vent rib.

Added to Savage's line of Model–311 side-by-side doubles is a "Waterfowler" version which has a dull, "Parkerized" type finish and 28-inch 12-gauge barrels chambered for the 3-inch 12-gauge shell. Choking is Modified and Modified, for best performance with steel shot.

Savage's Model–110 bolt-action centerfire rifle has a couple of new dresses; one is laminated construction and the other is a tough synthetic number made of DuPont Rynite. As always, the Savage 110 is a lot of rifle for the money. Savage Arms, Springdale Road, Westfield, MA 01085.

SIGARMS

Very few rifles have had such an immediate impact on the big-game hunting scene as the Colt Sauer. Made by the famed German firm of Sauer, the Colt rifle was big and bright with glossy wood and metal and rear locking bolt that was icy slick. It caught on with big-time hunters and for a while was considered quite a status symbol. Then Colt stopped distributing them and they became something of a collector's item.

Now the Sauer is back, but without the Colt prefix. It's called the Model–90 and in Supreme Grade appears unchanged from the way it was a decade ago. Now there are other grades too: the Lux, Stutzen, and Safari. The Lux has a satin oil finish, as does the Safari (.458 Win. Mag.). And the Stutzen has full-length, European-style stocking with an oil finish. Altogether there are 10 calibers available in the Sauer M–90 rifles being imported by Sigarms, 470 Spring Park Place, Unit 900, Herndon, VA 22070.

SKB

Last year we announced the return of the popular SKB shotguns. This was joyous news to the legion of shooters who had suffered a decline when SKB disappeared several years back. SKB's U.S. importer, Ernie Simmons, is still on track and dead on target with a full line-up of shotguns ranging from autoloaders to fast-handling side-by's on up to lavishly engraved over/unders with sideplates and detachable triggers. I've tried to count the different models and variations in SKB's catalog, but I lose track after page seven, so you'll have to get your own catalog. Pay particular attention to the multi-barrel sets and the field models with screw-in choke tubes. Ernie Simmons Enterprises, 719 Highland Ave., Lancaster, PA 17603.

SMITH & WESSON

S&W's newest revolver doesn't have a model number. As company officials put it, no mere number could represent the effort they put into creating this handgun. So it earned a name; the .44 Magnum Classic Hunter. Out of the box it looks like one of those expensive revolvers that has been specially reworked by a custom pistolsmith. The cylinder is unfluted and the ejector rod housing extends for the full length of the barrel. This adds weight and steadiness and lends an especially wicked look to the Classic Hunter. Finish is bright blue and contoured grips add comfort and control. I'm told that the Classic Hunter will be offered as a limited issue, but I hope a production model will be offered, with an integral scope mounting system. Smith & Wesson, 2100 Roosevelt Ave., P.O. Box 2208, Springfield, MA 02102.

THOMPSON/CENTER

I have long since lost track of the number—and the names—of the muzzleloading guns marketed over the past couple decades or so. The reason I've lost track is that most of them were forgettable. The *modus operandi* of many distributors seemed to be to sell a bunch of cheap guns then disappear before the complaints start pouring in. Amid all this black-powder flim-flamming one company in particular, Thompson/Center, continued to make solid and dependable equipment that shooters could count on. Thompson/Center's black-powder guns have become the standard of quality and performance by which production grade muzzleloaders are judged. And, if anything, the T/C's are better than ever. When black-powder shooters express a particular need, the guys at T/C try to fill the need in straightforward fashion. A case in point is their new Pennsylvania Hunter, which comes in .50 caliber and either flint or cap ignition. The 31-inch barrel, which is half round and half octagon, has a rifling twist of one turn in 66 inches for best accuracy with a round ball. This is significant because some shooters prefer the traditional patched round ball and because the hunting regulations in some areas specify round balls only for hunting with black-powder guns. So Thompson/Center offers the rifle for the job. Of course they also have muzzleloaders for just about every other black-powder game, and every gun comes with a 64-page booklet on how to get the best performance from your muzzleloader. T/C wants shooters to be happy with their products. Thompson/Center Arms, P.O. Box 5002, Rochester, NH 03867.

WEATHERBY

There are some guns so irresistible that they almost sell themselves. One such shotgun is the Weatherby Athena Grade over/under. It's one of those rare guns that not only pleases the eye but also feels so good to your cheek and shoulder that you just know you can't miss. There are about five shotguns in my "permanent" rack and a 20-gauge Athena Skeet is one of them. (There are some things a man can't live without.)

This year the Weatherby line has been made even sweeter by a .410 over/under. Trying to write about it is like trying to describe the spots on a setter puppy; the only way is to see it for yourself. When you pick it up you'll know what I mean. Weighing about 7 pounds, the .410 comes with screw-in choke tubes and despite the name, the Weatherby finish, engraved sideplates and beautiful wood, it doesn't cost as much as you'd think. If you're a trapshooter, take a look at Weatherby's new single barrel trap gun. Weatherby, 2781 E. Firestone Blvd., South Gate, CA 90280.

U.S.R.A.C.

Now that the Olin Corporation no longer imports the Winchester line of over/unders, the only place you'll see the legendary trademark is on guns made at the original Winchester factory in New Haven. The company name is U.S. Repeating Arms but the products are still pure Winchester.

Something else that is very much still a part of the Winchester tradition is their custom shop. This is where the Model-20 doubles are hand-crafted and where special features and deluxe engraving can be ordered on a custom basis.

When you look at the new production grade Winchester, you're going to see expanded use of their Win-Tuff and Win-Cam stocks. These stocks are of laminated wood with the Win-Cam camouflage feature being achieved by varying the colors of the laminates. For example, the stocks on their pump-action Model-1300 Turkey Gun are made up of alternating shades of browns and greens for a very striking camouflage effect. Just about every gun in the Winchester line, from Model-70s, to lever guns, rimfires and shotguns, is available with laminated as well as traditional stocking. Something the line doesn't have, that I wish they did, is a varmint rifle with a stiff barrel in a Win-Tuff stock. With their short Model-70 action in, say, .223 caliber, this could be a very serious piece of equipment. U.S. Repeating Arms Co., 275 Winchester Avenue, New Haven, CT 06511.

Index

Aberration
    chromatic, 108
    lens, 111
    spherical, 113
Achromatic, 108
Accuracy
    factory vs. handloaded ammuni-
        tion, 148–52
    of lightweight rifles, 53–54
    of muzzleloaders, 118, 199
    of synthetic stocks, 44–45,
    .22 handgun ammunition, 91
Actions
    in custom guns, 37
    rifle, 55
    Ultra Light, 56
Adventures of an Elephant Hunter,
    James Sutherland, 35
African Safaris, Maj. Anderson, 35
Air guns, 24–30
    ballistics, 30
    CO₂, 28–29
    early, 24
    manufacturers of, 26–27
    pneumatics, 27–28
    Quackenbush air rifle, 25
    spring-piston, 27
    systems, 24
American Custom Gunmakers
    Guild, 36
American Engraved Powder Horns,
    Stephen V. Grancsay, 138
Ammunition
    factory loads
        accuracy of, 148
        velocity of, 151
        vs. handloaded, 147–52
    handloading, for dangerous
        game, 153–56
    muzzleloading, 117, 188
    for Sporting Clays, 68
    .22 handgun, 91
Anderson, Gary, 124
Anderson, Maj. 35
Annual Custom Gun Show, 36
Arisaka, Nariake, Col., 57
Arisaka rifles, See Rifles,
    Japanese
Askins, Charles, Col., 70, 164
Astigmatism, 108
Axite. See Powder, smokeless

Barrels
    in custom guns, 37–39
    Gardonese, 8
    for handguns, varmint-shooting,
        long-range, 80–81
    length and choke, for Sporting
        Clays, 67
    and muzzleloader accuracy, 119
    shotgun, overboring, 70
Baker, Samuel, Sir, 32, 35
Ballistics
    air gun, 30
    of handgun cartridges, varmint
        shooting, long-range, 80
    of muzzleloading calibers, 117
    terminal, bullet, 154
BB guns. See Air guns
Bears, shotguns for, 150
Becker, Burt, 72, 76
Bedding, fiberglass, 42
    See also Stocks, synthetic
Beecham, Greg, 19
Beecham, Tom, 19
Bell, 108
Benchrest shooting, and develop-
    ment of synthetic stocks, 43
Berretta
    history of, 6–13
    World Sporting Championships,
        64
Bieson, Al, 54
Big game
    bullets, 48
    cartridges, 47–50
    hunting, handgun, 99
    rifles, 48, 166
        lightweight, 52–56
Black powder, 118
    granulation sizes, 118–19
    substitute, 118
Black-powder shooting. See Muzzle-
    loaders
Bogardus, A. H., Capt., 140
Bogardus
    Glass Ball, 140
    trap, 140
Book of Rifles, The, W. H. B. Smith,
    131
Bore sighter, 172
Boron. See Stocks, synthetic
Boxer Rebellion, guns of, 128–34

Boxlock double rifles, 35
Boyd, David I., 123
Buckingham, Nash, 72, 76
    and "Bo Whoop," 76
Bullets
    for big game, 48
    core-bonded, 155
    expanding, 155
    jacketed, development of, and
        double rifles, 32
    Keith .44 caliber, 95
    knockdown power, 155
    performance, 154–56
    rifle, for hunting, 154–55
    solids, 154
    for varmint shooting, long-range,
        79–80
    weight loss of, 155
Briarbank Ballistic Laboratory, 156
Brightness, relative of optics, 13
Brown, Chet, 43
Browning, John M., 21
Browning Automatic-5 shotgun, 21

Cable, Lee, 19
Calibers
    handgun, for varmint shooting,
        long-range, 79–80
    muzzleloading, ballistics, 117
Caras, Roger, 14
Carlisle, Dan, 67
Carlisle, G. L., 69
Carmichel, Jim, 157
Cartridges
    big game, 47–50, 166
    in custom guns, 36–37
    .44 Magnum, 92, 96, 98–99
        as a defense cartridge,
        98–99
    rifle
        CHeetah Mark II, 157–61
        double, 32–33
        .338 Winchester Magnum
        varmint shooting, long-range,
        78–80
        ballistics, 80
        handloading, 83
    for waterfowl hunting, 142
Checkering
    on custom guns, 39–40
    Japanese, 59

China in Convulsion, A. H. Smith, 131
Chromox, 73
Clay Pigeon Marksmanship, Percy Stanbury, and B. L. Carlisle, 69
Clay Pigeon Shooting Association, 69
Cleaning, firearms, 173–77
  action, 177
  bore, 173–77
  tools and accessories, 174–75
    manufacturers of, 177
Coheleach, Guy, 19
Collimation, binocular, 108
Collimator, 108
Coma, 109
Competition shooting
  Sporting Clays, 62–69
  See also Wigger, Lones
Conseil Internationale du Sport Militaire (CISM), 126
Cordite, *See* Powder, smokeless
Cradock, Chris, 69
Crosshairs, 109
Crossman, Edward C., 75
Curvature of field, 109
Custom guns, 36–40

Dangerous game
  ammunition for, handloading, 154
  bullets for, 154
Dawson, Peter, 35
Death as a Way of Life, Roger Caras, 17
Diaphragm, 109
Diopter, 109
Distortion, 109
Double rifles
  "Baby," 32
  boxlocks, 35
  British makers of, 35
  cartridges for, 32–33
  extractors vs. ejectors, 35
  and development of jacketed bullets, 32
  and development of smokeless powder, 32
Dry firing, 104
Ducks Unlimited, 21

Ejectors, vs. extractors, 35
Elephant Hunting in East Equatorial Africa, Arthur Neumann, 35
Engraving, 14–23
  Japanese, 59
  process, 23
Everett, Marshall, 133
Exit pupil, 110
Extractors, vs. ejectors, 35
Eyepiece, 110
Eye relief, 110

Fabricca d'Armi Pietro Beretta. See Beretta
Federation Internationale de Tir aux Armes Sportif de Chasse (FITASC), 69
Fiberglass stocks. *See* Stocks, fiberglass
Field of view, 110
Firearms Engravers Guild of America, 36
Flare, 110–11
Focal plane, 111
Focus, 111
  center, 108
  individual, 111
Focusing scale, 110–11
Forbes, Melvin, 56
Fox, A. H., Gun Co., 72
Fox, Ansley, 70
Francolini, Leonard, 17

Gardonese barrels, 8
Glass bedding. *See* Bedding, fiberglass
Golden Powder. *See* Black powder
Grancsay, Stephen V., 138
Graphite. *See* Stocks synthetic
Gunmakers, Japanese, 59–60

Handguns
  .44 Magnum, 92–101
    hunting with, 99
  revolvers
    double-action, 85–88
    single-action, 88–89
  .22, 84–91
  varmint shooting, long-range, 78–83
    accuracy, 81–82
    barrel length, 80–81
    cartridges, 78–80
    scopes, 83
Handloading
  ammunition, for dangerous game, 153–56
  the CHeetah Mark II rifle cartridge, 157–61
  handgun cartridges
    .44 Magnum, 100
    for varmint shooting, long-range, 83
  the .338 Winchester magnum, 165–66
Hawken rifles. *See* Muzzleloaders
Haze, 111
Holland & Holland Shooting School, 65
Hunter, John, 35
Hunting
  with muzzleloaders, 116–17, 120
  waterfowl, cartridges for, 142
Huntington, Fred, 157

International Hunters' Convention, 19

International Olympic Committee, 126
International Shooting Union (UIT), 125
Ithaca Model No. 37 shotgun, 21

Jacketed bullets. *See* Bullets, jacketed

Keith, Elmer, 95
Kentucky rifles. See *Muzzleloaders*
Krilling, Bill, 124
Kuhn, Bob, 19

Lens
  catadioptric, 108
  erector, 110
Lens coating, 111
Letoff. *See* Triggers, pull
Ligowski, George, 140
Lock. *See* Muzzleloaders, firing mechanism
Luminosity, 111–12

McKenzie, Lynton, 19
Magnification, 112
Mains, William H., 21
Manual of Clayshooting, A, Chris Cradock, 69
Marktl, Franz, 19
Mirage, 112
Monobloc system, 13
Muzzleloaders, 114–21
  accessories for, 118
  accuracy of, 118, 119
  ammunition for, 117, 118
  calibers for, ballistics, 117
  firing mechanisms, 119
  Hawken-style, 121
  for hunting, 116–17
    loading process, 121
  Kentucky, 120–21
  kits for, 119
  information and equipment for, sources of, 121
  manufacturers of, 121
  sights, 120
  trigger mechanisms, 120

National Matches, Camp Perry, 127
National Shooting Sports Foundation, 21
National Skeet Shooting Assocation, 69
National Rifle Association
  International Shooter Development Fund, 126
  Shooting Programs Department, 123
National Sportsman, 75
National Wild Turkey Federation, 21
Neumann, Arthur, 35
No More The Hunter, Rushby, George, 35

Objective, 112
O'Connor, Jack, 54
Ocular, 112
Olin, John, 70
Optical terms, 107–13
Outdoor Life, 54

Parallax, 112
Parcours de chasse. See Sporting
    Clays
Parson, Leon, 19
Perkins, Andrew, 65
Petersen, Robert E., 99
Plinking, 89–91
Powder, smokeless
    development of, and double
        rifles, 32
    See also Black powder
Powder horns, 135–39
    engraved, 137–38
Prism
    porro, 112
    roof, 113
Puckel, Dan, 124
Pyrodex. *See* Black powder

Quackenbush, Henry Marcus, 25
Quackenbush air rifle, 25

Recoil
    of lightweight rifles, 56
    reducer, for shotguns, 67
Reproduction guns, 185
Resolution. *See* Resolving power
Resolving power, 113
Reticle, 113
Rifles
    big game, 48, 166
    black-powder, 114–21
    double, 31–35
    .44 Magnum, 98
    Japanese, 57–61
    lighweight, 52–56
        accuracy of, 53–54
        recoil of, 56
    Ruger No. 1, engraved, 19
    See also Double rifles
Rigby, John, 32
Rowlands Ward's *Records of Big
    Game*, 164
Ruger, Bill, 96
Rushby, George, 35

Safari Club International, 19
    Conservation Fund, 19
Sanchez-Arino, 35
Scopes
    handgun, 83
    rifle
        mounting, 170–72
        mount systems, 168
Selous, Frederick Courtney, 31
Sheldon, Harold, 76
Shooting positions
    international skeet, 66
    for varmint shooting, 83
Shot, size, positioning of, in duplex
        loads, 143–44
Shotguns
    for bear, 50
    bore, 74
    Japanese, 57–61
    Super-Fox, 70–77
Shotshells
    design, 70–72
    duplex loads, 142–44
    pellet stringing, 72
    steel loads, 144, 145, 146
    target loads, 146
Sidelock double rifles, 35
Sights, on muzzleloaders, 120
Skeet, international shooting posi-
        tion, 66
Skennerton, Ian, 133
Smith, A. H., 131
Smith, W. H. B., 131
Smithsonian Institution, 21
Smokeless powder. *See* Powder,
        smokeless
Sporting Clays, 62–29
    accessories, 69
    ammunition, 68
    clubs and associations, 68, 69
    field layouts, 63–64
    information, sources of, 69
    shooting stands, 65
    shotguns for, 67
    shots, 64–65
    targets, 64–65, 66–67, 69
    traps, 64, 69
Sporting Goods Dealer, The, 73, 75
Stanbury, Percy, 69
Steigers, Bill, 155
Stocks, fiberglass. *See* Stocks, syn-
        thetic

Stocks
    shotgun, for Sporting Clays, 68
    synthetic, 41–46, 55, 165
    wood, laminated, 45, 186
Sutherland, James, 35
Swanson, Gary, 19
Sweeley, E. M., 70

Targets
    plinking, 90
    Sporting Clays, 64–65, 66–67
    trapshooting, early, 140
Taylor, John "Pondoro," 35
Traps, for Sporting Clays, 64
Trapshooting targets, early, 140
Trigger control, 102–04, 106
Triggers
    backlash, 105
    creep, 105
    double-set ("hair"), 104
    pull, weight of, 103–06
    squeezing technique, 103
    See also Dry Firing; Trigger Con-
        trol
Twilight factor, 113

U.S. Army Marksmanship Unit,
    123, 124
U.S. Olympic Training Center, 123
U.S. Sporting Clays Association, 69

Vande Zande, Ernie, 123
Variable power, 113
Varmint shooting
    handguns and cartridges for,
        78–83
    handloading for, 83
    shooting position for, 83
Velocity, .44 Magnum, 99–100

Wide-field, 113
Wigger, Lones, W., Jr., Lt. Col.,
    122–27
Winchester
    Model 70 Featherweight, 52
    Model 70 "Leopard Gun," 19
Wood, stock
    for custom guns, 39
    laminated, 45
World Shooting Championships,
    126